D0945261

William Carlos Williams's
Paterson

A Critical Reappraisal

Facsimile 1

William Carlos Williams's
Paterson

A Critical Reappraisal

Margaret Glynne Lloyd

Rutherford • Madison • Teaneck
Fairleigh Dickinson University Press
London: Associated University Presses

© 1980 by Associated University Presses, Inc.

Associated University Presses, Inc.
Cranbury, New Jersey 08512

Associated University Presses
Magdalen House
136–148 Tooley Street
London SE1 2TT, England

Library of Congress Cataloging in Publication Data

Lloyd, Margaret Glynne.
William Carlos Williams's Paterson.

Bibliography: p.
Includes index.
1. Williams, William Carlos, 1883-1963. Paterson.
2. Paterson, N. J., in literature I. Title.
PS3545.I544P335   811'.5'2   77-98775
ISBN 0-8386-2152-X

In memory of my father

Are facts not flowers
                and flowers facts
or poems flowers
                or all works of the imagination,
                            interchangeable?

                —William Carlos Williams,
                "Asphodel, That Greeny Flower"

Contents

Acknowledgments

I would like to thank Mrs. William Carlos Williams and Mr. James Laughlin of New Directions Publishing Corporation for kindly granting me permission to quote from Williams's unpublished worksheets in the Poetry Collection of the Lockwood Memorial Library, State University of New York at Buffalo, and in the Collection of American Literature of the Beinecke Rare Book and Manuscript Library, Yale University. I am also indebted to Mr. K. C. Gay, Curator of Buffalo's Poetry Collection, and to the staff of the Beinecke Library, for their interested assistance during my visits to study Williams's unpublished *Paterson* manuscripts and for their assistance in obtaining the facsimile reproductions of Williams's worksheets. Thanks are also due to the members of the University of Leeds, University of Toronto, and Smith College library staffs for their help.

I am deeply grateful to Mr. Geoffrey Hill for being such a conscientious and inspiring supervisor of my Ph.D. thesis on *Paterson* at the University of Leeds, England. This book has benefited immeasurably from his countless invaluable suggestions and rigorous standards. I owe a large debt of gratitude to Dr. Norman O. Brown, both scholastically and spiritually. Dr. Brown not only first kindled my interest in *Paterson*, he also initially introduced me, both directly and indirectly, to a number of the secondary sources used in this study. I would like to take this opportunity to thank my mother, brothers, and friends who have cheered me on in my work at a number of critical times. It is difficult to acknowledge the extent of my indebtedness to my husband, John K. Bollard. He read and astutely commented upon many drafts of the manuscript, talked with me endlessly on various issues, and provided me with constant, loving support and encouragement.

M.G.L.

Abbreviations

Throughout the text the following standard abbreviations will be used for primary sources by William Carlos Williams cited parenthetically:

AUTO   *The Autobiography of William Carlos Williams.* New York: New Directions, 1967.

BUFFALO   Unpublished manuscripts in the Poetry Collection of the Lockwood Memorial Library, State University of New York at Buffalo. Used by permission.

CEP   *The Collected Earlier Poems.* London: MacGibbon & Kee, 1967.

CLP   *The Collected Later Poems.* London: MacGibbon & Kee, 1965.

IAG   *In the American Grain.* London: MacGibbon & Kee, 1966.

IMAG   *Imaginations: Five Experimental Prose Pieces.* Ed. Webster Schott. London: MacGibbon & Kee, 1970.

IWW   *I Wanted to Write a Poem.* Ed. Edith Heal. London: Cape Editions, 1967.

KORA   *Kora in Hell: Improvisations.* San Francisco: City Lights Books, 1969.

ML   *Many Loves and Other Plays.* Norfolk, Conn.:
            New Directions, 1961.
PB   *Pictures from Brueghel and Other Poems.* Lon-
            don: MacGibbon & Kee, 1968.
SE   *Selected Essays of William Carlos Williams.* New
            York: New Directions, 1969.
SL   *The Selected Letters of William Carlos Williams.*
            Ed. John C. Thirlwall. New York: McDowell,
            Obolensky, 1957.
YALE   Unpublished manuscripts in the Collection of
            American Literature, Beinecke Rare Book and
            Manuscript Library, Yale University. Used by
            permission.

Quotations from *Paterson* are cited by parenthetical refer-
ence to the book, section, and page number from the New
Directions edition of 1963. Quotations from the "Author's
Note" will also be documented parenthetically.

The abbreviation "WCW" is used in the footnotes instead of
Williams's full name each time it occurs in a title.

Introduction

In the course of this study of William Carlos Williams's *Paterson*, there have emerged three distinct but related contexts within each of which the position of the poem is evaluated. *Paterson* is first introduced by considering the poem's significance in the context of the twentieth century's aesthetic ambivalence. This is further developed during a brief review of the negative criticism of *Paterson*, which primarily derives from the fact that the poem was written as an assault upon the hieratic tradition and as a reply to *The Waste Land.* The context of controversy also plays a part in Chapter 6, which examines the import of the poem as a whole. Secondly, throughout the discussion of various aspects of *Paterson*, the poem is placed within the context of Williams's corpus of work, not only to better our understanding of the poem, but also to demonstrate that it is a natural development of Williams's material, ethical, and structural concerns. Chapter 2 begins with an investigation of the city in Williams's shorter poems before turning to the city in *Paterson.* In Chapter 3 the concept of images of empathy is developed through examples derived from Williams's shorter poetry and a number of his prose works, and their specific function in *Paterson* is then considered. Chapter 4 is exclusively devoted to Williams's experiments with extended structures from *Kora in Hell* to *Many Loves,* providing an important background for the discussion of

Paterson's structure in Chapter 5. Finally, in the last chapter, the poem is viewed within a much broader literary context (from Homer to Eliot) as the poem is considered in terms of the epic tradition.

There is certainly room for further *Paterson* criticism and it is clear that the poem has not yet received the critical response it deserves. Each chapter of this book considers aspects of the poem which either have not been dealt with at all by *Paterson*'s critics, or which have been dealt with inadequately. For example, Williams's initial conception of the poem was "that a man in himself is a city" and yet scarcely any of the existing criticism centers on the nature of the city which is presented or attempts an investigation of the man/city image. The fact that Williams was concerned with the creation of larger structures throughout his poetic career has also largely been ignored and thus it has proven difficult for the critics to come to terms with the structure of *Paterson* and to see its validity as a modern epic.

During the investigation of the topics which are the main concerns of each chapter, a number of other aspects of the poem are dealt with indirectly. For example, Chapter 3's discussion of the conceptual presence of the city in *Paterson* brings to the surface themes such as usury, divorce, and the search for a redeeming language. In the course of the analysis of *Paterson*'s organization, many of the details, factors, and events of the poem are interpreted.

In the introduction to the *Selected Writings* of Charles Olson, Robert Creeley asserts that "criticism is not only a system of notation and categorization—it is an active and definitive engagement with what a text proposes. It is not merely a descriptive process."[1] The negative criticism of *Paterson* largely revolves around the fact that the poem's critics do not always see the cohesion between its many diverse elements and it has thus been described as structurally chaotic. However, *Paterson* proposes a new kind of unity and Chapters 2, 3, 5, and 6 examine various aspects of the poem which contribute to an understanding of the significance of that unity as well as its implementation. Since it is primarily the idiom and structure of *Paterson* which articulates the poem's dominant theme of unity, a considerable amount of space is devoted to "Theme and Structure" in Chapter 5, which considers from a variety of points of view the unity of city, man, and poem achieved in *Paterson*.

NOTES TO INTRODUCTION

1. Robert Creeley, "Introduction," *Selected Writings of Charles Olson* (New York: New Directions, 1966), p. 2.

William Carlos Williams's
Paterson

A Critical Reappraisal

1 The Literary Context of *Paterson*

In twentieth-century American literary criticism two areas of viable tradition emerge, although they have, of course, historical origins. Many modern critics and poets indicate their poetic inclinations by aligning themselves specifically with either T. S. Eliot or William Carlos Williams, and Williams's long poem *Paterson* was, from its very conception, intended to be a "detailed reply" (SL, 239) to the Eliot bias of modern poetry. In order to understand more fully the implications of this fact, as well as the particular shapes which American literature has assumed, this chapter examines the vocabulary through which a number of critics and poets have chosen to express the split in modern sensibility and continues with a discussion of Williams's position and *Paterson*'s role in the continuing controversy. Having established a critical and an aesthetic context for *Paterson*, the ground for further criticism of the poem is then delimited.

In *The Well-Tempered Critic* Northrop Frye discusses two tendencies in literature which originate in the perennial disagreement among poets as to the relationship of literature to ordinary speech. The first, established in Aristotle, Frye calls the hieratic:

> The hieratic tendency seeks out formal elaborations of verse and
> prose. The hieratic poet finds, with Valéry, that the kind of poetry

he wants to write depends, like chess, on complex and arbitrary rules, and he experiments with patterns of rhythm, rhyme and assonance, as well as with mythological and other forms of specifically poetic imagery.[1]

On the other hand is the demotic tendency, which goes back to Plato but whose chief spokesman is Longinus. According to Frye,

> The demotic tendency is to minimize the difference between literature and speech, to seek out the associative or prose rhythms that are used in speech and reproduce them in literature.[2]

As might be expected, the hieratic and the demotic traditions also involve differing attitudes toward reality. For example, the demotic stance can be perceived in the preface to the *Lyrical Ballads*, in which Wordsworth advocates the employment of the "real language of men,"[3] the avoidance of poetic diction, as well as the use of "incidents and situations from common life."[4]

As Frye indicates, the terms "Romantic" and "Classical" have often been used to refer to these two literary modes. Such notation has been carried through to twentieth-century literary criticism as exemplified by *Prose Keys of Modern Poetry*, edited by Karl Shapiro, a collection of highly significant essays that provide a background for modern British and American poetry. The essays are classified under two headings— "Modern Classicism" and "Modern Romanticism." Shapiro does betray, however, momentary doubts concerning the schematic arrangement of his book. For example, he includes Gerard Manley Hopkins in the Romantic section because of his experiments with prosody but is then forced to concede that "any attempt to classify Hopkins as a Classicist or a Romantic will reveal the essential absurdity of these terms."[5] In 1933 T. S. Eliot stated that "in the interest of clarity and simplicity I wish myself to avoid employing the terms Romanticism and Classicism, terms which inflame political passions, and tend to prejudice conclusions."[6] Similarly, in his introduction to *The New Writing in the USA* Robert Creeley asserts that

> the usual critical vocabulary will not be of much use in trying to locate the character of writing we have now come to. If one depends on the dichotomy of *romantic* and *classical*, he is left with, too simply, an historical description, itself a remnant from an earlier "period."[7]

That there is a dichotomy in modern American poetics can hardly be doubted. The difficulty lies in its exact characterization. If, as has been suggested, the terms "Romantic" and "Classical" have survived beyond their applicability, perhaps the most expedient way in which to obtain a sense of the modern polarity is to consider, with a degree of objectivity, how it has been expressed by a number of twentieth-century critics and poets.

In the 1919 introduction to the American edition of his *New Poems*, D. H. Lawrence proposes that, in addition to poetry of the past and poetry of the future which express in their form "perfect symmetry," there "is another kind of poetry: the poetry of that which is at hand: the immediate present."[8] The form of this poetry is never finished, is without symmetry or permanence, attesting to a "naked contact" with reality: "Whitman's is the best poetry of this kind. . . . The clue to all his utterance lies in the sheer appreciation of the instant moment, life surging itself into utterance at its very wellhead."[9] Kenneth Burke similarly differentiates between the "Contact writer" and the "Culture writer:"

> The Contact writer deals with his desires; the Culture writer must erect his desires into principles and deal with those principles rather than with the desires; the *Ur-phenomen*, in other words, becomes with the man of Culture of less importance than the delicate and subtle instruments with which he studies it.[10]

Burke treats one as the counterpart of the other, not as

necessarily antithetical, although he perceives that the difference in emphasis between them is critical. The difference, for Burke, resides in the physicality and immediacy of the poet of "Contact" as contrasted with the more idea-oriented "Culture" poet.[11] Karl Shapiro's "just poetry" is fairly close to Burke's "Contact writer:"

> If we posit two types of poetry, culture poetry and just *poetry*, the first type is that which attempts to explain culture. It can do this in the manner of the Metaphysical poets, who were troubled by scientific knowledge and who wished to compete with science; by rewriting history according to a plan; by tracing the rise and fall of a particular belief, and so forth. Culture poetry is always didactic, as indeed most modern poetry is. It is a means to an end, not an end, like art. Culture poetry is poetry in reverse; it dives back into the historical situation, into culture, instead of flowering from it. And there is remains to enrich the ground for criticism.[12]

It is clear that Shapiro considers the two approaches to be in complete opposition.

Roy Harvey Pearce uses the terms "Adamic" and "mythic" to indicate the "insistent opposition," claiming that the poets have used these same terms to sort "out in the American poet's work the components of innocence and experience, past and present, self and other, freedom and limitation."[13] Robert Langbaum opposes the "poetry of experience" to the "poetry of meaning:"

> In the poetry of experience, the idea is problematical and incomplete because it must give way before the need of the life flow to complete itself. But in Greek tragedy—if Aristotle's analysis is correct—the life flow, as it appears in the forces exerted by the agents, is problematical and incomplete because it must give way before the need of the idea or meaning to complete itself.[14]

In "Projective Verse" (1950), Charles Olson sets up what he calls "Projective" verse against the "non-Projective." In this manifesto Olson explains what projective verse means as far as the composition of a poem is concerned and also deals with the "stance toward reality [that] brings such verse into being."[15] The theory behind projective verse is that "FORM IS NEVER MORE THAN AN EXTENSION OF CONTENT,"[16] and this results in the creation of new forms for each occasion. This emphasis is also to be found in Lawrence's introduction, with his assertion that in the poetry of the present "the law must come new each time from within."[17] The nature of the relationship of the poet to experience becomes of the utmost importance:

> If he sprawl, he shall find little to sing but himself, and shall sing, nature has such paradoxical ways, by way of artificial forms outside himself. But if he stays inside himself, if he is contained within his nature as he is participant in the larger force, he will be able to listen, and his hearing through himself will give him secrets objects share. And by an inverse law his shapes will make their own way.[18]

In this essay Olson is dealing specifically with the central issues of the polarity. As Robert Creeley observes, "a division of method appears between those who make use of traditional forms, either for discipline or solution, and those who, as Olson, go 'By ear . . . ,' by, in effect, the complexly determined response to work literally in hand."[19]

In 1971, Donald M. Kartiganer published an essay entitled "Process and Product: A Study of Modern Literary Form," in which he uses the terms "product" and "process" to refer to

> two distinct kinds of illusion possible in literary form: the sense of rigorous control and that of comparative looseness and fragmentation; the work which appears to contain experience within a deliberately structured frame, and the work which creates an impression of unmodified spontaneity, of experience met more "directly" by the refusal to impose traditional notions of form on it.[20]

Kartiganer goes on in his essay to consider a number of modern American and British writers in the light of these two modes of literature. He illustrates process literature through a discussion of Williams's poem *Paterson,* "in which process operates in a comparatively pure form."[21] Following a theoretical discussion of process literature, reinforced with a number of literary examples from the past and present,[22] Kartiganer asserts that *Paterson* "brings to a kind of ultimate stage most of the techniques already referred to. . . . *Paterson* is clearly the poem wrenching itself into form."[23]

In his *Autobiography* Williams reveals that "Keats, during the years at medical school, was my God" (AUTO, 53). During that time he had labored over a poem which he describes as an "*Endymion*-like romantic poem" (AUTO, 106) which dealt with castles, kings and princes, a "romantic past." It was not long, however, before he "quit Keats" altogether, "just at the moment he himself did—with Hyperion's scream" (AUTO, 61). Keats provides the following explanation for his abandonment of the second *Hyperion* in a letter to his friend John Hamilton Reynolds:

> I have given up Hyperion—there were too many Miltonic inversions in it—Miltonic verse cannot be written but in an artful or rather artists' humour. I wish to give myself up to other sensations. English ought to be kept up. It may be interesting to you to pick out some lines from Hyperion and put a mark X to the false beauty proceeding from art, and one // to the true voice of feeling.[24]

Williams's affinity with Keats is further evidenced by the fact that during an interview with Walter Sutton he expresses an opinion of Miltonic verse which closely approximates that of Keats. Moreover, it is also of significance that he voices this opinion in the course of a criticism of T. S. Eliot. Williams asserts that

> he [Eliot] followed Milton. And I was particularly offended because in my reading of Milton, I found him to be using inversions of phrase which offended me, because I couldn't speak my own language without using, freely, inversions, which Shakespeare also does. But I wanted to get rid of using inversions of phrase—

Latinizations—and so, taking a backdoor approach, I was forced to consider a variation of the phrase in the manner of Whitman.[25]

In fact, at the same time that he was writing his Keats imitation, Williams was also writing down his "Whitmanesque 'thoughts'," but he eventually also outgrew Whitman: "Whitman was a romantic in a bad sense. He was the peak, in many ways, of his age, but his age has passed and we have passed beyond it" (SE, 218). Williams's poem "The Wanderer" (1914), which evinces the combined influence of his earlier Keatsian *Endymion* as well as Whitman's New York poems, is described by Kenneth Burke as "a kind of romantic allegorizing that he would later outlaw."[26] It is clear that after this initial period Williams no longer thought of himself as a "Romantic" poet either in aspiration or in execution.

Nevertheless Williams has been characterized as a "Romantic" in a number of critical writings. Wallace Stevens begins his preface to Williams's *Collected Poems, 1921–1931*, with the assertion that "there are so many things to say about him. The first is that he is a romantic poet. This will horrify him. Yet the proof is everywhere."[27] The "proof" as far as Stevens is concerned lies in his use of the sentimental and the anti-poetic and the constant interaction between the two in his poetry:

> What, then, is a romantic poet nowadays? He happens to be one who still dwells in an ivory tower, but who insists that life would be intolerable except for the fact that one has, from the top, such an exceptional view of the public dump.[28]

Yvor Winters also calls Williams an "uncompromising romantic" because of his "surrender to feeling and to instinct,"[29] his distrust of traditional form, and his repudiation of ideas in favor of the concrete. In *The Poetic World of William Carlos Williams*, Alan Ostrom asserts that

> Williams' position *is* Romantic. His belief that . . . there is a separation and opposition, and his conclusion that the main agent

of that disjuncture is the mechanical because it is a product almost
entirely of men's rational powers—this is a logical extension in a
more highly specialized technological world of the feelings of poets
like Wordsworth and Blake.[30]

Joseph Bennett observes that "as a poet, Williams is intensely
self-preoccupied, entranced with the image of his own ego.
This preoccupation has its roots in his Romanticism, as does the
concept of the self as hero."[31] Norman Holmes Pearson
comments on "the general romantic tradition in which . . .
Williams's poetry is so firmly established."[32] Peter Meinke
writes that Williams "is still in the major English lyric tradition,
representing the apotheosis of the Romantic tenets of organic
form, spontaneity as opposed to cerebration, and the language
of the common man."[33] In addition, Williams's major poem
Paterson has been variously described as in the "Romantic
tradition,"[34] a "Romantic epic,"[35] a "romantic cosmology,"[36]
and "one of those romantic epics of the self."[37] The poem has,
more than once, been compared with Wordsworth's *Prelude*.[38]

On the other hand, Vivienne Koch states in reference to
Stevens's preface to Williams's *Collected Poems* "that we never
get insight into the specific quality of a given poem if we
approach it by tabloid antithesis."[39] She suggests, for example,
that Eliot, despite his classical stand, is often a romantic in
practice.[40] As might be expected, there have been a number of
attempts at showing that Williams's work "registers a change in
sensibility which puts him, along with other writers in America
and abroad, beyond the characteristic assumptions of romanticism."[41]

J. Hillis Miller speaks of the absence of depth in Williams's
poems which is related to his avoidance of symbolism and
which results in an emphasis on the present moment:

> In romantic poetry, space frequently leads out to a "behind" or
> "beyond" which the poet may reach through objects, or which
> objects signify at a distance. In the Christian and Platonic tradi-
> tions, things of this world in one way or another stand for things of

this other world. Romantic poets inherit or extend this tradition.
. . . In Williams' poetry this kind of depth has disappeared and
with it the symbolism appropriate to it. Objects for him exist within
a shallow space, like that created on the canvases of the American
abstract expressionists.[42]

He also maintains that there is no attempt in Williams's poetry
to bring about a union between subject and object as "a
primordial union of subject and object is the basic presupposi-
tion of Williams' poetry."[43] Richard A. Macksay argues in a
similar vein that "Williams early dispossesses himself of his
romantic inheritance. . . . 'The dumfoundering abyss / Between us and the object' no longer exists for Williams."[44] At a
later point Macksay asserts that "the 'peculiar perfections'
which the poet discovers are born out of strenuous oppositions
(although never the romantic oppositions of subject and object)."[45] Kartiganer points out the difference between Coleridge's poetry with its "constant dualities of nature and
transforming poet" and Whitman's, "in which the fusion of
opposites is replaced by chaotic movement through a succession of distinct moments."[46] Tony Tanner, who generally
characterizes the modern American writer as a "Romantic,"
finds it necessary to differentiate between European and
American Romanticism in order to account for the unique
characteristics in American poetry: "That marriage between
subject and object, mind and nature, which is an abiding
Romantic dream, is seldom consummated in the work of the
American Romantics."[47] In his full-length study of Williams,
James E. Breslin discusses the rise of Imagism and its profound
effect on Williams. Breslin asserts that

in a deliberate reversal of the romantic tendency to dissolve the
object by looking through it, these poets [the Imagists] emphasized
the solid, independent existence of the thing and the need to
perceive its surface with care and precision. Modern poetry thus
began as a radical repudiation of the romantic ego and the idealistic
philosophy that supported it.[48]

Walter Sutton links Williams with the Romantics in his use of poetic diction and his rejection of conventional form, but makes the distinction that Williams does not adhere to the organic theory of form.[49]

The diversity of opinion reflected by the above critics further suggests the inadequacy of the terms "Romantic" and "Classical" as descriptive of the dichotomy in modern poetry. In fact, the controversy was dramatized *during* the Romantic period as documented by those chapters of the *Biographia Literaria* in which Coleridge criticizes Wordsworth's poetic theory. From Wordsworth's preface to the *Lyrical Ballads*, according to Coleridge, "arose the whole long-continued controversy."[50] A demotic tendency can be discerned in Wordsworth's preface and more recently in the use of such terms as "contact," "Adamic," "Projective," "process," etc., whereas the *Biographia*, in which Coleridge stresses the synthetic (i.e., unifying) properties of the imagination, reflects a hieratic tendency.[51]

Williams attempts to indicate the nature of the dichotomy in an anecdote related in his 1918 prologue to *Kora in Hell:* "One day Ezra [Pound] and I were walking down a back lane in Wyncote. I contended for bread, he for caviar. I became hot. He, with fine discretion, exclaimed: 'Let us drop it. We will never agree, or come to an agreement' " (SE, 24). As Williams commented at a later date, bread and caviar was a simplification of their positions as regards the art of poetry.[52] In "Letter to an Australian Editor" Williams writes that

> Ezra is one of my oldest friends. I shall not try to present his case. I wish only to say that for years we have been of opposite but friendly camps, touching the genesis of poetic genius. We parted years ago, he to move among his intellectual equals in Europe, I to remain home and struggle to discover here the impetus to my achievements, if I found myself able to write anything at all.[53]

Years later Williams was to acknowledge that he and Pound were not so far removed from each other as he had once thought.[54] T. S. Eliot was really his prime antagonist: "I know in my very bones, and not there only, that everything Eliot says is antagonistic to my viewpoint."[55]

The use of Eliot to represent the opposite of Williams is now a critical commonplace: "The new mode [Williams's] was a reconstitution of the old—that of Whitman and his peers—under the pressure of a kind of poetry—Eliot's—which would deny its relevance and worth."[56] Karl Shapiro and Sherman Paul describe their early admiration of Eliot and their subsequent championing of Williams.[57] Such comments as "I am of Eliot's party in this respect,"[58] or references to the "Williamsite bias"[59] in poetry, occur with an increasing frequency. When Robert Duncan presents us with a list of the poets that have been his masters, he ends by reminding us that "the two *sure* things—Frost and Eliot—are not there."[60]

Of course, Williams himself is partly responsible for this state of affairs. From the time of the appearance of *The Waste Land*, he never ceased inveighing against everything Eliot stood for. One of the most often quoted lines in this respect is from Williams's *Autobiography:* "Then out of the blue *The Dial* brought out *The Waste Land* and all our hilarity ended. It wiped out our world as if an atom bomb had been dropped upon it and our brave sallies into the unknown were turned to dust" (AUTO, 174). A year before his death he was still on the same tack:

> Eliot . . . was trying to find a way to record the speech and he didn't find it. He wanted to be regular, to be true to the American idiom, but he didn't find a way to do it. One has to bow down finally, either to the English or to the American.[61]

In his essay "Tradition and the Individual Talent" Eliot maintains that the poet enters into the structure of poetry as he has inherited it. The poet is the catalyzer of the poetic process, a "finely perfected medium."[62] Poems are begotten of other poems, not out of the poet's experience. In "Letter to an

Australian Editor" Williams proposes two kinds of poets. One is parallel with the poet in Eliot's essay. According to Williams, these are the poets who "think in terms of the direct descent of great minds," who experience a "mind to mind fertilization" and compose "in the forms of the past and even when they deviate from the fixed classic forms it is nevertheless precisely the established and accepted work of the masters from which they consciously deviate, by which they are asserting their greatest originality." Williams considers himself to be in direct opposition to this group of poets and goes on to explain the poetics of his platform. There is "another literary source continuing the greatness of the past which does not develop androgynetically from the past itself, mind to mind but from the present." The content and the form of this poetry "arise from the society about him of which he is (if he is to be fed) a part—the fecundating men and women about him who have given him birth."[63] In another essay, "Notes Towards a Definition of Culture," Eliot argues that

> there is no "culture" without "a culture," and no culture of a class or of an individual unless there is a living culture in the people to which that class or individual belongs. . . . What is desirable is an organic relationship of culture between the capital, the country, and also the provincial towns.[64]

Sherman Paul suggests that this essay put Williams "More than anything else . . . on trial as a poet and forced him to consider his past achievement,"[65] because in it Eliot presents a thesis similar, in many respects, to Williams's. What apparently antagonized Williams was that Eliot never mentions "a direct application of an American culture. . . . He has steadfastly ignored the application of the principles which he affects now to discover, the essential nature of local culture, while spouting at length upon its necessity" (SL, 224). In other words, Williams resented Eliot's presentation of an "abstract thesis" rather than a "specific study of American tendencies."[66] In a letter to Horace Gregory written on May 3, 1944, shortly after the appearance of Eliot's essay in the *Partisan Review,* Williams asked Gregory to be an "agent" working in his environment:

> I need help. I need you. There is a tremendous amount of work to be done here—and here better than elsewhere on earth, for it is the universal that we are after, nothing else than that and it is to that, in the particular, that Eliot in fact is defeating—as if he didn't dare acknowledge its presence, since that would show up his own defeat and emptiness. We are cultured as he himself says only when the environment we inhabit is cultured, etc., etc.[67]

In an essay on Williams, Robert Lowell observes that

> A seemingly unending war has been going on for as long as I can remember between Williams and his disciples and the principals and disciples of another school of modern poetry. The "beats"[68] are on one side, the university poets are on the other. . . . My own group, that of Tate and Ransom, was all for high discipline, for putting on the full armor of the past, for making poetry something that would take a man's full weight and that would bear his complete intelligence, passion and subtlety. . . . The struggle perhaps centered on making the old metrical forms usable again to express the depths of one's experience.[69]

There are two things emphasized here, as there were in "Letter to an Australian Editor," the "full armor of the past" as opposed to the present, and the attempt to create within forms and meanings established in the past as opposed to the making of new forms. These are the central issues about which the "unending war" is fought. According to Sherman Paul in *The Music of Survival:*

> A poet of culture (all that immediately environs us) is one who in his art responds to the living needs of his time and tries to make his art a force in the situation of his time. Eliot, Pound, and Williams try to do this; all are poets of culture. But Eliot and Pound offer Culture as a solution to the problems of culture; and each has a doctrine, the one religious, the other economic. Williams, however, offers only

poetry; the imaginative action of men in contact with their environment. [70]

Northrop Frye also acknowledges Williams's distinctive influence in modern poetry: "Many modern poets, with William Carlos Williams at their head, regard . . . concealing of a hidden design as gimmick-writing; for them, the image, the scene, the thing presented, the immediate experience, *is* the reality that the arts are concerned with, and to go beyond this is to risk dishonesty."[71]

As Charles Tomlinson suggests, Olson's *Projective Verse* "is a continuation of what was implicit in Williams' sense of the line, in his insistence on the line."[72] In fact in the beginning of his essay Olson states that the nonprojective is the kind of verse which had been operative in the United States up to 1950 "*despite* the work of Pound and Williams."[73] Williams's response to Olson's essay was immediate as evidenced by a letter to Robert Creeley:

> I share your excitement, it is as if the whole area lifted. It's the sort of thing we are after and must have. . . . Everything in it leans on action, on the verb: one thing *leads* to another which is thereby activated.[74]

He further demonstrated his high regard for the essay by reprinting a large portion of it in his *Autobiography*. Olson ends his discussion, appropriately, with a diatribe concerning the prime antagonist of projective verse, that is, T. S. Eliot:

> Eliot is, in fact, a proof of a present danger, of "too easy" a going on the practice of verse as it has been, rather than as it must be, practiced. . . . It is because Eliot has stayed inside the nonprojective that he fails as a dramatist—that his root is the mind alone, and a scholastic mind at that . . . and that, in his listenings he has stayed there where the ear and the mind are, has only gone from his fine ear outward rather than, as I say a projective poet will, down through the workings of his own throat to that place where

breath comes from, where breath has its beginnings, where drama
has to come from, where, the coincidence is, all act springs.[75]

Williams considered himself to be the spiritual heir of Walt
Whitman and thought of Whitman's accomplishment as the
dividing factor in subsequent developments in poetry:

> Since Whitman . . . the poems written in our circumference
> may be divided into two categories: those that have regressed from
> his bold stand and reverted to previous standards—with the
> prestige natural to such a position—or those that have constantly
> attempted to recombine the elements of a new verse (which he
> more envisaged than accomplished) into the poems he wanted to
> compose.[76]

According to Williams, Whitman's great achievement was his
break with traditional prosodic forms, his use of "free verse,"
which Williams saw as a transitional phase in which the
elements of composition were made free.[77] Nevertheless,
Whitman had been largely disregarded during his lifetime and
after. Robert Creeley calls him "a figure the New Critics and
the universities to this day have conspired to ignore."[78]
Williams suffered in much the same way at the hands of the
critics. In 1952 he was referred to as "still the most critically
neglected writer, in proportion to his importance of the first
half of the American century."[79] Thom Gunn also observes that
"it was Eliot who dominated poetry until the early 1950s and
such is literary fashion that apparently Williams could not but
suffer—being misunderstood or, more commonly, disregarded
under such dominance."[80] In a letter to Denise Levertov,
dated November 22, 1953, Williams wrote:

> You write well but you know what an advantage the poets who
> follow academic patterns possess . . . with their regularly arranged
> lines, their rhymes and stanzaic forms. Do not underestimate it.
> The world they represent is not your world but it is a world that
> occupies the driver's seat.[81]

This is no longer the state of affairs and, as we have seen above, the dialogue between the two traditions has increased in intensity.

In 1946 the first book of Williams's five-book poem *Paterson* appeared. The remaining four were published in 1948, 1949, 1951, and 1958. This poem is by far the longest and most ambitious undertaking of his literary career, a "big, serious

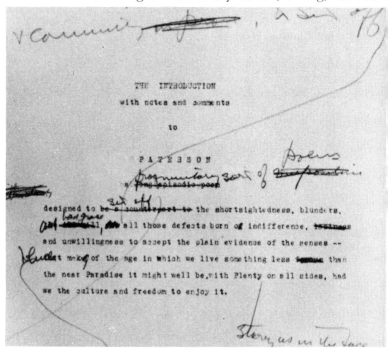

THE INTRODUCTION

with notes and comments

to

PATERSON

designed to be .... the shortsightedness, blunders, ... all those defects born of indifference, ... and unwillingness to accept the plain evidence of the senses -- .... make of the age in which we live something less .... than the near Paradise it might well be,with Plenty on all sides, had we the culture and freedom to enjoy it.

Facsimile 2

portrait" (SE, 62) of his time. In a letter to James Laughlin in 1943 he refers to the projected poem:

> "Paterson," I know, is crying to be written; the time demands it; it has to do just with all the peace movements, the plans for international infiltration into the dry mass of those principles of knowledge and culture which the universities and their cripples have cloistered and made a cult. It is the debasing, the keg-

cracking assault upon the cults and the kind of thought that destroyed Pound and made what it has made of Eliot. To let it into "the city," culture, the benefits of culture, into the mass as an "act," as a thing. [SL, 214]

Louis Martz maintains that "the more we read and reread *Paterson*, the more it emerges as a subtly devised protest against the cosmopolitan, the learned, the foreign aspects of such poems as *The Waste Land*, *Four Quartets*, and *The Cantos*."[82] Robert Lowell refers to *Paterson* both as "our *Leaves of Grass*"[83] and an "anti-Cantos rooted in America."[84] Eric Mottram observes that *Paterson* is

> distinctly unlike Eliot's fearful resentment of a city and more like Mumford's less agrarian, less Christian, but still wary, appreciation of the city as the major instance of what men have been able to achieve.[85]

Among Williams's unpublished papers may be found an early attempt at writing an introduction to the poem. This page provides further evidence that *Paterson* was intended as a counterpart to *The Waste Land*, a reaffirmation of Whitman's "myth of plentitude" which had been sharply contradicted by Eliot's myth of sterility"[86] (see facsimile 2).

There are a number of specific references to Eliot and Pound in *Paterson*:

> The rest have run out—
> after the rabbits.
> Only the lame stands—on
> three legs. Scratch front and back.
> Deceive and eat. Dig
> a musty bone (I, p. 11)
>
> Moveless
> he envies the men that ran
> and could run off
> toward the peripheries—
> to other centers, direct—

>   for clarity (if
>   they found it)
>   loveliness and
>   authority in the world—[I, iii, 48]

Pound and Eliot are chief among those whom Williams blames
for deserting America, "a local definition of effort" (SE, 32) in
favor of Europe and the academies, while he stayed at home
digging a "musty bone"—the equivalent of which Pound once
called the "bloody loam:" "Your interest is in the bloody loam
but what I'm after is the finished product" (I, iii, 50).[87]
Williams's solution as a writer lies not in running away, not in
"composition," but in an effort to "embrace/the/foulness" (III,
i, 126). Williams particularly resented Eliot because he felt that
Eliot was better equipped than he to further the revolution he
saw necessary: "And being an accomplished craftsman, better
skilled in some ways than I could ever hope to be, I had to
watch him [Eliot] carry my world off with him, the fool, to the
enemy. If with his skill he could have been kept here to be
employed by our slowly shaping drive, what strides might we
not have taken!" (AUTO, 174). Similarly, he lashes out against
the university poets and critics:

>   We go on living, we permit ourselves
>   to continue—but certainly
>   not for the university, what they publish
>
>   severally or as a group: clerks
>   got out of hand forgetting for the most part
>   to whom they are beholden.
>
>   spitted on fixed concepts like
>   roasting hogs, sputtering, their drip sizzling
>   in the fire [I, ii, 44]

In Book III there is a letter from Pound in St. Elizabeth's in
which he includes a reading list reminiscent of his earlier "How
to Read:" "re read *all* the Gk tragedies in/Loeb.—plus

Frobenius, plus/Gesell plus Brooks Adams" (III, iii, 165). The
following page of the poem consists of a tabular account of the
stone found in an artesian well in Paterson. The account ends
with "The fact that the rock salt of England, and of some of the
other salt mines of Europe, is found in rocks of the same age as
this, raises the question whether it may not also be found here"
(III, iii, 166). This is certainly intended as a commentary on the
expatriation of Pound and Eliot. The following four lines from
the preface to *Paterson* have been interpreted by a number of
critics[88] as a conscious echoing of Eliot's line from the *Four
Quartets*, "In my beginning is my end."

> For the beginning is assuredly
> the end—since we know nothing, pure
> and simple, beyond
> our own complexities [I, pp. 11–12]

Louis Martz writes that "the wry echo of Eliot's 'East Coker'
. . . suggests that the four books of *Paterson* may be considered
a deliberate counterpart of Eliot's *Quartets:* the eternal Pela-
gian's answer to the doctrine of original sin."[89] Later, in Book
III there is a direct reference to *The Waste Land:*

> Who is it spoke of April? Some
> insane engineer. There is no recurrence
> The past is dead. [III, iii, 169]

For Williams, "the roar of the present, a speech—/is, of
necessity, my sole concern" (III, iii, 172).

Some of the adverse criticism of *Paterson* derives from the
fact that the poem was written as an assault of the hieratic
tradition—"a reply to Greek and Latin with the bare hands" (I,
p. 10). Consequently a number of the poem's critics are
concerned with a defense of their particular aesthetic ground.
René Wellek observes that

> Criticism is discrimination, judgment, and hence applies and

implies criteria, principles, concepts, and thus a theory and
aesthetic and ultimately a philosophy, a view of the world.[90]

As Eliot points out, criticism can be thought of as "evidence of
the conception of the use of poetry in the critic's time."[91]
Considered in this light, such critical writing is of particular
interest in that it does bring out the ambivalence concerning
the "use of poetry" which characterizes the modern period.
The negative criticism of *Paterson* takes on additional
significance due to the fact that it is not only written by critics
who disapprove of Williams's poetic bias altogether, but also by
devotees of Williams who, for one reason or another, reject
Paterson, his major work. Karl Shapiro, for example, clearly
considers the poem to be a form of betrayal:

> *Paterson* is a typical culture poem, the only full-dressed one
> Williams ever wrote but, according to the critics, the real thing, a
> kind of New Jersey *The Waste Land.* Williams is so innocent that
> he would even do that. In writing his large bad poem Williams was
> perhaps trying to test the validity of works like the *Cantos* and *The
> Waste Land,* even to compete with them.[92]

Charles Olson presents us with the opposite point of view, in a
review of *Paterson V:*

> What looks like culture-talk, and that thinking the Doctor so
> long has said was not where it was, Not in ideas etc. (NOT
> prophecy, he exclaims here), isn't—by experience of the text of the
> poem, in what would appear to be its fussiest, or cutest (flowers &
> all that, and at the feet of the beloved) and least replica passage.
> Actually and solely, & quite exactly, the poem offers nothing but
> *the path* of itself. "Nothing else is real."[93]

Williams himself knew that *Paterson* would inevitably be
highly controversial: "already [1945] I have been informed that
Paterson will not be accepted because of its formlessness,
because I have not organized it into some neo-classic *recognizable* context" (SL,239). And, of course, he *meant* the poem to

be revolutionary and unacceptable to the critics—"I hope it cuts their hearts out" (SL,237).

The negative criticism of *Paterson* primarily revolves around the poem's alleged lack of organization, lack of measure, and inappropriate content. All three of these contentions will be severely challenged in the course of this study. Because Randall Jarrell's criticism of *Paterson* anticipated and influenced subsequent unsympathetic reactions to the poem and typifies much of the adverse criticism to which *Paterson* has been exposed,[94] we will briefly review his critical response to the poem.

Jarrell's criticism of Williams's poetry has always exhibited a marked tendency toward qualification. That is to say, he often undercuts the positive statements that he himself makes in reference to Williams's poetry in order to convey the impression of Williams as a poet of many limitations. It is not surprising, therefore, that Jarrell does not like *Paterson*, a poem in which he clearly believes Williams is overreaching himself:

> When one reads that no 'living American poet has written anything better and more ambitious' than *Paterson*, and that Dr. Williams is a poet who gives us 'just about everything,'[95] one feels that the writer has in some sense missed the whole point of William Carlos Williams. He is a *very* good but *very* limited poet, particularly in vertical range.[96]

Previously, however, Jarrell had given high praise to *Paterson I*. After its emergence in 1946 he published a brief appraisal of it in the *Partisan Review* in which his admiration was unequivocal: "*Paterson (Book I)* seems to me the best thing William Carlos Williams has ever written; I read it seven or eight times, and ended lost in delight."[97] Apparently he must have felt that Book I stayed within a sufficiently narrow compass. No doubt the book's reiteration of "no ideas but in things" contributed to this impression. In the same article he also expresses his admiration for the organization of the book, describing it as "musical to an almost unprecedented degree."[98]

After the publication of the following three books of the poem, Jarrell published another article in 1951 in the *Partisan Review* denouncing Books II, III, and IV. Of the organization of Book I he now writes, "Of course, Book I is not organized quite so well as a long poem *ought* to be."[99] He goes on to state a number of reasons for his objection to the poem even though he is reluctant to do so: "Book IV is so disappointing that I do not want to write about it at any length; it would not satisfactorily conclude even a quite mediocre poem."[100] Jarrell's primary objection to the poem is its structure, which he calls the "Organization of Irrelevance," and goes on to explain that

> such organization is *ex post facto* organization: if something is somewhere, one can always find Some Good Reason for its being there, but if it had not been there would one reader have missed it? if it had been put somewhere else, would one reader have guessed where it should have "really" gone?[101]

He also asserts that the measure of the poem is unsatisfactory—"flatter than the flattest blank verse I have ever read."[102] Finally, he objects to its content, maintaining that too much space is apportioned to the evangelist and to Cress's letters and that the themes of credit and usury have already been overworked by Pound. In light of Jarrell's reversal in his treatment of *Paterson*, it is interesting to note that in a letter to Babette Deutsch, Williams suggests that Jarrell "reverted to his old instinctive antagonism" (SL,259) after his praise of *Paterson I*.

Because of its scope and length, *Paterson* was able to command from the critics the recognition and response that Williams's shorter lyrics did not. Critics who had heretofore successfully ignored the poet of "local interest perhaps" (SL,141)[103] found it necessary to come to terms with Williams's "epic": "In 1941 Williams was still far from being accepted as a major literary figure, a critical misconception which was corrected after *Paterson* was published by Laughlin."[104] Although response to *Paterson* was slow to begin, a substantial amount of critical material has now accumulated which, by all indications, will continue to grow apace.

It is perhaps surprising, in view of the considerable number of books which deal critically with *The Waste Land* and the *Cantos*, that there have only been three book-length studies of *Paterson* to date. The first, *An Approach to Paterson* by Walter Scott Peterson, is an undergraduate thesis printed in the Yale College series in 1967. The second, *William Carlos Williams' Paterson: Language and Landscape* by Joel O. Conarroe was brought out in 1970 and the most recent, which appeared in 1971, is *A Companion to William Carlos Williams's Paterson* by Benjamin Sankey. Aside from these three books on *Paterson*, there have been more than twenty book-length studies of Williams since 1950, some of which contain scattered references to *Paterson* while others devote whole chapters to the poem. The remaining *Paterson* criticism is to be found in periodicals which range from those dealing with a very specific aspect of the poem such as water imagery or the theme of usury, to those which attempt a more general analysis of the poem's "meaning."

It can be seen from the variety of approaches taken by the major *Paterson* critics that the poem has the range to support a heterogeneous response. Yet the controversial nature of the criticism even in the interpretation of the poem's details and component elements (where we might expect the highest rate of agreement), suggests that it has proven difficult for the critics to reach a deep understanding of Williams's tenet "no ideas but in things."

Paterson criticism in general is best characterized as mechanical and conservative in its approach. Williams no doubt would have labeled it as "traditional" and "academic," though he did not reject entirely the role of criticism, as he wrote in a letter to Denise Levertov in 1957:

Reading the poems it came over me how almost impossible it is to realize what it is that goes over from a writer into a (her) poem. And how it gets there. Even the alertest reader can miss it. The poet herself (himself) might miss it, and quit trying. And yet if it is important enough to her she will never quit trying to snare the "thing" among the words. Where does it lie among the words? That is the critics business to discover and reveal that.[105]

Paterson critics grope unsuccessfully for an adequate critical language through which to bring the poem to life, and there have been a number of rather unsuccessful attempts at designating or dealing with *Paterson*'s organization.[106] Sister Bernetta Quinn in her use of the term "metamorphosis,"[107] Louis Martz by making an analogy between Williams's technique and the mode of the Unicorn tapestries,[108] and James Breslin's discussion of the poem as a "poetic field,"[109] come the closest to an active engagement with what *Paterson* proposes.

NOTES TO CHAPTER 1

1. Northrop Frye, *The Well-Tempered Critic* (Bloomington: Indiana University Press, 1963), p. 94.

2. Ibid., p. 94.

3. William Wordsworth and Samuel Taylor Coleridge, *Lyrical Ballads 1805*, ed. Derek Roper (London: Collins Pub., 1968), p. 38.

4. Ibid., pp. 20–21.

5. Karl Shapiro, ed., *Prose Keys to Modern Poetry* (New York: Harper & Row, 1962), p. 192.

6. T. S. Eliot, *The Use of Poetry and the Use of Criticism* (London: Faber & Faber, 1933), p. 129.

7. Donald Allen and Robert Creeley, eds., *The New Writing in The USA* (Harmondsworth, Middlesex: Penguin Books, 1967), p. 19.

8. D. H. Lawrence, *The Complete Poems of D. H. Lawrence* (London: Heinemann, 1964), p. 182. See Walt Whitman, "Song of Myself," *Leaves of Grass* (New York: New American Library, 1958), pp. 50–51: "I am mad for it to be in contact with me. . . . / I have heard what the talkers were talking, the talk of the / beginning and the end; / But I do not talk of the beginning or the end."

9. Ibid., p. 183.

10. Kenneth Burke, "WCW: Two Judgments," in *WCW: A Collection of Critical*

Essays, ed. J. Hillis Miller (Englewood Cliffs, N.J.: Prentice-Hall, 1966), p. 50. *Contact* was the name Williams and Bob McAlmon chose for the literary magazine they began in 1921. In *Contact III* Williams contributed an essay, "Yours, O Youth," in which he attempted to explain their doctrine of contact: "We have said this in the conviction that contact always implies a local definition of effort with a consequent taking on of certain colors from the locality by the experience, and these colors or sensual values of whatever sort are the only realities in writing or, as may be said, the essential quality in literature" (SE, 32).

11. See Burke, "WCW: Two Judgments," p. 52, where Burke suggests that the essence of Williams's doctrine of "contact" "resides in the kind of physicality imposed upon his poetry by the nature of his work as a physician."

12. Karl Shapiro, *In Defense of Ignorance* (New York: Vintage Books, 1960), p. 22.

13. Roy Harvey Pearce, *The Continuity of American Poetry* (Princeton, N.J.: Princeton University Press, 1961), p. 421.

14. Robert Langbaum, *The Poetry of Experience* (New York: W. W. Norton, 1963), pp. 227–28.

15. Charles Olson, "Projective Verse," in *The New American Poetry,* ed. Donald M. Allen (New York: Grove Press, 1960), p. 386.

16. Olson, "Projective Verse," p. 387.

17. Lawrence, *Complete Poems,* p. 185.

18. Olson, "Projective Verse," p. 395.

19. Robert Creeley, "Olson & Others: Some Orts for the Sports," in *The New American Poetry,* ed. Allen, p. 411. See Charles Olson, "I, Maximus of Gloucester, to You," *The Maximus Poems* (New York: Jargon / Corinth Books, 1960), p. 2: "facts, to be dealt with, as the sea is, the demand / that they be played by, that they only can be, that they must / be played by, said he, coldly, the / ear!"

20. Donald M. Kartiganer, "Process and Product: A Study of Modern Literary Form," *The Massachusetts Review* 12, no. 2 (Spring 1971): 297.

21. Ibid., p. 298.

22. Laurence Sterne's *Tristram Shandy,* Walt Whitman's "Song of Myself," and Arthur Miller's *Tropic of Cancer.*

23. Kartiganer, "Process and Product," p. 308. Kartiganer's distinction between "process" and "product" literature is largely derived from Frye's essay "Towards Defining an Age of Sensibility" in *Fables of Identity* (New York: Harcourt, Brace, & World, 1963), pp. 131–32. There are a number of critics who similarly use the term "process" in relation to the structure of *Paterson.* See Gordon K. Grigsby, "The Genesis of *Paterson,*" *College English* 23, no. 4 (January 1962): 280; Sister Bernetta Quinn, "*Paterson:* Landscape and Dream," *Journal of Modern Literature* 1, no. 4 (May 1971): 532–33; Thomas R. Whitaker, *WCW* (New York: Twayne Pub., 1968), p. 132; John Malcolm Brinnin, "WCW," *Seven Modern American Poets,* ed. Leonard Unger (Minneapolis: University of Minnesota Press, 1967), p. 114.

24. John Keats, Letter to J. H. Reynolds, 21 September 1819, *The Letters of John Keats: 1814–1821,* ed. Hyder Edward Rollins (Cambridge: Harvard Univ. Press, 1958), 2:167.

25. Walter Sutton, "A Visit with WCW," *Minnesota Review* 1 (Spring 1961): 315.

26. Burke, *WCW; Two Judgments,*" in *WCW,* ed. Miller, p. 60.

27. Wallace Stevens, "WCW," in *WCW*, ed. Miller, p. 62.

28. Ibid., p. 63.

29. Yvor Winters, "Poetry of Feeling," in *WCW*, ed. Miller, p. 66.

30. Alan Ostrom, *The Poetic World of WCW* (Carbondale: Southern Illinois University Press, 1966), p. 59.

31. Joseph Bennett, "The Lyre and the Sledgehammer," *Hudson Review* 5, no. 2 (Summer 1952): 298.

32. Norman Holmes Pearson, "Williams, New Jersey," *The Literary Review* 1 (Autumn 1957): 30.

33. Peter Meinke, "WCW: Traditional Rebel," in *Profile of WCW*, comp. Jerome Mazzaro (Columbus, Ohio: Charles E. Merrill Pub. Co., 1971), p. 108.

34. Joel O. Conarroe, "The 'Preface' to *Paterson*," *Contemporary Literature* 10, no. 1 (Winter 1969): 42.

35. Walter Scott Peterson, *An Approach to Paterson* (New Haven, Conn.: Yale University Press, 1967), p. 49.

36. A. D. Van Nostrand, *Everyman His Own Poet* (New York: McGraw Hill, 1968), p. 20.

37. Louis L. Martz, "*Paterson:* A Plan for Action," *Journal of Modern Literature* 1, no. 4 (May 1971): 521.

38. See Robert Lowell, "*Paterson* I," *Sewanee Review* 4 (Summer 1947): 500–510; Thomas W. Lombardi, "WCW: The Leech-Gatherer of *Paterson*," *The Midwest Quarterly* 9 (July 1968): 348; Babette Deutsch, *Poetry in Our Time* (New York: Doubleday & Co., 1963), p. 114.

39. Vivienne Koch, *WCW* (Norfolk, Conn.: New Directions, 1950), p. 62.

40. See also C. K. Stead, *The New Poetic* (London: Hutchinson & Co., 1964), p. 15, where Stead attempts "to arrive at a fresh view of Eliot's criticism and poetry, to see them not so much as a strange new 'classicism' blooming in the desert of post-war melancholy, but as another attempt to solve those fundamental problems, rooted in Romanticism, which have confronted all English-speaking poets of this century."

41. J. Hillis Miller, ed., "Introduction," in *WCW*, p. 1.

42. Ibid., p. 3.

43. Ibid., p. 6.

44. Richard A. Macksay, " 'A Certainty of Music': Williams' Changes," in *WCW*, ed. Miller, p. 132.

45. Ibid., p. 136.

46. Kartiganer, "Process and Product," p. 304.

47. Tony Tanner, "Notes for a Comparison Between American and European Romanticism," *Journal of American Studies* 2, no. 1 (April 1968): 90.

48. James E. Breslin, *WCW: An American Artist* (New York: Oxford University Press, 1970), p. 34.

49. Walter Sutton, "Dr. Williams' *Paterson* and the Quest for Form," *Criticism* 2 (Summer 1960): 244.

50. Samuel Taylor Coleridge, *Samuel Taylor Coleridge: Selected Poetry and Prose*, ed. Elisabeth Schneider (New York: Holt, Rinehart and Winston, 1964), p. 270.

51. Ibid., p. 274. For a further discussion of the Romantic controversy as it relates to twentieth-century literature see Stead, *The New Poetic*, p. 13.

52. Sherman Paul, *The Music of Survival* (Chicago: University of Illinois Press, 1968), p. 34, n. 28.

53. William Carlos Williams, "Letter to an Australian Editor," *Briarcliff Quarterly* 3, no. 2 (October 1946): 205.

54. In a 1960 interview with Walter Sutton, Williams confessed, "I've written a letter to Pound saying that he is the first who has used in his writing as a poet the American idiom" (Sutton, "A Visit with WCW," p. 311).

55. John C. Thirlwall, "WCW as Correspondent," *The Literary Review* 1 (Autumn 1957): 18.

56. Pearce, *The Continuity of American Poetry*, p. 336.

57. Shapiro, *In Defense of Ignorance*, p. 143; Paul, *The Music of Survival*, pp. ix–x.

58. Denis Donoghue, "For a Redeeming Language," in *WCW*, ed. Miller, p. 126.

59. "Robert Creeley in Conversation with Charles Tomlinson," *The Review* 10 (January 1964): 24.

60. Robert Duncan, "Biographical Notes," in *The New American Poetry*, ed. Allen, p. 435.

61. Stanley Koehler, "The Art of Poetry VI, WCW," *The Paris Review* 8, no. 32 (Summer-Fall 1964): 124.

62. T. S. Eliot, "Tradition and the Individual Talent," in *Prose Keys to Modern Poetry*, ed. Shapiro, p. 69.

63. Williams, "Letter to an Australian Editor," pp. 205–208.

64. T. S. Eliot, "Notes Towards a Definition of Culture," *Partisan Review* 11 (Spring 1944): 145, 150.

65. Paul, *The Music of Survival*, p. 30.

66. Thirlwall, "WCW as Correspondent," p. 18.

67. Ibid., p. 19.

68. It should be pointed out that Williams did not wish to be associated with the "beats" in any way: "an anti-Beat tenet of mine would be the variable foot. But what do they know about the variable foot? They've never thought anything about it. They don't even know that poetry is written in measurable feet" (Sutton, "A Visit with WCW," p. 323).

69. Robert Lowell, "WCW," in *WCW*, ed. Miller, pp. 157, 158.

70. Paul, *The Music of Survival*, p. 31, n. 20.

71. Northrop Frye, *The Modern Century* (Toronto: Oxford University Press, 1967), pp. 71–72.

72. "Robert Creeley in Conversation with Charles Tomlinson," p. 31.

73. Charles Olson, "Projective Verse," in *The New American Poetry*, ed. Allen, p. 386.

74. Creeley, "Introduction," p. 6.

75. Olson, "Projective Verse," in *The New American Poetry*, ed. Allen, pp. 396–97.

76. Williams, "An Approach to the Poem," *English Institute Essays, 1947* (New York: Columbia University Press, 1948), p. 74.

77. See Williams, "Letters to Denise Levertov," *Stony Brook* 1/2 (Fall 1968): 166: "The mark of his times was on Whitman, he had rejected the older prosody but had nothing to take its place but formlessness which had laid him open to attack on formal grounds. When you see what the young poets are writing today, Whitman might never

have existed instead of having founded a memorable school that should have gone on influencing the writing of poems to this day. Maybe it is best so, a great poet is strongly an individual and not to be copied but if he does not link up with the prosodic process in some way he seems to me to have lost his major opportunity."

78. "Robert Creeley in Conversation with Charles Tomlinson," p. 35.

79. Robert Beum, "The Neglect of Williams," *Poetry* 80 (August 1952): 291.

80. Thom Gunn, "WCW," in *WCW*, ed. Miller, p. 171.

81. Williams, "Letters to Denise Levertov," p. 163.

82. Louis Martz, "The Unicorn in *Paterson*: WCW," in *WCW*, ed. Miller, p. 77.

83. Lowell, "WCW," in *WCW*, ed. Miller, p. 158.

84. Lowell, "*Paterson* I," p. 503.

85. Eric Mottram, "The Making of *Paterson*," *Stand* 7, no. 3 (1964): 20.

86. James E. Breslin, "WCW and the Whitman Tradition," *Literary Criticism and Historical Understanding: Selected Papers from the English Institute*, ed. Phillip Damon (New York: Columbia Univ. Press, 1967), p. 161.

87. Cf. Kartiganer, "Process and Product," pp. 308–15.

88. See Koch, *WCW*, p. 118; Sister M. Bernetta Quinn, *The Metamorphic Tradition in Modern Poetry* (New Brunswick, N.J.: Rutgers University Press, 1966), p. 90; Glauco Cambon, *The Inclusive Flame* (Bloomington, Indiana: Indiana University Press, 1963), p. 200; Conarroe, "The 'Preface' to *Paterson*," p. 49.

89. Louis L. Martz, *The Poem of the Mind* (New York: Oxford University Press, 1966), p. 143.

90. René Wellek, *Concepts of Criticism* (New Haven, Conn.: Yale University Press, 1963), p. 316.

91. Eliot, *The Use of Poetry and the Use of Criticism*, p. 129.

92. Shapiro, *In Defense of Ignorance*, p. 145.

93. Charles Olson, "*Paterson* (Book Five)," *Evergreen Review* 2, no. 9 (Summer 1959): 220–21.

94. See "Ways of looking at a poem and a poet," anon. rev., *Times Literary Supplement* 613, no. 3 (May 28, 1971): 611; Brinnin, "WCW," pp. 116–17; Vivienne Koch, "WCW: The Man and the Poet," *The Kenyon Review* 14, no. 3 (Summer 1952): 502–510; Bennett, "The Lyre and the Sledgehammer," pp. 295–307; Conrad Aiken, *A Reviewer's ABC* (New York: Meridian Books, 1958), pp. 385–86; Thom Gunn, "Poetry as Written," *Yale Review* 48, no. 2 (December 1958): 298; Leslie Fiedler, "Some Uses and Failures of Feeling," *Partisan Review* 15, no. 8 (August 1948): 930.

95. See Lowell, "*Paterson* I," p. 500.

96. Randall Jarrell, *Poetry and the Age* (London: Faber & Faber, 1955), p. 243.

97. Ibid., p. 203.

98. Ibid.

99. Ibid., 231.

100. Ibid., pp. 232.

101. Ibid., pp. 233–34.

102. Ibid., p. 232.

103. This is the phrase which Eliot used to dismiss Williams in England.

104. Williams, "Four Unpublished Letters by WCW," *The Massachusetts Review* 3, no. 2 (Winter 1962): 292.

105. Williams, "Letters to Denise Levertov," p. 167.

106. Although Linda Wagner's discussion of "transitional and symbolic metaphor" in *The Poems of WCW: A Critical Study* (Middletown, Conn.: Wesleyan University Press, 1964), pp. 90–116, is valuable to an extent, her terms tend to be misleading as they do not readily call to mind the definitions she has given them. Furthermore, despite avowals to the contrary, she appears anxious to force the poem's design into a logical sequence, to motivate it, by placing considerable emphasis on the sequential relationship she believes is implied through juxtaposition. James Guimond's analysis of *Paterson* in *The Art of WCW* (Chicago: University of Illinois Press, 1968), pp. 176–98, suffers from an attempt to schematize the poem into a vision of growth and decline. Walter Scott Peterson in *An Approach to Paterson* fails to take into consideration the structure of the poem in any part of his book, holding that "*Paterson*'s primary unity is a unity of theme" (p. 13). Similarly, Benjamin Sankey in *A Companion to WCW's Paterson* (Berkeley: University of California Press, 1971) does not adequately relate the poem's thematic concerns to its structure, weakly concluding that "the method of *Paterson*, is, I think a form of allegory" (p. 225)

107. Quinn, *The Metamorphic Tradition*, pp. 89–129.

108. Martz, *The Poem of the Mind*, pp. 147–61.

109. Breslin, *WCW*, pp. 168–202.

2   The City

An epic poet normally completes only one epic
structure, the moment when he decides on his
theme being the crisis of his life.[1]

1

Whenever Williams was called upon to make a statement in
reference to *Paterson* he invariably stressed his initial conception of the poem:

> that a man in himself is a city, beginning, seeking, achieving and
> concluding his life in ways which the various aspects of a city may
> embody—if imaginatively conceived—any city, all the details of
> which may be made to voice his most intimate convictions.
> [Author's Note]

Yet scarcely any of the existing criticism centers on the nature
of the city which is presented or attempts an investigation of
the terms of the poem's major image ("that a man in himself is a
city"), to any appreciable extent.[2] In addition, the criticism
touching on this important aspect of the poem is, for the most
part, derogatory.

In *Mayan Letters*, Charles Olson states, in reference first to
the *Cantos* and then to *Paterson*:

The materials of history which he [Pound] has found useful are not at all of use (nor are Bill's [Williams's]), despite the more apparent homogeneity: date 1917, not only did Yurrup (West, Cento, Renaissance) go, but such blueberry American as Bill presents (Jersey dump-smoke covering same) also WENT (that is, Bill, with all respect, don't know fr nothing abt what a city *is*).[3]

Robert Creeley, to whom the *Mayan Letters* were written, also indicates that his reaction to *Paterson* has always been "equivocal" and for substantially the same reason:

> Now Williams grew up when Rutherford was a small town. He saw the town change in his occupation as a doctor. But I don't think that he was either interested or equipped, in a sense, to deal with the recognition of the city that Rutherford became, and certainly Paterson is even more complicated—an instance of an industrial, ugly city, but nonetheless a very substantial one.[4]

A reviewer of *Paterson* in *The Times Literary Supplement* is of the opinion that

> the first limitation of the poem is that its locale is selected not because it offers an urban complex which is representative of modern America but rather because Williams felt it to have an "important colonial history" it invited further excavations in the American grain.[5]

Finally, David R. Weimer in his book *The City as Metaphor* maintains that Paterson never comes alive as a real city and that in fact two Patersons emerge but never fuse—one past and one present. He adds that, even if Paterson is meant to be a symbolic city, it is "too vaporous to work well as symbol, as allegory, or even as analogy."[6] In addition, Weimer is of the opinion that the man/city metaphor does not function successfully in the poem:

> His notion of a city that is seeking and achieving somehow failed to grow into a sustained or persuasive structure for the poem. It

seems to have served Williams as an inspirational source, but as an operative idea in the various books it is almost an excrescence.[7]

Yet it is clear that Williams's intention in the writing of *Paterson* was to discover in the local city a "world-city," to use the term which Allen Ginsberg employs in his letter which is a part of *Paterson IV:* "I know you will be pleased to realize that at least one actual citizen of your community has inherited your experience in his struggle to love and know his own world-city, through your work." (IV,ii,205). We do not have to look far to discover proof that this was indeed his intention. As Williams writes in his *Autobiography* in reference to *Paterson:* "If it rose to flutter into life awhile—it would be as itself, locally, and so like every other place in the world" (AUTO,392).[8]

The preface to the poem includes, in an encapsulated form, the method of the poem:

> To make a start,
> out of particulars
> and make them general, rolling
> up the sum, by defective means—[I,p.11]

Williams continues by developing an image of the essential unity of creation evolving out of chaos:

> Yet there is
> no return: rolling up out of chaos,
> a nine months' wonder, the city
> the man, an identity—it can't be
> otherwise—an
> interpenetration, both ways. Rolling
> up! obverse, reverse;
> the drunk the sober; the illustrious
> the gross; one. [I,p.12]

This is, in Mircea Eliade's terms, the *coincidentia oppositorum,* in which all things coalesce and in which past (profane) time is abolished and a new (sacred) time established.[9] As Williams writes in "A Novelette," "What I conceive is writing as an actual creation. It is the birth of another cycle" (IMAG,293), and in an early poem he proclaims that "destruction and creation/are simultaneous" (CEP,266).[10] This new time is also analogous to what J. Hillis Miller calls the realm of the twentieth-century poem—a perpetual present, the poetic space: "a space both subjective and objective, a region of copresence in which anywhere is everywhere, and all times are one time."[11]

Throughout the preface Williams employs the terminology of mathematics—multiplication, sum, numbers, addition, subtraction, division—and plays with the idea that the general is made up of particulars, but also that, paradoxically, innumerable particulars can be one. As Williams writes in Book I, "the/equation is beyond solution" (I,i,18). Having developed this concept of unity he concludes the preface by focusing on the specific subject of the poem, his representation of the universal: Paterson—the man and the city. This approach contrasts markedly with the eighteenth-century method as expressed by Imlac in Johnson's *Rasselas:* "The business of a poet . . . is to examine, not the individual, but the species; to remark general properties and large appearances."[12] Williams, in fact, accuses Eliot of using this method:

> All Eliot does is to evade the particular in the general and the
> more or less abstract. He will not come out for the thing but the
> shadow of the thing—the intellectual shadow.[13]

In contemplating his long poem Williams's first task was to decide on a specific city. He had thought seriously of New York City but felt that he was not sufficiently acquainted with its particulars. As he explains in his *Autobiography,* " 'The local is the only universal, upon that all art builds.' . . . I had no wish, nor did I have the opportunity to know New York in that way" (AUTO,391). Williams also felt that New York was "not local enough, not individual enough. New York City belongs to the

world."[14] At another time he says, "It couldn't be New York,
not anything as big as a metropolis" (IWW,82). However, in a
1964 interview he admits that "it [New York] was near enough,
God knows, and I was familiar enough with it for all my
purposes—but so was Leipzig, where I lived for a year when I
was young, or Paris. Or even Vienna or even Frascati. But
Manhattan escaped me."[15]. On the other hand, Rutherford,
where he lived most of his life, wasn't a city; it was a country
town, and "not distinguished or varied enough"[16] for his
purposes:

> I thought of other places upon the Passaic River, but, in the end,
> the city, Paterson, with its rich colonial history, upstream, where
> the water was less heavily polluted, won out. The falls, vocal,
> seasonal, vociferous, associated with many of the ideas upon which
> our fiscal colonial policy shaped us through Alexander Hamilton,
> interested me profoundly—and what has resulted therefrom.
> Even today a fruitful locale for study. I knew of these things. I had
> heard. I had taken part in some of the incidents that made up the
> place. I had heard Billy Sunday: I had talked with John Reed: I had
> in my hospital experiences got to know many of the women: I had
> tramped Garret Mountain as a youngster, swum in its ponds,
> appeared in court there, looked at its charred ruins, its flooded
> streets, read of its past in Nelson's history of Paterson, read of the
> Dutch who settled it. [AUTO,391–92]

As Williams himself notes, Paterson was a real "find" (IWW,82)
and it is significant that in his *Autobiography* he speaks of the
city in terms of a "discovery:"

> Even though the greatest boon a poet grants the world is to
> reveal that secret and sacred presence,[17] they will not know what
> he is talking about. . . . I took the city as my "case" to work up,
> really to work it up. It called for a poetry such as I did not know, it
> was my duty to discover or make such a context on the "thought."
> To *make* a poem, fulfilling the requirements of the art, and yet
> new, in the sense that in the very lay of the syllables Paterson as
> Paterson would be discovered, perfect, perfect in the special sense
> of the poem. [AUTO,390, 392]

Williams chose the city ("I chose it, deliberately chose it to write about"[18]) and then set out to discover and uncover its "secret and sacred presence." Jack Spicer writes in his "Letter to Lorca" that

> I would like to make poems out of real objects. The lemon to be a lemon that the reader could cut or squeeze or taste—a real lemon like a newspaper in a collage is a real newspaper. . . . Things do not connect; they correspond. That is what makes it possible for a poet to translate real objects, to bring them across language as easily as he can bring them across time. . . . One does not need to imagine that lemon; one needs to *discover* it.[19]

These words apply equally to place, to Paterson. Williams points out that we live in one place at one time. Rather than restricting us, it is only through that place that we can finally realize freedom: "In that place, if we only make ourselves sufficiently aware of it, do we join with others in other places."[20]

Williams refers to Paterson as a *provincial* city:

> But I want to see the unknown shine, like a sunrise. I want to see that overpowering mastery that will inundate the whole scene penetrate to that last jungle. It can be detected in the remote province of a Paterson as well as elsewhere. [SL, 313]

In a letter to Marianne Moore concerning the "idyl" in *Paterson IV,i,* he states, "*As far as the story goes, she* [the lesbian] represents the 'great world' against the more or less primitive world of the provincial city" (SL, 304). In a subsequent letter he explains that he "was looking for an image to typefy [*sic*] the impact of 'Paterson' in his young female phase [the nurse] with a world beyond his own." (SL, 305). Oswald Spengler's elaboration upon the designation "provincial" in *The Decline of the West* is helpful in understanding Williams's use of the term:

> A handful of gigantic places in each Civilization disfranchises and

disvalues the entire motherland of its own Culture under the contemptuous name of "the provinces." The "provinces" are now everything whatsoever—land, town, *and* city. . . . There are no longer noblesse and bourgeoisie, freemen and slaves, Hellenes and Barbarians, believers and unbelievers, *but only cosmopolitans and provincials.* All other contrasts pale before this one, which dominates all events, all habits of life, all views of the world.[21]

Williams attempts in *Paterson* to reestablish through his art the universal value of the provincial city in a metropolitan civilization:

But people live in provinces—provinces are just as much part of the world as the technique of the artist can make them live. If he cannot succeed in making them live, it's going to be provincial, but if he can make them surmount the life around them and come to more mature experiences, he will succeed in writing wherever he is. Provinces will become not provincial when the artists are big enough to make contributions to those who are remembered.[22]

As Williams wrote to Pound in 1933, "There's no taboo effective against any land, and where I live is no more a 'province' than I make it. To hell with youse. I ain't tryin' to be an international figure. All I care about is to write" (SL, 140).

In *I Wanted to Write a Poem* Williams told Edith Heal that "I was always a country boy, felt myself a country boy. To me the countryside was a real world but none the less a poetic world" (IWW, 33). And as might be expected, Williams often experienced an instinctive resistance to urban life, to the prosaic world. David Weimer suggests that "as projections of . . . anxiety ["fear for the artist's world"] the metropolis and the provincial city become one: they are Society, the Outer World, Reality threatening the Artistic Sensibility."[23] Spengler interprets the difference in degree and kind among country town (Rutherford), city (Paterson), and metropolis (New York):

The country town *confirms* the country, is an intensification of the picture of the country. It is the Late City that first defies the

land, contradicts Nature in the lines of its silhouette, *denies* all
Nature. . . . And then begins the gigantic megalopolis, the *city-
as-world*, which suffers nothing beside itself and sets about
annihilating the country picture.[24]

In light of Weimer's suggestion that "the metropolis and the
provincial city become one," it is significant that the "idyl" in
Book IV takes place in New York City, and Paterson himself has
come to the "Big City" (IV, i, 178). In reference to Book IV
Williams told Edith Heal that "I was getting up closer to the
city. . . . With the approach to the city, international character
began to enter the innocent river and pervert it" (IWW, 91).
The following section of this chapter concentrates on the image
of the city in Williams's poetry in general and the third
examines the city in *Paterson*. This inquiry demonstrates that
Williams's concept of city, which developed over a number of
years, is integral to the material thematic concerns[25] of his long
poem: "All the details [of the city] . . . may be made to voice his
most intimate convictions" (Author's Note).

2

If we examine Williams's city poetry apart from *Paterson*, we
are confronted with poems on Paterson and certain unspecified
cities, but the greatest number focus on New York City. The
attitudes, both emotional and intellectual, communicated by
these poems, as well as in his essay "The American
Background," enable us to formulate a vivid, if paradoxical,
picture of Williams's concept of city even before we turn to
Paterson.

Situated in Rutherford, New Jersey, Williams had ample
opportunity to observe the continual flow of people from the
country into the city. He was interested in the causes and the
results of this sociological phenomenon, in part because he
considered it as support for his theories of the local and
immediate: "Just as the city depends, literally, both for its men

and its materials on the country, so general ideas, if they are to be living and valid, to some extent depend (at least for their testing) on local cultures" (SL, 225). Lewis Mumford writes in *The City in History* that

> the chronic miscarriages of life in the city might well have caused their abandonment, might even have led to a wholesale renunciation of city life and all of its ambivalent gifts, but for one fact: the constant recruitment of new life, fresh and unsophisticated, from rural regions, full of crude muscular strength, sexual vitality, procreative zeal, animal faith. These rural folk replenished the city with their blood, and still more with their hopes. [26]

In the poem "A Place (Any Place) to Transcend All Places" the country replenishes and ennobles the city:

> there are channels
> above that, draining
> places from which New York
> is dignified, created [CLP, 113]

In his essay "The American Background" Williams attributes two main causes to this centripetal tendency. The first is the desire for money: "Wealth went on. The cities were its seat. By its centralization of money men flocked to them" (SE, 147). This basic connection between the city and money is found in "A Morning Imagination of Russia."

> the walls
> against desire save only for him who can pay
> high, there were no cities—he was
> without money—[CEP, 305]

The second cause is the "growing spiritual impoverishment of the outlying districts, a breakdown which brought a moral breakdown in its train" (SE, 151):

We cannot go to the country

for the country will bring us
    no peace . . . .

        Love itself a flower
with roots in a parched ground.
Empty pockets make empty heads. [CLP, 52]

Williams analyzes the consequences of this migration to the city in "The American Background." Here he states that the city embodies a "secondary culture," cut off from its roots. People went to the cities "leaving the already hardpressed and often failing culture of immediate references still farther behind" (SE, 147). As Spengler maintains, "Money has become, for man as an economic animal, a form of the activity of waking-consciousness, having no longer any roots in Being."[27] The corruption which sets in as a consequence of the worship of filthy lucre is evoked in "Perpetuum Mobile: The City:"

                Money! in
                armored trucks—
                two men
                    walking
                at two paces from
                    each other
                their right hands
                    at the hip—
                on the butt of
                an automatic—
                till they themselves
                hold up the bank
                and themselves
                    drive off
                for themselves
                    the money
                in an armored car—[CEP, 386–87]

Whitman commented on this aspect of the city in his *Democratic Vistas:* "The great cities reek with respectable as much as

nonrespectable robbery and scoundrelism. . . . Money-
making is our magician's serpent, remaining to-day sole master
of the field."[28]

In "A Place (Any Place) to Transcend All Places" Williams
lists the particulars of the country from which the city is created
but from which it is cut off. After a catalogue of natural,
immediate life, he goes on to list aspects of the synthetic,
unrelated culture of the city:

>   a museum of looks
> across a breakfast
> table;   subways of dreams;
> towers of divisions
> from thin pay envelopes. [CLP, 114]

In the last verse paragraph of this poem the excremental
character of the city is emphasized. "Lettuce" is perhaps used
here as a slang term for money:

>   Obscene and
> abstract as excrement—
> that no one wants to own
> except the coolie
> with a garden of which
> the lettuce particularly
> depends on it—if you
> like lettuce, but
> very, very specially, heaped
> about the roots for nourish-
>   ment. [CLP, 115]

In "A Morning Imagination of Russia" the city is depicted as an
obstacle in the way of a natural, emotional life:

>   There were no cities
> between him and his desires
> his hatreds and his loves were without walls
> without rooms, without elevators
> without files, delays of veiled murderers

muffled thieves, the tailings of
tedious, dead pavements [CEP, 305]

In a New York City poem Williams writes, "In my life the
furniture eats me/the chairs, the floor/the walls" (CEP, 253).
In these poems the city eclipses the natural life of the country.
Spengler observes that cities imitate nature with parks, foun-
tains, flower beds, clipped hedges, etc. In "Rapid Transit" the
city is suffocating and claustrophobic and a voice exclaims, "Ho
for the open country" (CEP, 282), but the people do not get any
further than a park for relief.

The ascendency of a "secondary culture" in the city is
emphasized by the physical presence of the urban population:

> There came crowds walking—men as visions
> With expressionless, animate faces;
> Empty men with shell-thin bodies
> Jostling close above the gutter
> Hasting—nowhere!   .   .   .
>
> Dogged, quivering, impassive— [CEP, 5]

Whitman, too, reflects upon the inhabitants of the city,
describing them as "petty grotesques, malformations, phan-
toms."[29] According to Mumford, urban man is more unhappy
because of his removal from the sources of life and his
concentration on power and wealth. He postulates Nekropolis
as the last stage of the city. Spengler asserts that the "*sterility of
civilized man*" is not a matter of causality but "an essentially
metaphysical turn towards death."[30] In "The Wanderer,"
Williams pleads, "May I be lifted still, up and out of terror, /Up
from before the death living around me—" [CEP,6]. "Rumba!
Rumba!" begins with the lines,

> No, not the downfall
> of the Western World
> but the wish for its
>   downfall   .   .   .

melted in a wish to die. [CLP,34]

Finally Williams observes that the inevitable consequence of the movement toward the city is the eventual impoverishment of the country:

> The cities had at least population and a quickened pulse, but in getting this, as in everything where the secondary culture predominates, the cost was severe. It involved the decay of the small community. And the decay of the small community was a primary cultural decay. It would seem as if the city has as its very being the raising of the cultural level, as if it were in the very stream of the great flow. Quite the opposite is true, unless the place of the city, as a sort of turntable and that only, be clearly realized. [SE,147]

Mumford similarly maintains that "once we allow the village to disappear, this ancient factor of safety [replenishment of the city] will vanish."[31]

In a number of his city poems Williams focuses upon the "silhouette," the architectural forms of the city:

> Above
> the darkness of a river upon
> winter's icy sky
> dreams the silhouette of the city [CEP, 447]

In another poem he confesses his seduction by the city's visage at night:

> I have watched
> the city from a distance at night
> and wondered why I wrote no poem. [CEP,216]

His poem "The Forgotten City" provides a catalogue of those physical aspects of a city which intrigue and haunt him: avenues, monuments, institutions, parks, and apartments. He refers to the "great towers of Manhattan" in "The Wanderer," and in "January Morning" these tall buildings become the "water-loving giants of Manhattan." In "The Flower" the towers are "oblong" and all lit up. In a later poem they become "towers of divisions." Bridges, labyrinthine streets, factories, lights provide the content for many of Williams's poems. Whitman similarly reacted to the forms of the city:

> These, I say, and the like of these, completely satisfy my senses of power, fulness, motion, etc., and give me, through my esthetic conscience, a continued exaltation and absolute fulfilment.[32]

Mumford points out that the city performs the "function of materialization," that is, "the buildings speak and act, no less than the people who inhabit them; and through the physical structures of the city past events, decisions made long ago, values formulated and achieved, remain alive and exert an influence."[33] The city is a container which holds together a large body of people and institutions. By means of various "symbolic methods of storage" the city is able to maintain and transmit

> a larger portion of their lives than individual human memories could transmit by word of mouth. . . . Through its durable buildings and institutional structures and even more durable symbolic forms of literature and art, the city unites times past, times present, and times to come.[34]

Marshall McLuhan claims that "the human city in all its complexity of functions is thus 'a center of paralysis,' a waste land of abandoned images."[35] Accordingly, the city's forms speak to Williams of power and complexity, a power and complexity which both attract and repel him.

As historians inquiring into the forms and functions of the city in history, Lewis Mumford and Oswald Spengler provide a background for the specific and general content of Williams's city poetry. They also set forth from a historical point of view many of the same issues confronting modern urban society with which Williams is grappling in a more creative mode. The fact

that Williams's reflections on the city touch upon issues raised
by both Mumford and Spengler suggests quite the opposite to
Creeley's criticism that Williams was not either "interested or
equipped . . . to deal with the recognition of the city."

Mumford and Spengler, of course, held divergent points of
view, yet both are relevant to *Paterson* because of Williams's
ambivalent attitude toward the city. In an interview with John
Thirlwall concerning *Paterson*, Williams asserts that "you may
think of individual men as being perhaps from a country
district, but the concept of city, as I conceived it, was man at his
most accomplished."[36] However, in the actual poem Williams
includes numerous depressing and disturbing portraits of
urban people such as the following found in Book IV:

                              At the
        sanitary lunch hour packed woman to
        woman (or man to woman, what's the difference?)
        the flesh of their faces gone
        to fat or gristle, without recognizable
        outline, fixed in rigors, adipose or sclerosis
        expressionless, facing one another, a mould
        for all faces (canned fish) this   [IV, i, 196]

Similarly, Spengler emerges with a pessimistic pronounce-
ment for the future of urbanites, betrayed from the beginning
by the title of his major work—*The Decline of the West:* "The
Culture-man whom the land has spiritually formed is seized
and possessed by his own creation, the City, and is made into
its creature, its executive organ, and finally its victim."[37]
Mumford, however, is more optimistic: "In the end, the city
itself became the chief agent of man's transformation, the organ
for the fullest expression of personality."[38] The dialectics of the
city also function in Whitman's works. In "Democratic Vistas"
he states "that not Nature alone is great in her fields of freedom
and the open air . . . but in the artificial, the work of man too is
equally great."[39] In *Aurora* he writes that New York City is
"the great place of the western continent, the heart, the brain,

the focus, the main spring, the pinnacle, the extremity, the no
more beyond, of the New World."[40] And yet such lines as the
following are common in his poetry:

> Inside of dresses and ornaments, inside of those wash'd and
>   trimm'd faces,
> Behold a secret silent loathing and despair. . . .

> Smartly attired, countenance smiling, form upright, death
>   under the breast-bones, hell under the skull
>   bones[41]

Williams's self-contradictory attitude, his ambivalence
whereby the city at once attracts and repels him, is present in a
number of his pre-*Paterson* city poems. Conceivably, it is the
creative force generated by this dialectic opposition that led, in
part, to *Paterson*[42]:

> Dissonance
> (if you are interested)
> leads to discovery. . . . [1V,ii,207–208]

> Love, the sledge that smashes atom? No, No! antagonistic
> cooperation is the key, says Levy   . [IV,ii,208]

In "To a Friend Concerning Several Ladies," the city calls
for him to "Come!" and he becomes "confused, twisted/four
ways and—left flat" (CEP,216). If he doesn't respond to the
call, he remains stale to himself, but if he goes, he returns
"filled/with a bad poem" (CEP,217). In "Approach to the City"
the city possesses the ability to refresh the poet's spirit:

> I never tire of these sights
> but refresh myself there
> always for there is small holiness
> to be found in braver things. [CLP,177]

As Weimer aptly comments: "the city represents a power over

experience the artist both craves and scorns, his regard for which distresses him either way."[43] In "The Flower" Williams witnesses "the great bridge stanchions" in the process of being erected and complains,

> It
> makes me ill to see them run up
> a new bridge like that in a few months
>
> and I can't find time to get
> a book written. [CEP, 237]

A woman reminds him that the city has power, "That's what you all/want." In "Perpetuum Mobile: The City," the city is a dream of love and desire which suffers diminution and disillusionment. Alan Ostrom comments on this poem that

> not only as itself, but also as it represents modern society, the city is a dream or an illusion in two senses: as we see its beauties expressing our desires and as we refuse to see the ugliness of much of its reality, its perversions of the human spirit.[44]

In a number of poems Williams's ambivalence toward the city is associated with his involvement with women. In his *Autobiography* Williams speaks of "*The Wanderer*, featuring my grandmother, the river, the Passiac River . . . my first 'long' poem, which in turn led to *Paterson*" (AUTO, 60–61). He also confided to Thirlwall in reference to the early poem that

> I identified my grandmother with my poetic unconscious: she was the personification of poetry. I wanted to identify myself with something good and philosophic—with a perfect knowledge of the world. I thought of myself as all-good and all-wise. So the grandmother as the spirit of the River, led to the Passaic.[45]

However, there is also a definite suggestion in the poem that the old woman is, in some sense, a whore:

> And then for the first time

> I really saw her, really scented the sweat
> of her presence and—fell back sickened!
> Ominous, old, painted—
> With bright lips, and lewd Jew's eyes
> Her might strapped in by a corset
> To give her age youth .   .   .   .
>
> To you, O mighty, crafty prowler
> After the youth of all cities   .   .   .   .
>   All the youth
> That come to you, you having the knowledge
> Rather than to those uninitiate— [CEP, 5–6]

In an unpublished version the old woman is described as possessing "eyes of the street sort."[46] In addition to being "the personification of poetry," she is also representative of his environment, the greatest part of which is city. Guimond suggests that the old woman is Demeter:

> In the myth Demeter disguises herself as an ugly, barren crone to mourn the loss of Kora, but she remains a powerful goddess capable of conferring great benefits upon mankind—just as winter "disguises" the earth's fruitfulness but contains the seeds of spring. Similarly Williams was convinced that, beneath its growing ugliness and squalor, his environment possessed as much potential significance and beauty as any age or locale.[47]

The poem "To a Friend Concerning Several Ladies" begins by cataloguing Williams's simple desires. Between him and these desires enter the distractions of the city which are associated with the attractions exercised by women and

> There is
> no good in the world except out of
> a woman and certain women alone
> for certain things. [CEP, 216]

The city disrupts and preoccupies him in the same way as women do. Weimer comments that in this poem "the city occupies its ancient site as the locus of sexual temptation, and there are overtones in the poem of the seduced provincial."[48] In *I Wanted to Write a Poem* Williams speaks of his book *Sour Grapes,* in which this poem is included:

> I was very late, very slow, to find out about the world. This book is all about that sort of thing. The people in the Village could show me so I spent time in the Village. They wanted me to share. I was curious, I'll admit, very curious, but I was having none of it. They wanted me to go to bed just to amuse *them.* I knew it must be at my own time, in my own place. [IWW, 45]

In "A Morning Imagination of Russia," the city is a barrier between a man and the natural joys and necessities of life:

> There were no cities
> between him and his desires. . . .
>
> A city, fashion
> had been between—
>
> Nothing between now. [CEP, 305; 307]

In "The Flower" Williams imagines a flower whose petals extend to encompass the aspects of his life which have been of importance to him, one petal of which is Manhattan. At the flower's center is a woman who advises him to admit that the city has power even if he has no part in it: "She it was put me straight/ about the city" (CEP, 237). In "Young Love" Williams's thoughts of Manhattan are irrevocably tied up with remembrances of an unsatisfactory affair with "Miss Margaret Jarvis,"

> But I merely
> caressed you curiously
> fifteen years ago and you still
> go about the city, they say
> patching up sick school children [CEP, 255]

Likewise, in "A Marriage Ritual" a similar, if happier, connection is made:

> and my heart goes out to it [the city]
> dumbly—
>
> but eloquently in
> my own breast for you whom I love
> —and cannot express what
> my love is, how it varies, though
> I waste it— [CEP, 447]

Williams acknowledges that the city affects him even when
he is not able to comprehend or possess it. Leslie Fiedler
suggests that Whitman, Williams, and Ginsberg "are bounded
by a small circle . . . their imaginations made in the world
defined by the shadow which New York City casts one way
toward New Jersey, the other toward Long Island."[49] And
Kenneth Burke observes that

> when the sun rises behind "the moody/water-loving giants of
> Manhattan," eight miles to the east, they must cast their shadows
> for a time on the houses west of the Meadows. And in any case the
> troublous monsters at a distance, magical in the morning or
> evening mist, did unquestionably cast their shadows on his work.[50]

Williams himself confesses:

> For years I've been tormented by
> that miracle, the buildings all lit up—
>
> unable to say anything much to the point
> though it is the major sight
>
> of this region [CEP, 238]

In "The Flower" he proclaims that "Nothing/of it [the city] is
mine, but visibly/for all that it is petal of a flower—my own"
(CEP, 236). A similar metaphor is found in a later poem:

> This is my own! a flower,
> a fruit, an animal by itself—
>
> It does not recognize me
> and never will. Still, it is my own
> and my heart goes out to it
> dumbly— [CEP, 447]

In "Conquest" the poet becomes the creator of his environment. It is only through this function that the city can finally be his:

> Lie there, blue city, mine at last—
> rimming the banked blue-grey
> and rise, indescribable smoky-yellow
> into the overpowering white! [CEP, 172]

Paterson is clearly Williams's most ambitious attempt to possess, conceive, and discover his environment. *In the American Grain* was his first attempt, as he wrote to Horace Gregory in 1939:

> Let me begin by telling you something of how I came to write the book. Of mixed ancestry, I felt from earliest childhood that America was the only home I could ever possibly call my own. I felt that it was expressly founded for me, personally, and that it must be my first business in life to possess it; that only by making it my own from the beginning to my own day, in detail, should I ever have a basis for knowing where I stood. [SL, 185]

Gradually Williams developed the image of a man who is a city which was "large enough to embody the whole knowable world" (AUTO, 391) about him and this image led to *Paterson*.

3

Turning to an investigation of the city as a motif in *Paterson*, we find that every concept and attitude in his shorter city poems appears, in one form or another, in Williams's long poem as well. A few of these correspondences will be noted in order to establish, to some degree, the conceptual presence of the city in *Paterson*, which, as we have seen, has been challenged several times.

According to the unpublished worksheets of *Paterson* in Buffalo, the poem was originally to begin with a conversation between "Doc" and "Willie," who, we are told, is really Paterson: "The Doc called everyone Willie when he was drunk." They begin to talk about David Hower, an unemployed shoemaker with a large family, and Willie comments, "There's your economic thesis" (BUFFALO). Although Williams eventually dropped this dramatic structure, he kept the thesis: Paterson owes its existence as a city solely to its ability to produce wealth—"the mills had drawn a heterogeneous population" (I, i, 19):

> Even during the Revolution Hamilton had been impressed by the site of the Great Falls of the Passaic. His fertile imagination envisioned a great manufacturing center, a great Federal City, to supply the needs of the country. Here was water-power to turn the mill wheels and the navigable river to carry manufactured goods to the market centers: a national manufactury. [II, ii, 87]

In Book IV Phyllis writes to her father living in the small town of Ramapo: "I'm having a fine time in the Big City as a Professional Woman, ahem! Believe me there's plenty of money here—if you can get it" (IV, i, 178). Ramapo is shown to be an economically as well as spiritually impoverished area which explains why Phyllis left:

> Look, Big Shot, I refuse to come home until you promise to cut out the booze. . . . Maybe your family did once own the whole valley. Who owns it now? What you need is to be slapped down. . . . With your brains and ability this [city life] should be your meat. But you'd rather hit the bottle. [IV, i, 178]

Paterson is the embodiment of a "secondary culture," a culture in which all things are divorced from their origins:

                    a bud forever green
          tight-curled, upon the pavement, perfect
          in juice and substance but divorced, divorced
          from its fellows, fallen low—

                              Divorce is
          the sign of knowledge in our time,
          divorce! divorce! [I, ii, 28]

The Patersonians do not know the "sources nor the sills of
their/disappointments" (I, i, 14), nor do they know how to
inhabit their own bodies. Man is divorced from woman and
from the insistence of place. Universities are divorced from
knowledge and even nature suffers from dislocation:

          —flowers uprooted, columbine, yellow and red,
          strewn upon the path; dogwoods in full flower,
          the trees dismembered; its women
          shallow, its men steadfastly refusing—at
          the best   . [II, iii, 100]

Corydon comments similarly on New York City:

                    —and then
          the three rocks tapering off into the water.
          all that's left of the elemental, the primitive
          in this environment. I call them my sheep. [IV, i, 180]

On another worksheet for *Paterson*, dated May 22, 1942 and
entitled "Library," is typed

     The wheel turns. Within a comparative few years the entire
     character of the country altered. The ethnologic and social changes
     of the region may be summarized as follows, dramatic in its
     implications.

A catalogue of Indian names follows—"Every name described
the locality to which it was affixed:"

Assenmaykapuck—place of the big rock
Assenmaykapulig—pure Big Rock Spring
Moonachie—the place of the ground hog
Ompsk—the standing or upright rocks
Perrymus—the place of the Wild Turkeys [BUFFALO]

Williams associates the advent of a "secondary culture" with
the debasement of language, the separation of words from
things, and consequently the unreal language of the city is a
predominant theme in *Paterson:* "—the language/is divorced
from their minds" (I, i, 21); "The word had been drained of its
meaning" (I, i, 27); "The terms/foreign, conveying no immediacy" (II, iii, 102). Williams apparently agrees with Pound that
financial practices and the language arts are the most useful
referents for determining the health of a society. The effect of
polis on language does not escape Spengler either:

> Rootless, dead to the cosmic, irrevocably committed to stone
> and to intellectualism, it develops a form-language that reproduces
> every trait of its essence—not the language of a becoming and
> growth, but that of a become-ness and completion, capable of
> alteration certainly, but not of evolution. Not now Destiny, but
> Causality, not now living Direction, but Extension, rules.[51]

Similarly in Wordsworth's London "the whole creative powers
of man" are asleep and poetry cannot be written because love
cannot "thrive with ease/Among the close and overcrowded
haunts/Of cities, where the human heart is sick,/and the eye
feeds it not, and cannot feed."[52] In *Paterson* there is

> A voice calling in the hubbub (Why else
> are there newspapers, by the cart-load?) blaring
> the news no wit shall evade, no rhyme
> cover. Necessity gripping the words .   scouting
> evasion, that love is begrimed, befouled   . [IV, i, 194]

In a number of the prose pieces in Books I and II we are
given the background for usury which makes the "Difference

between squalor of spreading slums/and splendor of renaissance cities" (III, ii, 218). Among these are the Notch Brook
pearls incident—"A large round pearl, weighing 400 grains
which would have been the finest pearl of modern times, was
ruined by boiling open the shell" (I, i, 17). Money is also a
corruptive influence upon the churches: "Cash is mulct of them
that others may live/secure" (II, ii, 78), and Billy Sunday, the
evangelist, is one of the most flagrant abusers of his position:

> —getting his 27 Grand in the hotel room
> after the last supper (at the *Hamilton*)
> on the eve of quitting town, exhausted
> in his efforts to split (a split
> personality)   the plate [IV, ii, 203]

The reference to the "last supper" brings to mind Judas's
betrayal. John Johnson is a specific example of a man who even
kills for money. The Federal Reserve System on the national
level, and the Society for Useful Manufacturers on the local
level, are primarily institutions of usury. In Book IV there is a
vision of a megalopolis created by the lust for filthy lucre:

> while in the tall
> buildings (sliding up and down) is where
> the money's made
>   up and down
>   directed missiles
> in the greased shafts of the tall buildings.
>   [IV, i, 195]

The synthetic culture of the city is also emphasized—"a
comb and nail-file/in an imitation leather case" (I, iii, 49),
"Plaster saints, glass jewels/. . . paper flowers" (I, iii, 51). The
city discourages natural, spontaneous experience, the most
striking example of which is the scene in the park where rural
vitality survives amidst urban indifference:

                         The big guy
in the black hat is too full to move   .
                              but Mary
   is up!
            Come on! Wassa ma'? You got
   broken leg? . . .

        —lifts one arm holding the cymbals
   of her thoughts, cocks her old head
   and dances! raising her skirts [II, i, 73]

Williams juxtaposes this scene with thoughts of a peon in an old
Eisenstein film drinking with abandon from a wineskin. Like
Mary, the film was "suppressed   :   but . persistent" (II, i,
74). The following is Williams's interpretation of the scene,
found in his worksheets:

   The old living still, the old! Not a painting
   but living, all needed being recognition
   waking! and the old lives, is here—
   outmoded but alive. The new harder, colder—
   but the old still lives, here [BUFFALO]

The city encompasses time past and time present not only in its
architectural structures but also in its very inhabitants. The
citizens of Paterson are generally depicted as aimless, indifferent, lazy, bored, amnesiac. The park is merely an unsatisfactory substitute for the countryside: "At nine o'clock the park
closes. You/must be out of the lake, dressed, in/your cars and
going" (II, iii, 98), and there are "NO DOGS ALLOWED AT
LARGE IN THIS PARK" (II, i, 77).
   Spengler's concept of a "metaphysical turn towards death"
also pervades the poem in the form of Mrs. Cumming's fall,
Sam Patch's leap (see Chap. 5B.) and Paterson's thoughts:

   The thought returns: Why have I not
   but for imagined beauty where there is none
   or none available, long since
   put myself deliberately in the way of death? [I, ii, 30–31]

In Book IV a student commits suicide in New York:

>   pressed together
>   talking excitedly   .   of the next sandwich
>   reading, from one hand, of some student, come
>   waterlogged to the surface following
>   last night's thunderstorm   . [IV, i, 196]

The Library in Book II has "a smell of its own/of stagnation and death" (III, i, 123) while the Patersonians possess "the indifference of certain death/or incident upon certain death" (III, i, 129).

It would, of course, be possible to multiply these correspondences and references; however, this would undoubtedly lead to the type of thematic criticism of which we already have an abundance. Our inquiry into the city in Williams's shorter poems as well as in *Paterson* has accomplished two main functions. In the first place, we have shown that Williams did indeed know what a city is and that, in fact, he had been intimately concerned with the city throughout his poetic career. We have also seen that not only is Paterson "representative of modern America," it has much in common with cities throughout the world. Secondly, our investigation into the city has brought to the surface many of the material themes of the poem such as usury, divorce, and language, without the necessity of resorting to the isolation of each theme from its context. The themes have emerged *ex post facto*, as it were, from our discussion of a larger element of the poem. This fact substantiates how exactly right Williams was to use a city as the major focal point of his long poem. Even an objective, literal examination of the concept of the city as it emerges in *Paterson* reveals the relevance of Williams's minor thematic preoccupations. As we shall see, however, the essence of *Paterson* can never be captured by strictly conceptual methods:

> There is a fallacy in always insisting that poetry shall "mean" what some little stinker thinks it should. . . . What is sorely

needed is poetic construction, ability in among the words, to
invent there, to make, to make well and new. [SL, 219]

Among Williams's worksheets for *Paterson* is a letter to "Ken"
dated 2/5/47. "Ken" is presumably Kenneth Burke as the
letter begins with the statement—"Your difficulties (as
philosopher) begin where mine (as poet) end." The letter
continues, "Of course there is meaning (I myself often forget
that) but in a poem (when alive & not fossilized) it lies in the
structure or at least it is *in*structed by the fact of the poem itself
as a structure" (BUFFALO). Reestablishment of the provincial
is a matter of idiom and structure as well as of idea.

4

Before leaving our discussion of the conceptual presence of
the city in *Paterson*, a word or two might well be said in
reference to Williams's general choice of subject matter for the
poem, not only because he has been repeatedly attacked for his
"insularity" and because an understanding of his firm belief
that the local is the only universal is absolutely vital to an
appreciation of his poetry, but also because the content of any
poem inevitably affects its form. As Denise Levertov asserts, "I
believe content determines form, and yet that content is
discovered only *in* form. Like everything living, it is a mystery."[53] Unfortunately, it is precisely this aspect of Williams's
theory that has been the most widely misunderstood. In
Chapter 1 it was noted that Williams himself was partly
responsible for the so-called Eliot/Williams controversy.
Eventually, however, Williams was able to admit that he did
indeed admire the *Four Quartets* and John Thirlwall suggests
that "not only 'The Wasteland' [*sic*] but the 'Four Quartettes'
[*sic*] give him not only pleasure but profit."[54] As this apparent
reversal indicates, Williams was rather prone to exaggeration
in his critical statements, particularly in the early years when
he was almost singlehandedly engaged in an attempt at reviv-

ing Whitman's influence and waging a war against what he considered to be the foreign and intellectual pursuits of Eliot and Pound. Williams wrote to Marianne Moore that "each must free himself from the bonds of banality as best he can. . . . I, being perhaps more timid or unstable at heart, must free myself by more violent methods. . . . And so I have made the mistake of abusing the very thing [rhetoric] I most use" (SL, 52). Likewise, Williams's theory of the local has been continually misunderstood because of his own misleading insistences. As Burke comments,

> it [doctrine of contact] seemed to imply the problematical proposi-
> tion that one should live in a small town like Rutherford rather than
> in the very heart of Babylon (or in some area that, if not central to
> the grass roots of the nation, was at least close to the ragweed).[55]

At times, however, Williams does make his meaning clear, as when he admits that any city, such as Leipzig, Paris, Vienna, or even Frascati, could as readily have been the city in his long poem.
In 1932 he wrote the following to Marianne Moore after reading some of her poems:

> And to me especially you give a sense of triumph in that it is my
> own scene without mistaking the local for the parochial. Almost no
> one (or very few) has felt the full and conclusive impact of that
> necessity in the writing. The meaning of the objective, the
> realization of its releasing quality, instead of its walling effect when
> badly comprehended, has been nowhere so well forced to the light.
> It is the underlying reality as well as the supreme difficulty of an
> art. [SL, 123]

More light is shed on this aspect of Williams's theory when a comparison is made between his theory and that of the Anglo-Welsh poet David Jones. Although at first such a comparison might appear rather bizarre, quite the contrary is the case. Such a comparison also carries with it the added

advantage of establishing that Williams was not so narrow
minded and dogmatic as might superficially be supposed. In a
letter to Pound dated April 12, 1954, Williams writes:

> What you want is something to help break down the barriers to
> ignorance. There's a Welsh poet named Jones to whom we have
> just given, by we I mean the National Institute of Arts and Letters,
> the Loines award. It's a poem. Believe me, if you want something
> tough but rewarding, tackle that. [SL, 325]

The poem Williams is undoubtedly referring to is David Jones'
The Anathemata, for which he was presented the Russell
Loines Memorial Award for Poetry in 1954. It is interesting
(though hardly consequential) to note that *The Anathemata* was
written between the years 1946 and 1951—the same span of
years also witnessed the emergence of the first four books of
Paterson in the United States. In his preface to the poem Jones
explains that "part of my task has been to allow myself to be
directed by motifs gathered together from such sources as have
by accident been available to me and to make out of those
mixed data."[56] Similarly, in his Introduction to "The Wedge,"
Williams states:

> All that an artist or a Sperry can do is to drive toward his purpose,
> in the nature of his materials; not to take gold where Babbit metal is
> called for; to make: make clear the complexity of his perceptions in
> the medium given to him by inheritance, chance, accident or
> whatever it may be to work with according to his talents and the
> will that drives them. [CLP, 4]

Despite the wide gulf between the deposits known to Jones and
those known to Williams, *The Anathemata* and *Paterson*
represent a similar attempt: both poets are trying to make a
shape out of the things of which they are made. Jones refers to
the "necessarily insular" character of his writing, and so it is
with Williams. Jones maintains that only what is actually loved
and known can be seen *sub specie aeternitatis*, which is to say

that the local is the only universal: "(For men can but proceed from what they know, nor is it for/the mind of this flesh to practice poiesis, *ex nihilo*.)."[57]

NOTES TO CHAPTER 2

1. Northrop Frye, *Anatomy of Criticism*, (Princeton, N.J.: Princeton University Press, 1971), p. 318.

2. Sister Macaria Neussendorfer's article "WCW's Idea of a City," *Thought* 40 (Summer 1965): 242–74, is the only inquiry into this aspect of *Paterson* to date. Despite the astuteness of much of her discussion, she still leaves considerable territory unexplored.

3. Charles Olson, *Mayan Letters*, ed. Robert Creeley (London: Cape Editions, 1968), p. 30.

4. "Robert Creeley in Conversation with Charles Tomlinson," *The Review* 10 (January 1964): 27.

5. "One Man's River," anon. rev., *Times Literary Supplement* 263, no. 3 (September 10, 1964): 842.

6. David Weimer, *The City as Metaphor* (New York: Random House, 1966), p. 118.

7. Ibid., p. 119.

8. Cf. "The Men," CEP, p. 459.

9. Mircea Eliade, *Patterns in Comparative Religion*, trans. Rosemary Sheed (Cleveland: The World Pub. Co., 1963), p. 399. Also see p. 379: "The creation of the world is the exemplar for all constructions. Every new town, every new house that is built, imitates afresh, and in a sense repeats, the creation of the world. Indeed, every town, every dwelling stands at the 'centre of the world', so that its construction was only possible by means of abolishing profane space and time and establishing sacred space and time."

10. Cf. Ezra Pound, "Dr. Williams' Position" in *WCW: A Collection of Critical Essays*, ed. J. Hillis Miller, (Englewood Cliffs, N.J.: Prentice-Hall, 1966), p. 33, where Pound comments upon the two poetic traditions of which we spoke in Chapter 1: "Art very possibly *ought* to be the supreme achievement, the 'accomplished'; but there is the other satisfactory effect, that of a man hurling himself at an indomitable chaos, and yanking and hauling as much of it as possible into some sort of order (or beauty), aware of it both as chaos and as potential."

11. J. Hillis Miller, *Poets of Reality* (Cambridge: Harvard University Press, 1965), p. 288.

12. Samuel Johnson, *History of Rasselas* (Oxford: Clarendon Press, 1927), p. 62.

13. John C. Thirlwall, "WCW as Correspondent," *The Literary Review* 1 (Autumn 1957): 19.

14. John C. Thirlwall, "WCW's *Paterson*," *New Directions in Prose and Poetry 17* (Norfolk, Conn.: New Directions, 1961), p. 308.

15. Koehler, "The Art of Poetry VI: WCW," *The Paris Review* 8, no. 32 (Summer-Fall 1964): 130.

16. Thirlwall, "WCW's *Paterson*," p. 263.

17. Cf. Lewis Mumford, *The City in History* (New York: Harcourt, Brace & World, 1961), p. 9: "Two of the three original aspects of temporary settlement have to do with sacred things, not just with physical survival: they relate to a more valuable and meaningful kind of life, with a consciousness that entertains past and future, apprehending the primal mystery of sexual generation and the ultimate mystery of death and what may lie beyond death." In "WCW's Idea of a City" Sister Macaria Neussendorfer comments that the city has always had "a significance beyond the mere sum of dwelling places gathered for security and convenience" (p. 248).

18. Thirlwall, "WCW's *Paterson*," p. 308.

19. Jack Spicer, "Letter to Lorca," in *The New American Poetry*, ed. Donald Allen (New York: Grove Press, 1960), pp. 413–14 (italics mine). Also cf. Eliade, *Patterns in Comparative Religion*, p. 369: "In actual fact, the place is never 'chosen' by man; it is merely discovered by him; in other words, the sacred place in some way or another reveals itself to him."

20. William Carlos Williams, "In Praise of Marriage," *Quarterly Review of Literature* 2, no. 2 (1944): 145.

21. Oswald Spengler, *The Decline of the West*, trans. Charles Francis Atkinson (New York: Alfred A. Knopf, 1947), 2: 98–99.

22. Thirlwall, "WCW's *Paterson*," p. 282.

23. Weimer, *The City as Metaphor*, p. 121.

24. Spengler, *The Decline of the West*, p. 94.

25. See Chapter 5 for a discussion of the distinction between the "material" and "dominant" themes of *Paterson*.

26. Mumford, *The City in History*, p. 54.

27. Spengler, *The Decline of the West*, p. 98.

28. Walt Whitman, "Democratic Vistas," in *The Collected Writings of Walt Whitman: Prose Works 1892* (New York: New York Univ. Press, 1964), 2:370.

29. Whitman, "Democratic Vistas," p. 372.

30. Spengler, *The Decline of the West*, p. 103.

31. Mumford, *The City in History*, p. 54.

32. Whitman, "Democratic Vistas," p. 371.

33. Mumford, *The City in History*, p. 113.

34. Ibid., p. 98.

35. Marshall McLuhan, *From Cliché to Archetype* (New York: Pocket Books, 1971), p. 20.

36. Thirlwall, "WCW's *Paterson*," p. 307.

37. Spengler, *The Decline of the West*, p. 99.

38. Mumford, *The City in History*, p. 110.

39. Whitman, "Democratic Vistas," p. 371.

40. *Walt Whitman of the New York Aurora*, ed. Joseph Jay Rubin and Charles H. Brown (Pennsylvania: Bald Eagle Press, 1950), p. 19.

41. Whitman, "Song of the Open Road," in *Leaves of Grass* (New York: New American Library, 1958), p. 143.

42. See Eliade, *Patterns in Comparative Religion,* p. 13: "Everything unusual, unique, new, perfect or monstrous at once becomes imbued with magico-religious powers and an object of veneration or fear according to the circumstances (for the sacred usually produces this double reaction)."

43. Weimer, *The City as Metaphor,* p. 109.

44. Ostrom, *The Poetic World of WCW* (Carbondale, Ill.: Southern Illinois University Press, 1966), p. 90.

45. Thirlwall, "WCW's *Paterson,*" p. 257.

46. Thirlwall, p. 258. Guimond suggests that Williams deleted a number of lines "when he realized that the old woman symbolized his grandmother" (*The Art of WCW,* p. 14, n. 19). This is unlikely as there is sufficient suggestion in the remaining lines to make the meaning clear.

47. Guimond, *The Art of WCW,* p. 17.

48. Weimer, *The City as Metaphor,* p. 109.

49. Leslie Fiedler, *Waiting for the End* (New York: Stein and Day, 1964), p. 241.

50. Burke, "WCW: Two Judgments," in *WCW,* ed. Miller, p. 55.

51. Spengler, *The Decline of the West,* p. 107.

52. Quoted in Guimond, *The Art of WCW,* p. 20.

53. Denise Levertov, "Statements on Poetics," in *The New American Poetry,* ed. Allen, p. 412.

54. Thirlwall, "WCW's *Paterson,*" p. 298, n. 17.

55. Burke, "WCW: Two Judgments," in *WCW,* ed. Miller, p. 52.

56. David Jones, *The Anathemata* (London: Faber & Faber, 1955), p. 9.

57. Ibid., p. 79.

3 The Man/City

1

Having dealt with the concept of the city in *Paterson,* our attention may now be turned more profitably to the major image in the poem—"that a man in himself is a city." This image first appears in Williams's 1926 poem "Paterson" on which he "based the later and more extended poem" (AUTO, 243). In fact, more than half of the lines of this poem are used verbatim in *Paterson I.* The image next occurs in *The Broken Span* (1941), which includes a section entitled "For the Poem Patterson" [*sic*] prefaced by the following lines:

> A man like a city and a woman like a flower—who are in love. Two women. Three women. Innumerable women, each like a flower. But only one man—like a city.[1]

These words are written in Williams's handwriting on an unpublished *Paterson* worksheet to be found in Buffalo (see facsimile 1, frontispiece). They obviously provided a source of inspiration for his long poem and appropriately found their way into *Paterson I* in a slightly different form (I, i, 15). In "A Marriage Ritual," written in 1928 and also found in *The Broken Span,* there is a metaphorical use of the particulars of a landscape to reflect the poet's psychic state:

                    It is
        a river flowing through refuse
        the dried sticks of weeds
        and falling shell-ice lilac
        from above as if with thoughts
        of you—

        This is my face and its moods
        my moods, a riffled whiteness
        shaken by the flow
        that's constant in its swiftness
        as a pool—[CEP, 447]

Vivienne Koch finds this poem "interesting chiefly as a pre-
liminary exercise of the later *Paterson* theme."[2] *Paterson* is
further foreshadowed in "A Sort of a Song:"

            —through metaphor to reconcile
            the people and the stones.
            Compose. (No ideas
            but in things) Invent!
            Saxifrage is my flower that splits
            the rocks. [CLP, 7]

Not only is the phrase "No ideas/but in things" first found in
this poem, the lines "—through metaphor to reconcile/the
people and the stones," prefigure many of Williams's later
statements in reference to the method of *Paterson*. As he wrote
on a rough draft for the poem, "The poet's weapon is
metaphore [*sic*]/his strength is marriage. Marry us, the/
stream cries. Marry us, give us blood" (BUFFALO).

An examination of Williams's writing even apart from *Paterson* brings to light numerous images in which the poet enters
into sympathy with his environment:

    The inevitable flux of the seeing eye toward measuring itself by
    the world it inhabits can only result in himself crushing humiliation
    unless the individual raise to some approximate co-extension with
    the universe [*sic*]. This is possible by aid of the imagination. Only

through the agency of this force can a man feel himself moved largely with sympathetic pulses at work—[IMAG, 105]

At times Williams internalizes his surroundings to the extent that he experiences its facts as his flesh; his body becomes the universe. Williams contends that poets should be "possessors of knowledge in the flesh as opposed to a body of knowledge called science or philosophy" (SL, 137). In his book of prose poems *Kora in Hell* he states that "a thing known passes out of the mind into the muscles." (KORA, 71). In his short essay on "How to Write" he claims that poets

> are in touch with "voices," but this is the very essence of their power, the voices are the past, the depths of our very beings. It is the deeper, not "lower" (in the usually silly sense) portions of the personality speaking, the middle brain, the nerves, the glands, the very muscles and bones of the body itself speaking.[3]

We shall refer to those images in which Williams sympathizes with, identifies with, or internalizes his environment as images of empathy. "Empathy" is defined by the *OED* as "the power of entering into the experience of or understanding objects or emotions outside ourselves." Our use of the term "empathy" is appropriate, for extreme empathy leads to identification and finally to an apprehension of the profound unity of existence. According to Gaston Bachelard in his study of the phenomenology of the poetic image, *The Poetics of Space*, "Grandeur progresses in the world in proportion to the deepening of intimacy"[4]; Williams's doctrine of contact is the necessary basis for his "co-extension with the universe." Despite the large number of Williams's poems which are often read simply as vignettes of objective description,[5] the images of empathy which we are about to consider testify to the fact that "there is *something else* to be expressed besides what is offered for objective description. What should be expressed is hidden grandeur, depth."[6] Williams observes in *The Great American Novel* that "men and women cannot be content, any more than

children, with the mere facts of a humdrum life—the imagination must adorn and exaggerate life, must give it splendor and
grotesqueness, beauty and infinite depth" (IMAG, 200), and in
his prose to *Spring and All* he writes that "imagination is not to
avoid reality, nor is it description nor an evocation of objects or
situations, it is to say that poetry does not tamper with the
world but moves it" (IMAG, 149).

In Williams's 1914 poem "The Wanderer" the poet witnesses the brutality which is the result of a labor strike and
exclaims, "But in me, more sensitive, marvelous old queen/It
sank deep into the blood" (CEP, 7). Here, in the earliest poem
which he wished to preserve, Williams experiences an objective situation in physical terms. In the following section of the
poem the old queen, who is identified with his poetic unconscious as well as with his environment, charges him to "speak
to men of these, concerning me!" and Williams then shouts to
the inhabitants of the country,

> "Waken! my people, to the boughs green
> With ripening fruit within you!
> Waken to the myriad cinquefoil
> In the waving grass of your minds!
> Waken to the silent phoebe nest
> Under the eaves of your spirit!" [CEP, 8]

Here it is his poetic unconscious which prompts him to waken
the masses to the boughs, fruit, flowers, grass, and nests which
are in them. In this poem the young Williams is discovering
one of his proper functions as a poet. As Bachelard contends,
"Poets will help us to discover within ourselves such joy in
looking that sometimes, in the presence of a perfectly familiar
object, we experience an extension of our intimate space."[7] At
the end of "The Wanderer" the poet becomes one with the
filthy Passaic river: "And I knew all—it became me" (CEP, 12).
In a considerably later poem, Williams employs a similar
image:

Sometimes the river
becomes a river in the mind
or of the mind
or in and of the mind

Its banks snow
the tide falling a dark
rim lies between
the water and the shore

And the mind hesitant
regarding the stream
senses
a likeness which it

will find—a complex
image: something
of white brows
bound by a ribbon

of sooty thought [CLP, 118]

Here the poet simultaneously internalizes the river ("the river/becomes a river in the mind") and creates it ("or of the mind"). Williams writes in the prose to *Spring and All* that "taught by the largeness of his imagination to feel every form which he sees moving within himself, he [the poet] must prove the truth of this by expression" (IMAG, 105).

In "A Morning Imagination of Russia" Williams's persona is in perfect harmony with nature because he has "gotten—touch" (CEP, 308):

When the sun rose it rose in his heart
It bathed the red cold world of
the dawn so that the chill was his own [CEP, 305]

He begins to feel that "the world was himself" (CEP, 306). Similarly, in "Notes in Diary Form" the protagonist is naturalized: "And an oak tree grows out of my shoulders. Its roots are my arms and my legs" (SE, 63). In *Kora in Hell* Williams states that "I confess freely there's not a bitch littered in the pound but my skin grows ruddier" (KORA, 20) and in the poem "Every Day" he empathizes with a rose:

> But it is a rose, rose
> pink. One can feel it turning slowly
> upon its thorny stem [CLP, 147]

Bachelard, in reference to similar images, comments that "Such images . . . must be taken, at the least, in their existence as a *reality of expression*. For they owe their entire being to poetic expression, and this being would be diminished if we tried to refer them to a reality, even to a psychological reality."[8] In Williams's novel *A Voyage to Pagany* (1928) the night becomes the body of the poet: "It is ourselves—And he felt that his body extended to the horizon. . . . The night is the body of someone else. Into which we have come."[9] Perhaps the most striking of Williams's images of empathy is found in his late love poem, "Asphodel, that Greeny Flower:"

> Every drill
>   driven into the earth
> for oil enters my side
>   also. [PG, 168]

Williams also sympathizes with and at times identifies himself with the inhabitants of his environment, to which his numerous "portrait" poems testify. He also assumes, as did Whitman before him, that "in the imagination, we are from henceforth (so long as you read) locked in a fraternal embrace, the classic caress of author and reader. We are one. Whenever I say 'I' I mean also, 'you.' And so, together, as one, we shall begin" (IMAG, 89). In a chapter on Williams in *The Incarnate Word* Cary Nelson observes that "Williams . . . pulls us down to his page, his white field, where we *do* something together."[10] In this way the reader becomes the poet: "In the resonance we hear the poem, in the reverberations we speak it, it is our own. The reverberations bring about a change of being. It is as though the poet's being were our being."[11] In *The Great American Novel,*

> his great heart had expanded so as to include the whole city, every woman young and old there he having impregnated with sons and daughters [*sic*]. For everyone loved him. And he knew how to look into their eyes with both passion and understanding. [IMAG, 198]

In his 1926 "Paterson" poem, the poet asks, "But who! who are these people?" and the poem continues, "It is/his flesh making the traffic, cranking the car/buying the meat—" (CEP, 234). Williams believed that Shakespeare, above all others, possessed this ability to empathize and identify:

> Shakespeare had that mean ability to fuse himself with everyone which nobodies have, to be anything at any time, fluid, a nameless fellow whom nobody noticed—much, and *that* is what made him the great dramatist. . . . When he speaks of fools he is one; when of kings he is one, doubly so in misfortune. He is a woman, a pimp, a prince Hal—. [IMAG, 253, 258]

In light of the fact that Keats was an early mentor of Williams (see Chap. 1), it is interesting to note that in a letter to Richard Woodhouse, he expresses a similar point of view:

> The poetical Character . . . is not itself—it has no self—it is every thing and nothing—It has no character—it enjoys light and shade; it lives in gusto, be it foul or fair, high or low, rich or poor, mean or elevated—It has as much delight in conceiving an Iago as an Imogen.[12]

2

Since images of empathy can be found in Williams's writing throughout his career, from "The Wanderer" to "Asphodel," it is not at all surprising, therefore, that the crisis to which

Northrop Frye referred (see epigraph to Chapter 2) was reached in Williams's "metaphysical conception" (IWW, 81) of a man identified with a city. On a Yale worksheet for *Paterson* Williams writes that

> the birth and life of a city is likened in many respects with the birth, infancy, growth and development of a human being. First the period of infancy, when it knew no recognition from the outside world, but was confined to a little world of its own. [YALE]

The frequency and the dispersion of images of empathy further refute those critics who consider *Paterson* to be a radical departure from Williams's customary poetic preoccupations. We have seen that Williams's intention was to find in Paterson a "world-city," and that his concept of the city in general and of Paterson in particular encompasses all the essential aspects of his contemporary environment—the city is a world in miniature. The man/city image becomes, by extension, the image of a man who is the world: *pars pro tota. Paterson* is, in fact, Williams's most ambitious attempt both to internalize his environment and to externalize his imagination in terms of a verbal structure. In *Kora in Hell* Williams wishes that he could "stand . . . where the largest town might be taken in my two hands." (KORA, 77), and in his *Autobiography* Paterson is described by a friend as "something you could visualize so distinctly, practically hold it in the hollow of your hand" (AUTO, 393). Bachelard writes that "the cleverer I am at miniaturizing the world, the better I possess it. . . . One must go beyond logic in order to experience what is large in what is small."[13] *Paterson* is also an attempt to provide that which Whitman calls for in his "Democratic Vistas":

> America demands a poetry that is bold, modern, and all-surrounding and Kosmical, as she is herself. . . . America needs, and the world needs, a class of bards who will, now and ever, so link and tally the rational physical being of man, with the ensembles of time and space, and with this vast and multiform show, Nature,

surrounding him, ever tantalising him, equally a part, and yet not a part of him, as to essentially harmonize, satisfy, and put at rest.[14]

The image of a man who is a city is not, by any means, new. This image has, in fact, what might be called "historical" and "political" precedents as well as the more obvious mythological and literary ones. Lewis Mumford maintains that at the very origin of the city in history there was an identity between the king and the community. The king was considered to be the representative of a god and therefore the sacred powers of the god were transferred to his own person. Because the welfare of the community was dependent on divine favor, the king, as god's representative, became essentially equated with the existence of the community:

> The king gathered to himself extraordinary sacred powers; he not only incarnated the community, but by his very assumptions held its fate in his hands. . . . With the rise of the city the king incarnated a new idea of human development, and the city became nothing less than the corporate embodiment of this evolving idea. One by one, the privileges and prerogatives of kingship were transferred to the city, and its citizens.[15]

From its very beginnings, the city was a body through which the mind of the king expressed itself. In *Paterson V* Paterson refers to himself as "the king-self" (V, iii, 272), and when *Paterson III* was published in 1949 Williams explained his conception of the poem:

> I began thinking of writing a long poem upon the resemblance between the mind of modern man and a city. The thing was to use the multiple facets which a city presented as representative for comparable facets of contemporary thought, thus to be able to objectify the man himself as we know him and love him and hate him.[16]

For the proem to Book III Williams uses a passage from

Santayana's *The Last Puritan* to elucidate the connection between the mind, and its second body, the city:

> Cities, for Oliver, were not a part of nature. He could hardly feel, he could hardly admit even when it was pointed out to him, that cities are a second body for the human mind, a second organism, more rational, permanent and decorative than the animal organism of flesh and bone: a work of natural yet moral art, where the soul sets up her trophies of action and instruments of pleasure. [III, i, 116]

Our human bodies are a diagram of the functions of inhabiting our environment because of the build up of reflexes and organic habits and, as Cary Nelson observes, "The body which ripens and decays is the space where temporal events are truly simultaneous."[17] The city, too, is a diagram of our inhabitation of the world in the past and in the present. Both are "our bodies, which do not forget."[18] Mumford points out that

> The city, as Emerson well observed, "lives by remembering." . . . Within the historic precincts of the city time clashes with time: time challenges time. Because the structures of the city outlast the functions and purposes that originally molded them, the city sometimes preserves for the future ideas that have been wantonly discarded or rejected by an earlier generation; but, on the debit side, it transmits to later generations maladaptations that might have been cast off, if they had not materialized in the city and left their imprint there—just as the body itself transmits as a scar or a recurrent rash some painful long-past injury or disorder.[19]

There is also a notable correspondence between the man/city image and the "body politic." For example, in *Titus Andronicus* Shakespeare images civil strife as dismemberment:

> Oh, let me teach you how to knit again
> This scattered corn into one mutual sheaf,
> These broken limbs again into one body;[20]

Paterson, whose very name contains within it father and son, is one man and yet all men, and thus analogous to the concept of representation in politics which is the essence of social contract. Thomas Hobbes describes a commonwealth or state as a great Leviathan, an "Artificiall Man" with a soul, joints, nerves, etc., and he maintains that "the *Pacts* and *Covenants*, by which the parts of this Body Politique were at first made, set together, and united, resemble that *Fiat*, or the *Let us make man*, pronounced by God in the Creation."[21] A body politic is created when "A Multitude of men, are made *One* Person, when they are by one man, or one Person, Represented. . . . For it is the *Unity* of the Representer, not the *Unity* of the Represented, that maketh the Person *One*."[22] Coleridge also maintains that a state is an idea intermediate between an organic and an inorganic body—" the whole being a result from, and not a mere total of, the parts, and yet not so merging the constituent parts in the result, but that the individual exists integrally within it."[23] This is Paterson: one man and yet all men; one man, and yet a city. The man Paterson is, in Hobbes' words, a person, a persona, "*whose words or actions are considered, either as his own, or as representing the words or actions of an other man, or of any other thing to whom they are attributed, whether Truly or by Fiction.*"[24]

The first reference to the man/city image in the poem can be found in the preface to *Paterson*. This reference is made in the form of a factual statement:

> Yet there is
> no return: rolling up out of chaos,
> a nine months' wonder, the city
> the man, an identity—it can't be
> otherwise—an
> interpenetration, both ways. [I, p. 12]

According to the unpublished manuscripts for the poem, the image was originally to be included in the catalogue which precedes the preface. Williams experimented with various combinations to express the image (one man a city; a man a city; a city as one man [BUFFALO]), and eventually decided against incorporating any of them in the catalogue. The same preoccupation with the form of the explicit expression of the image is also evident in Williams's drafts for the lines from the preface which we have quoted above:

> The city is the man, rolling up knowledge
> is the city fulfilled and it cannot
> be otherwise
> the man the city of equal parts
>
> The end is in the beginning, the city
> in the man as the man, in the city, is
> the city
>
>   and the city lacking knowledge is
> knowledge brought together in one and so
> no one. A man old and young, centirfugal [*sic*]
> in the present phase, one man, he [BUFFALO]

These lines from the rough drafts to the preface finally resolved into the simple statement, "the city/the man, an identity . . ./an interpenetration, both ways," but the discarded lines are of interest because they substantiate the centrality of the relationship of man to city in Williams's long poem; the man/city image was obviously extremely meaningful and important to him in a number of ways. It was not necessary, however, for Williams to say explicitly more than he eventually chose to say in the preface regarding the image because, as we shall see in Chapter 5, its ultimate being and validity can only be established by the poem itself.

Book I of *Paterson*, "The Delineaments of the Giants," begins with an evocation of a male and a female giant. The male is the city of Paterson, who

> lies in the valley under the Passic Falls
> its spent waters forming the outline of his back. He

lies on his right side, head near the thunder
of the waters filling his dreams! Eternally asleep
his dreams walk about the city where he persists
incognito. [I, i, 14]

His female counterpart is the surrounding landscape:

And there, against him, stretches the low mountain.
The Park's her head, carved, above the Falls, by the quiet
river. . . .

                    facing him, his
arm supporting her, by the Valley of the Rocks, asleep.
Pearls at her ankles, her monstrous hair
spangled with apple-blossoms is scattered about into
the back country, waking their dreams—where the deer run
and the wood-duck nests protecting his gallant plumage. [I, i, 17]

In the poem "Paterson: The Falls," which purports to be an
outline for the long poem, Williams refers to the giants as "the
archaic persons of the drama" (CLP, 10). Etymologically, the
first element ἀρχή of "archaic" signifies beginning, origin,
cause, primal source and principle. The giant Paterson is the
"source" and the "sill" of the inhabitants of the city; he is also
the body out of which the city is made.

    The personification of the city as a giant and the country as a
giantess fulfills the role of myth as defined by Northrop Frye:

    A myth is a simple and primitive effort of the imagination to
    identify the human with the non-human world, and its most typical
    result is a story about a god. . . . The containing framework of the
    mythology takes the shape of a feeling of lost identity we had once
    and may have again.[25]

In the beginning of Book I Williams is affirming, through the
use of myth, his apprehension of a lost unity and identity, and
the poem is an attempt to repair the damage caused by
disunity. As Williams asserts, "The brunt of the four books of
Paterson . . . is a search for the redeeming language."[26] To

redeem is to rescue, save, deliver, or "to make good a loss" (*OED*). In *William Carlos Williams et le Renouveau du Lyrisme*, Hélène Dupreyron-Marchessou stresses the reality of myth in *Paterson:*

> Le souffle racque qui anime la "caverne" de Paterson est une manifestation de l'âme primitive, et le poème qui en résulte est, dans une certaine mesure, une actualisation des anciens mythes. Quand le poète a répudié la culture sous la forme d'idées générales, il atteint aux couches les plus profondes de la conscience, là où gisent les sédiments des images primaires qui Jung nomme les "archétypes de l'inconscient collectif.[27]

Williams's use of myth becomes more accessible when a comparison is made with actual recorded myth. Fortunately it is not necessary to resort to an indiscriminate juxtaposition. In Williams's early book of prose poems, *Kora in Hell,* is found the line, "Of Ymir's flesh the earth was made and of his thoughts were all the gloomy clouds created" (KORA, 44). According to Williams's manuscripts for *Paterson,* this line was originally to be included in I, i, placed directly after the first verse paragraph. Although the line was subsequently deleted, it is of use in understanding certain aspects of the poem. In Icelandic mythology it is believed that the physical world was created out of the body of the giant Ymir after his fall: "They [Oðinn and his brothers] made sea and lakes of his blood, earth of his flesh and the sky of his skull. . . . The clouds were made of Ymir's brains."[28] Ymir is thought to be not only the progenitor of all the terrible tribe of giants but also the ancestor of the gods. The world is thus the scattered and broken body of a human giant or god. The giant Paterson is the general myth translated into particular terms. The epigraph to the poem's preface states that "rigor of beauty is the quest. But how will you find beauty/ when it is locked in the mind past all remonstrance?" Williams maintains that " 'beauty' is related not to 'loveliness' but to a state in which reality plays a part" (IMAG, 117). In an early draft of the opening lines of *Paterson* Williams makes his meaning more explicit and also adds an injunction to himself:

> Beauty is the quest and how will you find beauty when it is locked in the mind? It is not in those things unless transfigured by employment. Make it free to live here also, by the art you have, to enter these starved and broken pieces to transform them. [BUF-FALO]

The poem strives to transform the starved and broken pieces of the world, to give them reality, to make the Patersonians aware of their unity in Paterson as well as their unity with the world.

There is also a correspondence between Williams's use of myth and that of William Blake. As Richard Ellman observes, Paterson is "a giant on the order of Blake's Albion."[29] In Blake's mythology, when Albion fell, the unity of the human race was lost. According to Northrop Frye, Blake's central myth is

> that in a perfectly imaginative state all individuals are integral units of a race, species or class, related to it as tissues and cells are to a body. This larger unit is not an abstraction or aggregate, but a larger human body or human being. . . . Whether we see the larger unit as one man or as a multitude of individuals is a matter of perspective.[30]

Perhaps a closer literary comparison is afforded by James Joyce's *Ulysses* and *Finnegans Wake*. In *I Wanted to Write a Poem* Williams told Edith Heal in reference to his original conception of *Paterson* that he "may have been influenced by James Joyce who had made Dublin the hero of his book. I had been reading *Ulysses*. But I forgot about Joyce and fell in love with my city" (IWW, 82). According to a list of correspondences which Joyce gave to Stuart Gilbert in 1938, each episode in *Ulysses* (except the first four) is associated with an organ of the human body and "together these compose the whole body, which is thus a symbol of the structure of *Ulysses*, a living organism, and of the natural interdependence of the parts between themselves."[31] Dublin is, therefore, not simply

the setting for the action but also a giant body, a "hero." As
Hélène Cixous writes in *The Exile of James Joyce* in reference
to *Ulysses*, "Dublin exists, but much more as an animate
object, a giant body, a corporate character, than as a stage."[32]
Sister Bernetta Quinn, Vivienne Koch, and Glauco Cambon
among others assert that *Paterson* also has elements in common with *Finnegans Wake:*

> The conception of Paterson formulated in Book One is that of
> giant lying on his back, asleep in the valley under the Passaic Falls
> like Finnegan laid out for his wake. Paterson is both myth and the
> maker of myth; he is, like Humphrey Chimpden Earwicker, both
> subject and self-creating object. Like HCE in relation to Dublin,
> Paterson's identity shifts and metamorphoses into that of the poet,
> the citizen, and the city. Like HCE he is both a particular and a
> universal and his essential energy is procreative, himself the
> miraculous child of his own imaginings.[33]

Hugh Kenner observes that "the very title is a Joycean pun:
Paterson is a city, a man (sometimes a doctor), and Pater-son,
the molecule of generative succession."[34] Glauco Cambon
suggests that the mythical origins in *Paterson* have "something
to do with Viconian giants."[35] According to *A Skeleton Key to
Finnegans Wake,*

> the comical Finnegan episode is only the prologue to the major
> action. It is related to the later episodes as prehistory is related to
> history; or (to use a Viconian image) as the giants of the dawn-chaos
> are related to the patriarchs of orderly history.[36]

Analogously, Williams told John Thirlwall that *Paterson* was
"to show the life of the people beginning with giants and ending
with the most sophisticated people I know."[37] In *Kora in Hell*
he describes the people as "giants in the dirt. The gods, the
Greek gods, smothered in filth and ignorance. . . . It's all of
the gods, there's nothing else worth writing of. They are the
same men they always were—but fallen" (KORA, 50–51). In

Book I of *Paterson* Williams refers to "The giant in whose apertures we/cohabit," of whom we sometimes have vague intimations and who can "live again" in us (I, ii, 34, 36). James Breslin's observation concerning *In the American Grain* can be applied equally to *Paterson*. He writes that the book "grows out of the tension between Williams's reverence for literal, individuating detail and his desire to discover mythic recurrences amid the welter of facts. . . . Individuals, in context, become archetypes."[38]

"Ymir . . . was at once father and mother of the giants and was, in other words, bisexual."[39] Paterson is also both male and female:

> *Paterson* is a man (since I am a man) who dives from cliffs and the edges of waterfalls to his death—finally. But for all that he is a woman (since I am not a woman) who *is* the cliff and the waterfall.[40]

Williams was aware of the male and the female elements inside himself, the acceptance and recognition of which he believed was vital to any artistic production: "It is the woman in us/That makes us write—/Let us acknowledge it—/Men would be silent" (CEP, 34). He thought of his unconscious faculties as female (see "The Wanderer"), which explains, to some degree, his interest in the myth of the rape of Persephone or Kora. Breslin maintains that Kora is "the generative principle, whose yearly round signifies the burial and sprouting of the seed. Internally, she is the dark, unknown region of the unconsciousness—a bodily force; she is the dark core of our being, the buried creative principle that Williams is striving to release."[41] The giant Paterson can be characterized as an androgyne for, as Eliade explains,

> *androgyny extends even to divinities who are preeminently masculine, or feminine.* This means that androgyny has become a general formula signifying *autonomy, strength, wholeness;* to say of a divinity that it is androgyne is as much to say that it is the ultimate being, the ultimate reality.[42]

Williams's poem "For Eleanor and Bill Monahan" sheds
further light on this important point by indicating that it is the
vital interdependence of male and female that allows them to
be, in a special sense, spoken of as one; if one is destroyed then,
the other is also:

> I do not come to you
> > save that I confess
> > > to being
> > > half man and half
> woman. I have seen the ivy
> > cling
> > > to a piece of crumbled
> wall so that
> > you cannot tell
> > > by which either
> stands: this is to say
> > if she to whom I cling
> > > is loosened both
> of us go down. [PB, 84]

Williams wrote that *Paterson* is

> a search for the redeeming language by which a man's premature
> death, like the death of Mrs. Cumming in Book I, and the woman's
> (the man's) failure to hold him (her) might have been prevented.[43]

According to his drafts for the catalogue which precedes the
poem, Williams also experimented with phrases to do with
man and woman: man and a woman; a man among women; a
woman among many; man and woman (BUFFALO). In the
beginning of *Paterson* the male element is identified with the
city, a man-made landscape, while the female element is
identified with the mountain and the park, a predominantly
natural landscape. Such identification is highly appropriate as
according to Mumford,

> In the new proto-urban milieu, the male became the leading

figure; woman took second place. . . . Woman's strength had lain in her special wiles and spells, in the mysteries of menstruation and copulation and childbirth, the arts of life. Man's strength now lay in feats of aggression and force, in showing his ability to kill and his own contempt for death: in conquering obstacles and forcing his will on other men, destroying them if they resisted.[44]

The interdependence of Paterson and his female counterpart is implicit in the mythic scene in which Paterson's arm supports her in an embrace. On one level, this embrace signifies the necessity of a reciprocal relationship between the city and the country, which we have previously discussed (see Chap. 2). On his worksheets Williams wrote,

> The city is a husband [who] has lost
> his desire for husbandry, let the word
> lead! rushes away without finding
>
> It is the crime of husbands that they
> have lost the desire for husbandry, that
> rush away and do not build, that cannot
> love, that know no new women
> except as amputations—and are ashamed. [BUFFALO]

In addition, Leo Marx points out that

> the contrast between "city" and "country" in the pastoral design makes perfect sense as an analogue of psychic experience. It implies that we can remain human, which is to say, fully integrated beings, only when we follow some such course back and forth, between our social and natural (animal) selves.[45]

The mythic embrace also symbolizes Paterson's need to "marry" his particular female counterpart ("In the one woman/I find all the rest" [CEP, 31]). In his *Autobiography* Williams refers to his wife as "the rock on which I have built" and states that "men have given the direction to my life and women have always supplied the energy" (AUTO, 55). As Whitman wrote:

It is also good to reduce the whole matter to the consideration of a single self, a man, a woman, on permanent grounds. Even for the treatment of the universal, in politics, metaphysics, or anything, sooner or later we come down to one single, solitary soul.[46]

On another level, the female giant represents Paterson's environment with which he tries to establish a fertile contact.[47] Cary Nelson observes that "passive and open, feminine space permits both violation and inhabitation. All the metaphors for passivity in *Paterson* are also metaphors for this space and the process of inhabiting it."[48] On a draft for the beginning of Book II, "Sunday in the Park," Williams writes, "There is a world/—at rest!/female to my pro-, in-, re-, de-, seductions" (BUFFALO). In the foreword to his *Autobiography* he informs us:

What relations I have had with men and women, such encounters as have interested me most profoundly, have not occurred in bed. I am extremely sexual in my desires: I carry them everywhere and at all times. I think that from that arises the drive which empowers us all. Given that drive, a man does with it what his mind directs. In the manner in which he directs that power lies his secret.

Paterson's walk in the park has an intense sexual significance and represents his desire to explore and penetrate his world: "Sex becomes not only an object of thought but in some sense an imaginative method of comprehension."[49] His walk progresses by a series of images, sexual in connotation:

> Outside
>   outside myself
>   there is a world,
> he rumbled, subject to my incursions. . . .
>
>   The scene's the Park
>   upon the rock,
>   female to the city

—upon whose body Paterson instructs his thoughts
(concretely) [II, i, 57]

he rejoins the path and sees, on a treeless
knoll—the red path choking it—
a stone wall, a sort of circular
redoubt against the sky, barren and
unoccupied. Mount. Why not? [II, i, 68]

Thus she finds what peace there is, reclines,
before his approach, stroked
by their clambering feet—for pleasure [II, i, 70]

Loiterers in groups straggle
over the bare rock-table—scratched by their
boot-nails more than the glacier scratched
them—walking indifferent through
each other's privacy   . [II, i, 72]

In "Letter to an Australian Editor" Williams identifies society
as a "supplying female" with which he must attain conjunction:

> A man may live for a time on a gathered hoard of skills granted,
> but if he live his meat will run out unless replenished about him.
> He will continue to produce only if his attachments to society
> continue adequate. If a man in his fatuous dreams cuts himself off
> from that supplying female, he dries up his sources—as Pound did
> in the end heading straight for literary sterility.[50]

3

We began our inquiry into the man/city image in *Paterson*
by considering a few of the images of empathy found in
Williams's shorter poems which involved, in their creation, a
muscular and/or emotional identification on the part of the
poet. We also observed that it is through such an intimate or
carnal apprehension that the mind can spread its embrace.
We indicated that the man/city image was a natural culmination of Williams's desire for unity since the image incorporates

the many and the one, man and the world. On a worksheet for
Paterson Williams writes that "all metaphor, in the
Elizabethan sense, means the same thing. / No matter how you
vary it, what you say, the meaning remains un-/altered"
(BUFFALO); that is to say, two things are made one flesh. The
metaphor is to be discovered in *Paterson;* it is observable *there,*
in the facts and conditions of the place, as there are "no ideas
but in things." Williams refers to the image as initially a
"metaphysical conception"—"how to get that into a form
probably came gradually" (IWW, 81). Therefore we considered a number of correspondences to the man/city image in
the realms of history, politics, mythology, and literature in
order to give a sense of its complexity as well as its universality.
The widespread appearance of this metaphorical equation of
man and city tends to suggest that it is a primary image, an
archetype. We concluded with a discussion of the male/female
duality in *Paterson.* This is an important element in much of
Williams's poetry as can be seen in a conversation which he had
with a philosophy teacher concerning the origin of art:

> "There is one thing God Himself cannot do," I said. "He cannot
> raise the arm and lower it at the same time." "He could if He
> wanted to," said Stanley. "No, He couldn't. Not at the same time.
> Not at once raise the arm and lower it at the same time. Therefore
> duality, therefore the sexes. Sex is at the bottom of all art. He is
> unity, but to accomplish simultaneity we must have two, multi-
> plicity, the male and the female, man and woman—acting together,
> the fecundating principle." "Go on," he said. . . . "Therefore,
> everything we do is an effort to achieve conjunction, not to say
> unity." [AUTO, 373]

In *Paterson* especially, Williams is concerned with the expression of Paterson's sexual being in both its male and its female
aspects in order to make explicit the nature of the struggle
toward unity which the poem represents. This brings us to the
crux of the whole matter, which is that, in actual fact, "art has
nothing to do with metaphysics" (SL, 238), for "it isn't what he

says that counts as a work of art, it's what he makes, with such intensity of perception that it lives with an intrinsic movement of its own to verify its authenticity" (CLP, 4–5). In *Paterson*, as we shall see in Chapter 5, words are used not to interpret or describe the world but to *incarnate* it, and thereby to give it unity as it is perceived as "the flesh of a constantly repeated permanence" (SL, 130), and "as something alive—caught forever in the structure of words."[51]

NOTES TO CHAPTER 3

1. Emily Mitchell Wallace, *A Bibliography of WCW* (Middletown, Conn.: Wesleyan University Press, 1968), p. 52.

2. Vivienne Koch, *WCW* (Norfolk, Conn.: New Directions, 1950), p. 99.

3. Williams, "How to Write," in an appendix to Linda Welshimer Wagner, *The Poems of WCW: A Critical Study* (Middletown, Conn.: Wesleyan University Press, 1964), p. 146.

4. Gaston Bachelard, *The Poetics of Space*, trans. Maria Jolas (New York: The Orion Press, 1964), p. 195.

5. See Benjamin Sankey, *A Companion to WCW's Paterson* (Berkely: University of California Press, 1971), p. 18: "Williams is sometimes thought of as essentially a descriptive writer, and it's true that many of his unquestionably successful works are short poems in which the main work is done by descriptive means."

6. Bachelard, *The Poetics of Space*, p. 186.

7. Ibid., p. 199.

8. Ibid., pp. 177–78.

9. William Carlos Williams, *A Voyage to Pagany* (New York: The Macaulay Co., 1928), p. 127.

10. Cary Nelson, *The Incarnate Word: Literature as Verbal Space* (Urbana: University of Illinois Press, 1973), p. 203.

11. Bachelard, *The Poetics of Space*, p. xviii.

12. John Keats, Letter to Richard Woodhouse, 27 October 1818, in *The Letters of John Keats*, ed. Hyder Edward Rollins (Cambridge: Harvard University Press, 1958), pp. 386–87.

13. Bachelard, *The Poetics of Space*, p. 150.

14. Walt Whitman, "Democratic Vistas," in *The Collected Writings of Walt Whitman: Prose works 1892* (New York: New York University Press, 1964), 2:412, 421.

15. Lewis Mumford, *The City in History* (New York: Harcourt, Brace & World, 1961), pp. 40, 110.

16. Quoted in John C. Thirlwall, "WCW's *Paterson*," in *New Directions in Prose and Poetry 17* (Norfolk, Conn.: New Directions, 1961), p. 254.

17. Nelson, *The Incarnate Word*, p. 5.

18. Bachelard, *The Poetics of Space*, p. 15.

19. Mumford, *The City in History*, p. 98.

20. William Shakespeare, *The Tragedy of Titus Andronicus*, act 5, sc. 3, line 70, *The Complete Works*, ed. G. B. Harrison (New York: Harcourt, Brace, & World, 1952).

21. Thomas Hobbes, *Leviathan* (Cambridge: Cambridge University Press, 1904), pp. xviii–xix.

22. Ibid., p. 113.

23. S. T. Coleridge, 18 December 1831, *Specimens of the Table Talk* (London: John Murray, Albermarle St., 1858), p. 155.

24. Hobbes, *Leviathan*, p. 110.

25. Northrop Frye, *The Educated Imagination* (Bloomington: Indiana University Press, 1964), p. 110.

26. William Carlos Williams, "A Note on *Paterson:* Book III," on back flap of dust jacket of *Paterson* (Book Three) (Norfolk, Conn.: New Directions, 1949).

27. Hélène Dupreyron-Marchessou, *WCW et le Renouveau du Lyrisme* (Paris: Presses universitaires de France, 1967), p. 135.

28. E. O. G. Turville-Petre, *Myth and Religion of the North* (New York: Holt, Rinehart and Winston, 1964), p. 276.

29. Richard Ellman, "From Renishaw to Paterson," *Yale Review* 39, no. 3 (March 1950): 544.

30. Northrop Frye, *Fearful Symmetry* (Boston: Beacon Press, 1947), p. 125.

31. Stuart Gilbert, *James Joyce's Ulysses* (Harmondsworth, Middlesex: Penguin Books, 1963), p. 37, n. 1.

32. Hélène Cixous, *The Exile of James Joyce*, trans. Sally A. J. Purcell (New York: David Lewis, 1972), p. 696.

33. Koch, "WCW: The Man and the Poet," *The Kenyon Review* 14, no. 3 (Summer 1952): 505.

34. Hugh Kenner, "With the Bare Hands," in *WCW: A Critical Anthology*, ed. Charles Tomlinson (Harmondworth, Middlesex: Penguin Books, 1972), p. 196.

35. Glauco Cambon, *The Inclusive Flame* (Bloomington, Indian University Press, 1963), p. 190.

36. Joseph Campbell and Henry Morton Robinson, *A Skeleton Key to Finnegans Wake* (London: Faber & Faber, 1947), p. 15.

37. Quoted in Thirlwall, "WCW's *Paterson*," p. 272.

38. James Breslin, *WCW: An American Artist* (New York: Oxford University Press, 1970), p. 89.

39. Turville-Petre, *Myth and Religion of the North*, p. 277.

40. Williams, "A Note on Paterson: Book III."

41. Breslin, *WCW*, p. 58.

42. Mircea Eliade, *Myths, Dreams, and Mysteries*, trans. Philip Mairet (London: Collins, 1968) p. 177.

43. Williams, "A Note on Paterson: Book III."

44. Mumford, *The City in History*, p. 27.

45. Leo Marx, *The Machine in the Garden* (New York: Oxford University Press, 1964), p. 70.

46. Whitman, "Democratic Vistas," in *The Collected Writings*, pp. 393–94.

47. See Sister M. Bernetta Quinn, *The Metamorphic Tradition in Modern Poetry* (New Brunswick, N.J.: Rutgers University Press, 1966), pp. 102–103, and James Guimond, *The Art of WCW* (Chicago: University of Chicago Press, 1968), p. 164.

48. Nelson, *The Incarnate Word*, p. 198.

49. Norman O. Brown, *Love's Body* (New York: Random House, 1966), p. 249.

50. Williams, "Letter to an Australian Editor," p. 208.

51. Jack Spicer, "Letter to Lorca" in *The New American Poetry*, ed. Donald Allen (New York: Grove Press, 1960), p. 413. Since this book was written, I have come to the realization that a study of the images of men and women in *Paterson* from a feminist point of view would reveal not only much about Williams and *Paterson*, but much about the patriarchal nature of our society as well.

4
Experiments with Extended Patterns

Many of *Paterson*'s critics consider the poem to be a substantial departure from Williams's previous technical concerns, a completely unpredictable accomplishment. In a review of *Paterson I* Robert Lowell observes that "if the short poems show Williams as an excellent stylist, there is nothing in them to indicate that their thematic structure could be extended to a long poem."[1] Similarly A. Walton Litz in *The Literary Heritage of New Jersey* writes that "of all modern poets, Williams would seem at first thought to be least qualified for work on a long architectural poem. His emphasis on the moment of sensation, the timeless image, hardly makes for continuity in structure."[2] Vivienne Koch states that "the venture of the long poem is the single issue where he [Williams] comes closest to the interests and recommendations of other distinguished modern poets,"[3] implying, at the very least, that Williams's writing prior to *Paterson* has very little in common with his "epic."

Williams's long-standing reputation as an "entrenched imagist,"[4] "the master of the glimpse,"[5] as anti-idea and consequently not very "profound," was predicated and reinforced by the statements of important critics in the 1920s and 1930s. Years before there was any public intimation of *Paterson*'s appearance, these early assessments (some of which were later amended) prejudiced the poem's potential for acceptance. In 1922 Kenneth Burke observed:

His [Williams's] hatred of the idea in art is . . . pronounced, and very rightly brings in its train a complete disinterest [*sic*] in form. (Note: Form in literature must always have its beginnings in ideas. In fact, our word for idea comes from a Greek word whose first meaning is "form.")[6]

In 1928 Gorham B. Munson categorized Williams as a "Primitive" because he is not master of his environment: "He has no pattern for it, only uncoordinated perceptions, impressions, contacts."[7] He remarks that "profundity is scarcely the term to associate with Williams's writing."[8] Although Munson admits that Williams originated a vigorous school of writing, he finds it necessary to stress its limitations:

The school itself will require fertilization by elements not in Williams and not peculiar to America, elements to which America has not attained, elements that come out of general consciousness and not from the particular ground-contact, if its writings are to . . . pass from the category of minor to the category of major in aim, scope and power.[9]

Ezra Pound in "Dr. Williams's Position" printed in *The Dial* in 1928 declared his preference for those pages of Williams's work where "he has made the least effort to fit anything into either story, book, or . . . into an essay."[10] He goes on to maintain that plot, major form, or outline should only be used by those who feel an inescapable need for these things or when they issue naturally from the matter treated. Pound concluded his essay with the statement:

We retain a liberty to . . . ask whether for example Williams would have done better to have read W. H. Hudson than to have been interested in Joyce. At least there is place for reflection as to whether the method of Hudson's *A Traveller in Little Things* would serve for an author so concerned with his own insides as is Williams; or whether Williams himself isn't at his best—retaining interest in the uncommunicable or the hidden roots of the consciousness of people he meets, but confining his statements to presentation of their objective manifests.[11]

Yvor Winters in *In Defense of Reason*, originally published in 1937, states that one has to make "allowances for his [Williams's] somewhat narrow intellectual scope"[12] and goes on to maintain that Williams "is wholly incapable of coherent thought."[13] In 1939 R. P. Blackmur wrote "that his [Williams's] intellect is in him so badly proportioned that it interferes with the operation of his sensibility."[14]

It is true, of course, that Williams did adopt an "anti-idea" stance, which undoubtedly encouraged some of this critical commentary. His stance was directed toward what he referred to as "metaphysical" thought (i.e., unrelated to "things"), typified by the academy. Nevertheless, although Williams did not care for the term "intellectual" (because it makes you think of the thinker"[15]), he became increasingly conscious of the use of "intellect" in relation to his writing. However, this fact did not, for the most part, alter the general critical opinion of Williams as "anti-intellectual" because it did not affect the specific content (i.e., subject matter) of his compositions, so much as their form. In other words, Williams held that the proper use of a poet's intellect is to discover and refine new structures and techniques, rather than to develop a complex system of "profound" thought[16]:

> So that when I say, and some well-meaning critic attacks my intelligence for saying it, that art has nothing to do with metaphysics—I am aiming at the very core of the whole matter. Art is some form of an honest answer, the forms of art, the discovery of the new in art forms—but to mix that with metaphysics is the prime intellectual offense of my day. [SL, 238–39]

The fact that Williams's reputation as a writer has been based primarily on his short imagist and objectivist poems has obscured his concern with the creation of larger constructions. The reality, however, is that *Kora in Hell* was published in 1920, and subsequent novels, short stories, essays, plays, and improvisations reflect his search for forms on a larger scale. This chapter documents the years of experimentation with extended patterns which reached their culmination in *Paterson*.

During the years 1913–1920 Williams identified himself with and participated in a movement in poetry known as Imagism and was included in *Des Imagistes, An Anthology*, edited by Ezra Pound in 1914.[17] The words "imagist" was first used by Pound in 1912 in a note on five poems by T. E. Hulme printed at the end of *Ripostes*. In that same year Pound, H. D., and Richard Aldington formulated three principles which they believed to be basic to the new "school."[18] These general principles—"Direct treatment of the 'thing' whether subjective or objective," careful and economical word usage, and composition "in the sequence of the musical phrase,"[19]— remained with Williams to a certain but vital extent throughout his career.[20] For example, in the 1953 dialogue with Thirlwall concerning *Paterson* Williams explains that he

> made the thing insofar as possible happen on the page. The imagistic mood comes in there. You can't tell what a particular thing signified, but if you see the thing happening before you, you infer that that is the kind of thing that happens in the area. This is the imagistic method.[21]

However, Williams did not associate himself with the Imagist movement for very long. He explains the reasons behind his disassociation in a talk at Harvard University in 1941:

> Imagism, which had a use in focusing the attention upon the importance of concrete imagery in the poem, lost its place finally because as a form it completely lacked structural necessity. The image served for everything so that the structure, a weaker and weaker free verse, degenerated finally into a condition very nearly resembling that of the sonnet.[22]

Tony Tanner describes Williams's poem "The Red Wheelbarrow" as

> naive in a technical sense. To a man with a certain view of the world it might seem symptomatic of chaos (as Imagism did to some

critics). More likely it is a symptom of disorientation. In a world of
melting beliefs, of disintegrating systems, a universe which
seemed recalcitrant to one harmonious integrating explanation,
the bewildered poet might take refuge in examining only the
palpable fragment.[23]

After his break with Imagism, Williams concerned himself with
finding a literary means of synthesizing the various elements of
his world. He was no longer satisfied with "examining only the
palpable fragment"; he began to recognize that his "isolated
observations and experiences needed pulling together to gain
'profundity' " (AUTO, 391). In his 1930 essay "Caviar and
Bread Again" Williams writes of the necessity for "a magnificent organization of those materials his age has placed before
him [the poet] for his employment" (SE, 103). In the same
essay he talks of gathering "all the threads together that have
been spun for many centuries" and weaving them into a design
(SE, 103).

In "An Essay on *Leaves of Grass*" Williams calls free verse
"immoral,"[24] demonstrating his awareness that, for a writer,
moral concerns and technical concerns are intimately related.
A. Alvarez writes that

> in the States it is very easy to assume what an intelligent man does
> *not* believe in; the reverse is equally difficult. . . . They [the
> intellectuals] can . . . hardly be said to build up their moralities at
> all; they reach them by a process of sceptical reduction. They seem
> to judge less from what they believe in than from what they are not
> taken in by. In all their enthusiasms, they are responsible finally to
> an abiding core of scepticism, of common sense. . . . It is this
> kind of minimal sanity on which the best and least pretentious
> verse of William Carlos Williams . . . is built. As poetry it is not
> very profound, but it is occasionally impressive as a statement of
> the American negative virtues.[25]

Alvarez's observations are valid as far as Williams's imagistic
poems are concerned; these poems do originate in what might
well be termed "a process of sceptical reduction." Yet Alvarez

does not acknowledge that beginning with *Kora in Hell* in 1920 Williams was actively engaged in discovering some positive values upon which to base his constructions. In *In the American Grain* he writes:

> It is an extraordinary phenomenon that Americans have lost the sense . . . that what we are has its origin in what *the nation* in the past has been; that there is a source in AMERICA for everything we think or do; that morals affect the food and food the bone, and that, in fine, we have no conception at all of what is meant by moral, since we recognize no ground our own. . . . That unless everything that is, proclaim a ground on which it stand, it has no worth; and that what has been morally, aesthetically worth while in America has rested upon peculiar and discoverable ground. [IAG, 109]

As we shall see, Williams's search for a set of values, a ground on which to stand, is synonymous with his struggle to find a large, unifying structure.

Williams maintains that "on the poet devolves the most vital function of society: to recreate it—the collective world—in time of stress, in a new mode, fresh in every part" (SE, 103). The poet is essential to the preservation and development of society, endowing with identity the objects, people, and places of this world. As Williams writes in his introduction to Byron Vazakas' *Transfigured Night:* "No world can exist for more than the consuming of a match or the eating of an apple without a poet to breathe into it an immortality."[26] The poet is responsible for the creation of "culture," which, according to Williams, is not a thing, but an act: "the act of lifting these things [climate, sands, flowers, conditions of knowledge, etc.] into an ordered and utilized whole" (SE, 157). Thus Williams's ethical concern is also a technical concern: the making of "an ordered and utilized whole."[27]

Cesare Pavese, who wrote a degree thesis on Walt Whitman and who was very much involved with the problems and concerns of American literature, writes in *This Business of Living:*

It is easy to create a "momentary" work of art, a "fragment," just as it is easy to live a moment of morality, but to create a work that transcends the moment is difficult, just as it is difficult to live for longer than a single heartbeat in the kingdom of heaven. The art of organising the kingdom of heaven for longer than a moment (saintliness), is on the same level as organising a work of poetry beyond the fragmentary stage.[28]

Like Williams, Pavese was interested in the relation among art, life, and morality and also became dissatisfied with what he calls "real or presumed constructed lyrics" such as *Les Fleurs de Mal* or *Leaves of Grass*. It is noteworthy that Pavese was drawn to a similar solution as Williams and came to the conclusion that "one must have the courage and strength to conceive a major work all of a piece."[29]

René Taupin in *L'Influence du Symbolisme Français sur la Poésie Américaine* (1929) was the first critic to recognize that *Kora in Hell* was symptomatic of Williams's growing dissatisfaction with Imagism:

Cependant vers 1918, en écrivant *Kora in Hell* il s'évadait des rythmes imagistes pour donner la liberté au train de ses émotions. . . . Il est certain qu'après *Al Que Quiere*, Williams s'est posé le problème d'une plus fidèle traduction de ses émotions; il a alors douté du pur imagisme et du pur verbalisme, il a voulu trouver un moyen plus complet de communiquer avec ses semblables.[30]

Taupin maintains, despite the fact that Williams claims he was more influenced by the French painters than the French writers, that Williams "a trouvé sa tradition et son expressions dans la technique française,"[31] in particular Rimbaud. Whatever one may think of this thesis, Taupin was undoubtedly correct in his evaluation of the importance of *Kora* in Williams's literary development away from Imagism. James Breslin accurately observes in reference to the Improvisations that "the aim is not evocation of the Image but the release of a primitive force of imagination."[32]

Kora in Hell was actually written during 1917 and 1918 and the "Prologue" to the original edition ("which is really an Epilogue" [IWW, 41]) is dated September 1, 1918. In *I Wanted to Write a Poem* Williams talks about how the book was written:

> For a year I used to come home and no matter how late it was before I went to bed I would write *something*. And I kept writing, writing, even if it were only a few words, and at the end of the year there were 365 entries. . . . They were a reflection of the day's happenings more or less, and what I had had to do with them. [IWW, 38–39]

Williams rejected most of the entries because they were "pure nonsense" (IWW, 38), and when the book was published in 1920 it consisted of twenty-seven "chapters," most of which were further divided into three sections. Williams quite rightly felt that many of the improvisations were completely unintelligible and so he included interpretations of some of them within the text itself: "First came the Improvisations, those more or less incomprehensible statements, then the dividing line and, in italics, my interpretations of the Improvisations" (IWW, 39).[33] Some of the interpretations were included in the prologue in order to keep the text as uncluttered as possible and to add strength to the prologue's "fragmentary argument" (IMAG, 16). Williams's gesture of including interpretations does appear to indicate a desire on his part to make himself understood by his readers. However, the fact that as Williams himself admits, the explanations are "often more dense than the first writing" (IMAG, 29), coupled with his statement that "it reveals myself to me and perhaps that is why I have kept it to myself" (IWW, 38), suggests that "communication" was not a primary concern during his writing of the improvisations. *Kora* is the first large construction that Williams attempted and the "Prologue" is the first piece of continuous expository prose he remembers writing (IWW, 43).

In Williams's prologue to the City Lights edition of *Kora* in

1957 he denies any identity between his improvisations and the French prose poem. He also admits that they definitely cannot be described as verse and concludes with the statement that there was "nothing to do but put it down as it stood, trusting to the generous spirit of the age to find a place for it" (IMAG, 29). It is significant and fitting that Williams did not want his improvisations to be classified as either prose, verse, or as a prose poem, as his search for a satisfactory synthesis involved a struggle to define the relationship between, and the use of, prose and poetry. In his later prologue Williams indicates clearly that he thought of all the improvisations as comprising a unit, a whole: "The whole seemed satisfactory to me when I gathered it together" (IMAG, 29).

The improvisations have a certain, if limited, integrity as a unified construction simply by virtue of the fact that they are "thoughts put down like a diary" (IWW, 39). That is to say, *Kora* is a unit because it attempts to record and interpret imaginatively, the reality of Williams's life over the period of one year. Cesare Pavese writes:

> A century is an empiric, abstract unit, but a life, an individual, is something more than that.
> Certainly something more in that he lived and developed himself; but is there an implied unity of construction in his works as a whole, arising from the mechanical succession of days and his own self-criticism as each stage is completed? What one calls a metaphysical unity. [34]

Williams did in fact rely on what Pavese describes as an "implied unity of construction" to help unify certain of his compositions, of which *Kora* is the first example. Perhaps more to the point in this instance is that Williams *chose* 84 of the 365 entries and then "placed the . . . *Improvisations* in groups, somewhat after the A.B.A. formula, that one may support the other, clarifying or enforcing perhaps the other's intention" (IMAG, 28).

A greater sense of the nature of the *Improvisations* as a form is gained through a contemplation of certain of Williams's statements in the original "Prologue." Here Williams claims that *Kora* is a "Cubist work," and analogous to "a stained-glass window that had fallen out and lay more or less together on the ground" (IMAG, 8). Among the interpretations included in the "Prologue" are the assertions,

> By the brokenness of his composition the poet makes himself master of a certain weapon which he could possess himself of in no other way. . . . A poem is tough by no quality it borrows from a logical recital of events nor from the events themselves but solely from that attenuated power which draws perhaps many broken things into a dance giving them thus a full being. . . . The stream of things having composed itself into wiry strands that move in one fixed direction, the poet in desperation turns at right angles and cuts across current with startling results to his hangdog mood. [IMAG, 16–17]

Kenneth Burke and Gorham B. Munson reflect the early, general reactions to *Kora*. In 1922 Burke wrote in reference to the book:

> (How beautiful the association of ideas would have been in art if used in one work, by one man, for one page, and for some end other than that of a beautiful association of ideas). . . . Having twenty sentences of chaos to heighten one sentence of cosmos is too much like thanking God for headaches since they enable us to be happy without them.[35]

A few years later Munson wrote along similar lines, "Since the 'association of ideas' is accidental in the first place and in the second it is personal, private, excessively subjective, therefore whether or not it produces an intended effect upon an intended reader is purely a hit-or-miss proposition."[36] In retrospect, Williams himself was critical of his improvisations. Only three years after the publication of *Kora* he stated in a prose passage from *Spring and All* that "their [the Improvisations'] fault is their dislocation of sense, often complete," (IMAG, 117) and in

a letter to David Ignatow in 1948 he described the improvisations as "wild flights of the imagination. As I look at them now I
see how 'romantic' they were. I feel embarrassed. I was having
'dreams' at that time; I was having 'ideas' " (SL, 267).
Nevertheless, Williams recognizes the fundamental
significance of *Kora* in his development as a writer. In *Spring
and All* he implies that during the period of time prior to his
writing of *Kora*, his creative inspiration and imagination had
been steadily diminishing; consequently he resorted to the
expedient of letting "the imagination have its own way to see if
it could save itself. . . . It is the best I could do under the
circumstances. It was the best I could do and retain any value to
experience at all" (IMAG, 116–17). *Kora* was also a crucial work
because it represented a way out of Imagism and launched
Williams on his search for and experimentation with extended
structures. Furthermore, it is significant that Williams saw the
import of *Kora* in terms of the values the work enabled him to
discover:

> I found myself alleviated but most important I began there and
> then to revalue experience, to understand what I was at—
> The virtue of the improvisations is their placement in a world of
> new values—. . . . I find that the values there discovered can be
> extended. . . .
> I find that there is work to be done in the creation of new forms,
> new names for experience. . . .
> enlargment—revivification of values. [IMAG, 116–17]

In *Spring and All* Williams progresses to a slightly tighter form,
and persists in his move away from Imagism:

> It [work using "crude symbolism"] is typified by use of the word
> "like" or that "evocation" of the "image" which served us for a time.
> Its abuse is apparent. The insignificant "image" may be "evoked"
> never so ably and still mean nothing. [IMAG, 100–101]

Spring and All and *The Descent of Winter* belong together in
our discussion due to their similarity of construction as well as

their parallel treatment as far as publication is concerned. Three hundred copies of *Spring and All* (twenty-seven poems interspersed with prose) were published in 1923 by Robert McAlmon's Contact Publishing Company in Paris and many of these copies were not distributed.[37] Williams admits that "nobody ever saw it—it had no circulation at all" (IWW, 48). *The Descent of Winter* (twenty-one poems and eighteen prose pieces) was originally published by Ezra Pound in *The Exile*, no. 4 (Autumn 1928).[38] The verse sequences in each of these two works were later included in *The Complete Collected Poems 1906–1938* and in *The Collected Earlier Poems* (1951) and some of the poems of each sequence were reprinted elsewhere. The prose passages from *Spring and All* were published separately in *William Carlos Williams* (1966), a collection of critical essays edited by J. Hillis Miller; and the prose from *The Descent of Winter* appeared as "Notes in Diary Form" in Williams's *Selected Essays*, first published in 1954. Thus in spite of the fact that both works originally appeared as a unit composed of prose and verse, they had only a very limited circulation in the form in which they were written. Consequently, barring Linda Wagner's study *The Prose of William Carlos Williams* (1970), critics of these early works have not treated them as unified constructions—in intent or in execution. Until the publication of *Imaginations* in 1970, which reproduces both works in their original form, the vast majority of Williams's readers were completely unaware that *Spring and All* and *The Descent of Winter* are among Williams's first, tentative attempts at reaching a synthesis.[39] In these two works Williams tries to unify his isolated poems by interspersing them with prose segments, as an alternative to the "bare image haphazardly presented in loose verse" (AUTO, 265). Wagner's observation in relation to *Spring and All* applies equally to *The Descent of Winter:*

> Taken without the prose that so fittingly accompanied them, the
> poems of *Spring and All* are very different in effect than Williams

intended. Like halves of any book, any painting, the poems cannot be separated from the prose without reducing the whole to fragments. As conscious as Williams was about the unity of design in modern art, it seems grossly unfair to have disregarded the unity of his design in *Spring and All*. [40]

Williams describes *Spring and All* as "poems interspersed with prose, the same idea as IMPROVISATIONS" (IWW, 48). Such a comparison with the structure of *Kora* implies that either the prose passages present the literary principles to which the poems have been written or that the poems demonstrate the principles set forth in the prose. This is the way in which the interaction of the prose and poetry has been generally characterized. Yet the relationship between the two modes of writing within the work is primarily interesting as Williams's second attempt at the creation of a larger form. In one of the prose passages Williams explains that, although he has often known the "quickening of the sense" which comes of the imagination, he has not "always been able to complete the intellectual steps which would make . . . [him] firm in the position." As a result of this state of affairs, he writes that most of his life "has been lived in hell—a hell of repression lit by flashes of inspiration, when a poem such as this or that would appear" (IMAG, 116). The prose passages in *Spring and All* are the "intellectual steps" whereby Williams hoped to integrate the twenty-seven poems. In another prose passage Williams writes:

> I think often of my earlier work and what it has cost me not to have been clear. I acknowledge I have moved chaotically about refusing or rejecting most things, seldom accepting values or acknowledging anything. [IMAG, 115]

Williams is undoubtedly thinking in particular of the opacity of *Kora in Hell* and he equates this opacity with a lack of values. In

Spring and All he is more conscious of an obligation to his readers and he is also beginning to satisfy his "sense of inclusiveness without redundancy" (IMAG, 116).

Williams also describes *Spring and All* as a "travesty" on typographical form, which explains why the "chapters" are numbered out of order, a heading is printed upside down, Roman and Arabic numerals are used interchangeably. Williams recognizes that the kind of synthesis he is after will have little in common with the Aristotelian beginning, middle, and end. *Spring and All* is of fundamental importance, as it marks the beginning of Williams's lifelong concern with the relationship between prose and poetry:

> Prose: statement of facts concerning emotions, intellectual states, data of all sorts—technical expositions, jargon, of all sorts—fictional and other—poetry: new form dealt with as a reality in itself. . . . The cleavage goes through all the phases of experience. It is the jump from prose to the process of imagination that is the next great leap of the intelligence. [IMAG, 133–34]

The Descent of Winter is similar in origin to *Kora in Hell* as the prose and the poems were initially entries in a diary. Unlike *Kora*, however, they are presented in chronological order from 27 September to 18 December. Although Vivienne Koch comments that "there is a spurious unity given by entry dates above each poem,"[41] the prose and the poems cohere with more success as an imaginative construction than those in *Spring and All*. Whereas the prose in *Spring and All* is predominantly critical and expository, the subject matter of the prose entries in *The Descent of Winter* often runs parallel to that of the poetry.

The first prose passage of *The Descent* states Williams's intent for the work as a whole: "I will make a big, serious portrait of my time" (IMAG, 238). However, the sequence is little more than "notes" for such a portrait, as Williams was well aware since he titled the prose "Notes in Diary Form" in his

Selected Essays. Consistent with his tenet that the "local is the only universal," Williams's "portrait" of his time was to be a portrait of one person:

> Born, September 15, 1927, 2nd child, wt. 6 lbs. 2 ozs. The hero is Dolores Marie Pischak, the place Fairfield, in my own state, my own country, its largest city, my own time. This is her portrait. [IMAG, 241]

As Wagner observes, "Williams seems to be focusing here on one person who would synthesize the spirit of her locale."[42] Yet, other than the particulars already quoted, we do not learn much more of Dolores Marie. A certain element of coherence in *The Descent* is provided instead by brief glimpses into the life of "Fairfield," in both prose and verse. Though these glimpses are presented in a haphazard fashion ("Order-is dead" [IMAG, 241]), the story of Fairfield is also, in a sense, usurped by Williams's concern with himself and his problems as a writer. Vivienne Koch suggests (apropos of the verse) that "the idea seems to be to record the emotional biography of the poet through presenting a more or less sustained mood, a nucleus of experience grouped around a season, a season which is also a season of the soul."[43] The prose passages consist of musings, anecdotes, history, memories, etc., while the poems strive for "vividness," for "the truth of the object" (IMAG, 247). But the fact that many of the poems in *The Descent* were first written down as prose[44] tends to suggest that Williams is still uncertain as to the actual relationship between the two modes. In a prose entry toward the middle of *The Descent* he again attempts a definition similar to those in *Spring and All:* "The good poetry is where the vividness comes up 'true' like in prose but better. That's poetry" (IMAG, 247). Wagner writes that "Williams' artistic problem here becomes how to present the material to touch the reader as it touches him."[45] As the title of this sequence suggests, as well as the nature of its structure and

subject matter, Williams felt himself to be frustrated in his
search for a "ground" on which to stand:

> The difficulty of modern styles is made by the fragmentary
> stupidity of modern life, its lacunae of sense, loops, perversions of
> instinct, blankets, amputations, fullsomeness of instruction and
> multiplications of inanity. [IMAG, 259]

In 1922 Ezra Pound wrote to Williams asking him if he had a
prose work which he wanted to publish. In reply to Pound's
inquiry, Williams sent him his first extended piece of prose—
The Great American Novel—and Pound included it in the
series he was editing which came out in the summer of 1923. In
the "Postscript" to his own contribution, *Indiscretions*, Pound
wrote about the authors included in the series, "They have set
out from five very different points to tell the truth about *moeurs
contemporaines*, without fake, melodrama, conventional ending."[46]

Williams describes *The Great American Novel* as "a satire on
the novel form" (AUTO, 237) and in *I Wanted to Write a Poem*
he calls it "a travesty on what I considered conventional
American writing. People were always talking about the Great
American Novel so I thought I'd write it" (IWW, 50). Kenneth
Burke observes that the whole novel is "written incidentally
while the author searches for an opening sentence."[47] That
Williams concurred with this observation is evidenced by a
letter he wrote to Burke in the month following the publication
of his essay: "Yes, my *Great American Novel* never found a
beginning. It was that I must have wanted to say. . . . It is not
for me merely to arrange things prettily" (SL, 61–62). *The
Great American Novel* is primarily composed of short bits of
Americana—historical, personal, and imaginary. Webster
Schott remarks that "after starting with himself, Williams
gradually turns *The Great American Novel* into a discovery of
the United States of his time" (IMAG, 156). Some of the

passages are rough portraits of characters which later appear in *In the American Grain,* and there is also a prose version of Williams's later poem "The Last Words of My English Grandmother." The structure is arbitrary although, as Pound remarks,

> if one read it often enough, the element of form emerges in *The Great American Novel,* not probably governing the whole, but in the shaping of at least some of the chapters, notably chapter 7, the one beginning 'Nuevo Mundo.'[48]

In the prose passages of *Spring and All* and to a lesser extent in those of *The Descent of Winter,* Williams explicates his literary theories and in a sense becomes his own critic. In a similar fashion in *The Great American Novel,* he intersperses remarks on the difficulties involved in writing a novel and general critical observations on his work and the work of his contemporaries, with random observations and anecdotes. In the beginning of Chapter 5 Williams asks, "What then is a novel?," and replies, "It is a thing of fixed form. It is pure English" (IMAG, 173). He concludes that it is impossible for him to write one because he is "a beginner. I am an American. A United Stateser" (IMAG, 175).

In the "Prologue" to *Kora in Hell* Williams quotes portions from a letter written to him on April 9, 1918, by Wallace Stevens. In this letter Stevens directs his remarks toward Williams's book of poems *Al Que Quiere,* but Williams maintains that his criticism "holds good" for each of the improvisations as well as for the work as a whole. Stevens writes,

> My idea is that in order to carry a thing to the extreme necessity to convey it one has to stick to it; . . . Given a fixed point of view, realistic, imagistic or what you will, everything adjusts itself to that point of view; and the process of adjustment is a world in flux, as it should be for a poet. But to fidget with points of view leads always to new beginnings and incessant new beginnings lead to sterility. [IMAG, 15]

Of course, Williams includes this letter in his "Prologue" in order to clarify his *own* position at that time which was in radical opposition to Stevens's "ideas of discipline." However, from our retrospective vantage point, this letter from Stevens appears to foreshadow the direction in which Williams eventually did move. Bearing in mind Stevens's letter it is significant that Williams's next attempt at a larger structure after *Kora—The Great American Novel*—consists entirely of new beginnings; so much so that *a* beginning is never found. The appearance in 1925 of *In the American Grain* (Williams's first commercial publication), which not only finds a beginning but develops a definite "point of view," suggests that after his experience in writing *The Great American Novel* he began to concede the validity of Stevens's statement that "incessant new beginnings lead to sterility." He wrote to Horace Gregory in 1939 that "I must have a basis for orienting myself formally in the beliefs which activated me from day to day . . . to establish myself from my own reading, in my own way, in the locality which by birthright had become my own" (SL, 185). Munson, in one of the first critical essays written on Williams (1928), similarly recognizes that in *In the American Grain*

> Williams is grappling as hard as he can with the difficulties that frustrated his attempt to write the "great American novel." The past is made to put its weight directly and heavily upon the present: a vivid sense of historical determinism is constantly awake.[49]

Williams concludes the penultimate chapter of *In the American Grain*, called "Descent," with the words, "However hopeless it may seem, we have no other choice: we must go back to the beginning; it must all be done over; everything that is must be destroyed" (IAG, 215). These words bring to mind similar sentiments found in *Spring and All*—"To it [the imagination] we come to dedicate our secret project: the annihilation of every human creature on the face of the earth. . . . Then at last will the world be made anew" (IMAG,

91), as well as these lines from *The Great American Novel*—"I begin small and make myself into a big splurging word: I take life and make it into one big blurb. I begin at my childhood. I begin at the beginning" (IMAG, 160). Williams wants to put "language in a state of emergence, in which life becomes manifest through its vivacity,"[50] to return to a state where nothing has yet any names or values attached to it, where words are not "plastered with muck out of the cities" (IMAG, 175). In *In the American Grain* Williams is moving away, to a certain degree, from the highly personal and somewhat self-indulgent writing such as that found in *Kora in Hell* and *The Great American Novel*. In *In the American Grain* he does not turn to his own childhood for a "beginning," but instead to the discovery of the New World. His intent, as in *The Great American Novel*, is to "liberate the words" (IMAG, 166), as he writes in a statement in the beginning of *In the American Grain*:

> In these studies I have sought to re-name the things seen, now lost in chaos of borrowed titles, many of them inappropriate, under which the true character lies hid. In letters, in journals, reports of happenings I have recognized new contours suggested by old words so that new names were constituted. . . . It has been my wish to draw from every source one thing, the strange phosphorus of the life, nameless under an old misappellation.

Most of the twenty-one chapters of *In the American Grain* deal with a character from American history (the exceptions are the "Voyage of the Mayflower" and the "Advent of the Slaves"):

> The plan was to try to get inside the heads of some of the American founders or "heroes," if you will, by examining their original records. . . . I want to give the impression, an inclusive definition, of what these men . . . have come to be for us. That they have made themselves part of us and that is what we are. [AUTO, 178, 236]

In the American Grain gains a certain unity by virtue of its subject matter; each chapter deals with an aspect of American history and these are arranged chronologically. Yet the book also has a thematic structure which emerges from the juxtaposition, recollection, and anticipation of parallel or similar events and themes. Throughout *In the American Grain* Williams is interested in the exploration of people's response to the "new." Breslin observes that "the constant alternation of open and aloof character types makes recurrence a structural principle in *In the American Grain:* it is thus not just something we know abstractly, but a reality we *experience* in reading the book."[51] The unity of the book is further advanced by the fact that Williams wrote each chapter in a style appropriate to its contents, often quoting extensively from the original sources.[52] Williams was greatly pleased when his essay "Sir Walter Raleigh" was included in Selden Rodman's anthology *One Hundred Modern Poems:*

> It was a startling and original thought of yours to include my "Raleigh" as a poem. Yes, I've known from the first that it was exceptionally regular in its meter but I never looked at it as anything but what it set out to be: an "imitation" of Raleigh, Raleigh caught in the mesh of his own period's forms; to show Raleigh according to my conception of how, by form only, we must "make" our designs. Perhaps it is also an original poem. I hope so. What you have done is precisely what I call criticism. Merely to point the finger is criticism. [SL, 276]

In "The Legacy of Fenimore Cooper," Donald Davie observes that if Williams confounds the roles of poet and historian, he does so in the interest of the larger synthesis of myth; *In the American Grain* is a supplement to the myth of American history analogous to D. H. Lawrence's *Studies in Classic American Literature.* In this context Davie accepts Marius Bewley's definition of myth as "the incarnation of racial aspiration and memory"[53] and makes the astute observation that what Lawrence seems to have recognized is that, just because American history begins after the invention of print, printed literature has played a part in the forming of the national self-consciousness such as in older cultures has been played by folklore and legend.[54]

In *In the American Grain* Williams reevaluates and recreates various myths of American history; yet it is significant that he deals primarily with episodes and characters which relate to his own interior tensions or with which he can particularly empathize or mold to his own purposes. Therefore we are justified in speaking of Williams's "personal mythology." By "personal mythology" we are referring to the personal extension of a myth to such a degree that the interpretation becomes more important than the myth itself, as well as the conferring of mythical status on to personal elements by attaching these elements to ready-made myths. Each essay in *In the American Grain* centers around an established myth or legend from American history. Williams elaborates on the original stories, leaves certain things out, and generally manipulates the source material.[55] What actually happened, or the popular idea of what happened, thus gives way to Williams's personal interpretation: "All of the book's characters are versions of William Carlos Williams, the motives and values of his heroic types are identical to his own, and the conflict that he saw in American history *was* the conflict of his own soul."[56] Williams writes in his essay on Aaron Burr, "He's in myself and so I dig through lies to resurrect him" (IAG, 197). Glauco Cambon has commented on the fact that the dilemma of American history is paralleled by Williams's personal existence,

> which he owes to the spark-striking combination of a typical English father and a lively Latin mother. American history, American problems, are thus identical with Williams' ideal autobiography; the accident of his birth afforded him a direct, shocking confrontation with the basic issues of American history, which, being a poet, he could not help translating into myth.[57]

Notwithstanding the fact that *In the American Grain* is a development of Williams's personal mythology, this book of essays is far less subjective than his improvisatory work. He is no longer communicating only as an individual but is beginning to communicate as a "professional man with a social function."[58] He is searching throughout the writing of these essays, not only for a personal viewpoint, and personal values, but for a moral source for all Americans such as that which he recognizes in Daniel Boone:

> There was, thank God, a great voluptuary born to the American settlements against the niggardliness of the damming puritanical tradition; one who by the single log,c of his passion, which he rested on the savage life about him, destroyed at its spring that spiritually withering plague. For this he has remained since buried in a miscolored legend and left for rotten. Far from dead, however, but full of rich regenerative violence he remains, when his history will be carefully reported, for us who have come to call upon him. [IAG, 130]

or in Père Sebastian Rasles,

> It is *this* to be *moral:* to be *positive,* to be peculiar, to be sure, generous, brave—to MARRY, to *touch*—to *give* because one HAS, not because one has nothing. . . . In Rasles one feels THE INDIAN emerging from the pod of his isolation from eastern understanding, he is released AN INDIAN. He exists, he is—it is an AFFIRMATION, it is alive. [IAG, 121]

Thus, we can see that *In the American Grain* is not simply a collection of separate character studies; it is an integrated series. Yet this fact has often been ignored. For example, Yvor Winters praises "The Destruction of Tenochtitlan" but prefaces his appreciation with the remark that Williams's "experience is disconnected and fragmentary, but sometimes a fragment is wrought to great beauty."[59] Winters divorces the chapter from its context. However, each chapter does contribute to a definite view of American history and the American experience which is anything but "disconnected and fragmentary."

January, A Novelette, written in 1929 and published in 1932, is a continuation of Williams's search for a new form for the novel. This work is his last piece of improvisatory writing and Williams considers it to be the most successful:

> I returned to a more placid style than in *Spring and All* but it was still a tremendous leap ahead of conventional prose. An American reader would have been lost entirely. I had abandoned all hope of getting American readers of a special sort. I wrote for personal satisfaction. This was automatic writing. I sat and faced the paper and wrote. The same method as in the IMPROVISATIONS but the material has advanced; it is more sophisticated. [IWW, 60]

A Novelette presents the reader with what by now have become familiar techniques—the brief anecdotes and observations put forward without transitions, sometimes interspersed with expository prose and theoretic explanations of his arbitrary procedure. However, *A Novelette* is Williams's most effective improvisatory synthesis. In a letter to Ezra Pound, Williams told him that "the *Novelette* is very close to my heart. . . . [It] contains something I have been trying for half my life" (SL, 112). In all probability Williams is referring here to his attempt to fuse his roles as husband, doctor, and poet.[60] The central motivation for the conversations, events, images, and thoughts in *A Novelette* is an influenza epidemic. Williams found that due to the "seriousness of the moment" caused by the epidemic, all the extraneous things of life disappeared and what was truly of value came into focus and "stood out in all fineness" allowing him to perceive the "real" relationships between parts, their "design" (IMAG, 273)[61]:

> That singleness I see in everything—actual—which has been my life, because of the haste due to the epidemic, I see in you and so you become beautiful partly because you are so but partly because

of other women. . . . There is a single significance in every minutest gesture of my life of which I am a part only. . . . These and other things have a relationship with each other simply because both are actual. [IMAG, 283, 295, 297]

Williams here begins to recognize the terms of the intimate connection and interdependence of his writing with his marriage and medical profession:

You, I, we, cannot you see how in the singleness of these few days marriage and writing have been fused so that the seriousness of my life and common objects about me have made up an actuality of which I am assembling the parts? [IMAG, 294]

In "assembling the parts," he again rejects any conventional form which would impose order for the purpose of a story or for the "meaning" of the novel. Rather, he strives for a "novel that is pure design—like the paintings of Juan Gris" (IMAG, 288), a design made up of "actual" objects rather than "realistic" portrayal.

In 1927 Williams began to write a novel entitled "Fairfield" revolving around the birth of a baby girl. The first versions and notes for this novel are contained in *The Descent of Winter* and *A Novelette and Other Prose.* It was during the planning and writing of this novel that Williams finally became dissatisfied with his former improvisatory techniques, and found himself faced with a dilemma since he also did not want to revert to a conventional novel form: "In writing a new novel—a clear style—the dangers are on one side my formerly important irritability, diffuseness—and on the other the 'plain' novel style or stylelessness" (BUFFALO). Williams tried to resolve his dilemma by putting aside "Fairfield" in favor of a more impersonal approach in *White Mule* (1937) and its sequel *In the Money* (1940).

Williams states that he wrote *White Mule* "without too much forethought, the way I always wrote" (IWW, 70–71), and that as the book was printed serially he "was always just up to the publication deadline" (IWW, 71). Nevertheless *White Mule* did emerge as an integrated whole. Williams told James Laughlin, who offered to make *White Mule* the first publication of *New Directions*, "This book is a unit. It has a beginning and a fairly satisfactory end" (SL, 162). The critics obviously agreed as the novel was Williams's "first real success" (AUTO, 301). The novel's "plot" consists of a series of episodes held together by the passage of time:

> A "real" plot would have interfered with Williams's sense of truth to life: there are no parallel developments of groups of characters, no structural ironies, and Williams is uninterested in the knowing asymmetries of the *nouvelle vague*. [62]

Williams did not want to subordinate his characters to a conventional plot.

Williams's technique in *White Mule* and *In the Money* is best understood in relation to "Objectivism," which Williams, along with a number of other writers, [63] turned to in the 1920s. Objectivism involved two basic tenets. The first is the necessity for intense concentration on the "object" or "thing," free from subjective interpretations. The second is that "the poem, like every form of art, is an object, an object that in itself formally presents its case and its meaning by the very form it assumes" (AUTO, 264). In "*White Mule* Versus Poetry" Williams states that "to turn to the writing of 'White Mule' from my usual interests in poetry meant no more to me than the carrying over of the same concerns for language into new conditions." [64] Consequently, in writing *White Mule* and its sequel Williams strives to remain as objective as possible. Thomas Whitaker makes an important and revealing point in reference to Williams's Objectivism in *White Mule* and *In the Money*:

> Though in *White Mule* and *In the Money* the author seems almost refined out of existence, the fiction does not use strictly limited points of view or impersonal techniques of revelation. The result is no illusion of an independent world but a continuing sense

of a truly human point of observation that does not call attention to itself—one that has become as transparent as possible. It is this transparency rather than any technical substitution of impersonality for personality, that Williams later meant when he said: "we've got first to annihilate ourselves out of the way of what we have to do and to say."[65]

Williams was the main protagonist of *The Great American Novel, January, A Novelette* as well as *A Voyage to Pagany* (1928), which was his "first serious novel" (IWW, 56). In the *White Mule* trilogy, however, the main characters are Williams's wife and her family; he found a "beginning" this time with Flossie's birth:

> I'd heard a lot about Flossie's babyhood from her family and I thought it was a good true picture of a baby. Why not write about Floss' babyhood, combining all the material I had learned about her with all that I had learned about babies. [IWW 71]

Williams states in reference to *White Mule* that he uses conversation from his patients' speech verbatim and tries not to distort it or mold it to his purposes.[66] This approach is quite different from that of *In the American Grain* where Williams manipulates and edits the original source material to conform to his theme.[67] It is the words he uses which interests him most of all:

> The writing of the language is what interests me. So in writing *White Mule* my greatest concern was to write with attention to marshalling the words into an order which would be free from "lies."[68]

In accord with Objectivist belief, he also wanted to make his novels into "objects," into a part of the real world:

> I want to write it so that when I speak of a chair it will stand upon four legs in a room. And of course it will stand upon a four-legged sentence on a page at the same time. [SL, 312]

In 1942 Williams published a play in prose and verse whose title *Trial Horse No. 1* was later changed to *Many Loves*. This play is composed of three prose sequences and a "counter-plot" written in verse. In *I Wanted to Write a Poem* Williams explains how the play came into existence. He had written three short plays, which he was unable to get produced, and so, having been influenced by Noel Coward's play *Tonight at 8:30*, he decided to try to link his unrelated plays together. This he accomplishes structurally by using the play-within-a-play technique. The counter-plot concerns the rather complex relationship between the playwright (Hubert), the backer (Peter), and the leading lady (Alise). Alise plays the main female role in each playlet while Hubert and Peter look on. The playlets already have a thematic link which Williams describes as "love—of a sort" (ML, 3), but is more accurately described as the consequences of male inadequacy and general lack of communication. The synthesizing counter-plot takes place not only between the playlets but also during them. Williams's stage direction that "the roles of Alise, Serafina, Agnes Breen and Clara are to be played by the same actress" (ML, 2), further brings out the unity of theme in the play as a whole.

The situations in the playlets are taken from Williams's experiences in Rutherford with the people he had seen and known. In *The Descent of Winter* Williams writes that

> the drama is the identification of the character with the man himself (Shakespeare—and his sphere of knowledge, close to him). As it flares in himself the drama is completed and the back kick of it is the other characters, created as the reflex of the first, so the dramatist "lives," himself in his world. . . . It is the *natural* drama, which can't imagine situations in any other way than in association with the flesh. [IMAG, 261–62]

T.S. Eliot makes a distinction among three voices of poetry:

> The first is the voice of the poet talking to himself—or to nobody. The second is the voice of the poet addressing an audience,

whether large or small. The third is the voice of the poet when he attempts to create a dramatic character speaking in verse; when he is saying, not what he would say in his own person, but only what he can say within the limits of one imaginary character addressing another imaginary character.[69]

As an example of voice three, Eliot relates that in his creation of the chorus of *Murder in the Cathedral* "I had to make some effort to identify myself with these women, instead of merely identifying them with myself."[70] This statement is in radical opposition to Williams's claim that "the drama is the identification of the character with the man himself"; however, as Eliot further maintains, in poetic drama all three voices can be heard. Despite Williams's definition of drama in *The Descent of Winter*, three voices are transparently audible in *Many Loves.* Hubert and "Doc" (a character who appears in the third playlet) are clearly aspects of Williams in his dual roles as poet and doctor. In the creation of the remainder of the characters, however, Williams quite obviously makes an effort to identify himself with them and their situation and to transcribe accurately the words they would use.

Williams originally titled the play *Trial Horse No. 1* because he considered the play to be an experiment with language. He explains the function of the prose and the verse within the play in a letter to Vivienne Koch:

> Of course my chief interest as always where the theatre is concerned is the language, verse first of all if it can be swung. And so the theme grew. I wanted verse. I saw that ordinary verse was impossible. So I goaded myself to study a possible verse.
>
> The first coalescing idea was to fix the bastards in their places by commonplace prose playlets, something to hold their *first* attention after which I would have my try at them with the intermediate verse which was my deepest concern.[71]

Williams is not interested in conventional dramatic devices, although the counter-plot does have a definite climax which culminates in a marriage (the playlets are episodes without dramatic development). The kind of "climax" Williams is really interested in effecting would be a consequence of his ability as poet/playwright to uncover the "special dramatic structure of words:"

> What is the dramatic structure, as it occurs in words? Verse. That is the drama of words—words in love, hot words, copulating, drinking, running, bleeding! [ML, 33]

He wants to make all the words so real that the members of the audience can see themselves in the characters on stage: "And how you shall laugh to see yourselves/all naked, on the stage!" (CLP, 15); this would constitute the "climax" of the play. He conveys this concept directly in Hubert's explanations of his plays to Peter (the "counter-plot" also serves the same function as the expository prose which Williams intersperses throughout his earlier work); but he also conveys it indirectly by making the climax of the counter-plot a direct consequence of their watching of the three playlets.

This chapter has traced Williams's concern with the discipline of writing in larger forms, from *Kora in Hell* to *Many Loves*. We have seen that Williams's involvement with the writing of these longer works led toward, and also depended upon, a concern with aspects of literary creation which need not detain the writer of short, nonrelated lyrics. In the first place, Williams became increasingly conscious of a moral obligation, as a poet, to make a shape out of the heterogeneous pieces of his world because "when we name it, life exists" (IMAG, 115). Williams also gradually became aware of an "audience," and of a responsibility to make himself clear and understood. In a 1964 interview, Williams told Stanley Koehler that his short stories

> were written in the form of a conversation which I was partaking in. We were in it together. . . . I was placing myself in continuation of a common conversation. . . . When I was talking in front of a

group, I wasn't interested in impressing them with my power of speech, but only with the seriousness of my intentions towards them. I had to make them come alive.[72]

In addition, Williams began to remove himself, his ego, out of the way of what he had to say; to develop a sense of objectivity in relation to the world, as well as to his own experiences and the parts of his own life. Finally, Williams's making of larger structures runs a parallel course to his working out of the relationship between prose and poetry, until finally, in reference to certain criticisms of *Paterson I* he can write with conviction, "The truth is that there's an *identity* between prose and verse, not an antithesis. It all rests on the same time base, the same measure" (SL, 265).

The following chapter, "Theme and Structure in *Paterson*," will reveal that, rather than being a substantial departure from Williams's customary concerns as a writer, *Paterson* is a continuation and an almost predictable culmination of his attempts at reaching a satisfactory synthesis through the writing of longer works. Our examination of Williams's experiments with extended patterns has also laid the foundation for a discussion of *Paterson* as a "Modern Epic" in Chapter 6.

NOTES TO CHAPTER 4

1. Robert Lowell, "*Paterson* I," *Sewanee Review* 4 (Summer 1947): 501.

2. A. Walton Litz, "WCW," in *The Literary Heritage of New Jersey*, New Jersey Historical Series, vol. 20 (Princeton, 1964), p. 105.

3. Vivienne Koch, "WCW: The Man and the Poet," *The Kenyon Review* 14, no. 3 (Summer 1952): 507.

4. David Weimer, *The City as Metaphor* (New York: Random House, 1966), p. 104.

5. Kenneth Burke, "WCW: Two Judgments," in *WCW*, ed. J. Hillis Miller (Englewood Cliffs, N.J.: Prentice-Hall, 1966), p. 47.

6. Burke, "WCW: Two Judgments," p. 50.

7. Gorham B. Munson, "WCW, a United States Poet," in *WCW: A Critical Anthology*, ed. Charles Tomlinson, (Harmondsworth, Middlesex: Penguin Books, 1972), p. 107.

8. Ibid., p. 100.

9. Ibid., p. 114.

10. Ezra Pound, "Dr. Williams' Position," in *WCW*, ed. Miller, p. 35.

11. Ibid., p. 36.

12. Yvor Winters, *In Defense of Reason* (Denver: University of Denver Press, 1947), p. 84.

13. Ibid., p. 93. See Winters, "Poetry of Feeling," in *WCW*, ed. Miller, p. 69, where Winters intensifies his earlier remarks with the statement that "to say that Williams was anti-intellectual would be almost an exaggeration: he did not know what the intellect was. He was a foolish and ignorant man, but at moments a fine stylist."

14. R. P. Blackmur, "John Wheelwright and Mr. Williams," in *WCW*, ed. Tomlinson, p. 138.

15. Walter Sutton, "A Visit with WCW," *Minnesota Review* 1 (Spring 1961), p. 323.

16. Wallace Stevens found this conviction to be a "constant difficulty." See *Letters of Wallace Stevens*, ed. Holly Stevens (New York: Alfred A. Knopf, 1966), p. 544: "I have not read *Paterson*. I have the greatest respect for him, although there is the constant difficulty that he is more interested in the way of saying things than in what he has to say. The fact remains that we are always fundamentally interested in what a writer has to say. When we are sure of that, we pay attention to the way in which he says it, not often before." On the other hand, it is interesting to note that C. K. Stead writes that, for Eliot, "a poem is to be tested not by what it *says* but by what it *is*" (*The New Poetic*, [London: Hutchinson, 1964], p. 125).

17. Williams claims that he "was interested in the construction of an image before the image was popular in poetry" (IWW, 33).

18. In his *Autobiography* Williams writes that "the immediate image, which was impressionistic, sure enough, fascinated us all. We had followed Pound's instructions, his famous 'Don'ts,' eschewing inversions of the phrase, the putting down of what to our sense was tautological and so, uncalled for, merely to fill out a standard form" (AUTO, 148).

19. Ezra Pound, "A Retrospect," in *Prose Keys to Modern Poetry*, ed. Karl Shapiro (New York: Harper & Row, 1962), pp. 104–05.

20. A less succinct version of Pound's three tenets appeared in the anthology *Some Imagist Poets* (Boston: Houghton Mifflin Co., 1915).

21. Quoted in John C. Thirlwall, "WCW's *Paterson*," *New Directions in Prose and Poetry 17* (Norfolk, Conn.: New Directions, 1961), p. 309.

22. Quoted in Vivienne Koch, *WCW* (Norfolk, Conn.: New Directions, 1950), p. 13.

23. Tony Tanner, *The Reign of Wonder* (Cambridge: Cambridge University Press, 1965), pp. 91–92.

24. William Carlos Williams, "An Essay on *Leaves of Grass*," in *Leaves of Grass One Hundred Years After*, ed. Milton Hindus (Stanford: Stanford University Press, 1955), p. 24.

25. Alfred Alvarez, *The Shaping Spirit* (London: Chatto & Windus, 1958), p. 178.

26. Byron Vazakas, *Transfigured Night* (New York: Macmillan, 1946), p. xi.

27. Despite the fact that Eliot and Williams differ radically in their approach to

technique, it is worthwhile pointing out that Eliot, too, maintains that it is through the development of technique, rather than particular moral judgments, that a poet achieves a moral quality. See Stead, *The New Poetic*, p. 133.

28. Cesare Pavese, *This Business of Living: Diary 1935–1950*, ed. and trans. A. E. Murch (London: Peter Owen, 1961), p. 123.

29. Cesare Pavese, *Selected Poems*, trans. Margaret Crosland (Harmondsworth, Middlesex: Penguin Books, 1971), p. 14.

30. René Taupin, *L'Influence du Symbolisme Français sur la Poésie Américaine* (Paris: Librairie Ancienne Honoré Champion, 1929), p. 281.

31. Ibid., p. 180.

32. James Breslin, *WCW: An American Artist* (New York: Oxford University Press, 1970), p. 60.

33. According to Williams, he adopted this method from a book Ezra Pound had left at his house—*Varie Poesie* dell' Abate Pietro Metastasio, Venice, 1795 (IWW, 39).

34. Pavese, *This Business of Living*, p. 122.

35. Burke, "WCW: Two Judgments," in *WCW*, ed. Miller, p. 48.

36. Munson, "WCW, a United States Poet," in *WCW*, ed. Tomlinson, pp. 100–101.

37. Robert McAlmon writes in *Being Geniuses Together:* "Paris bookshops did not show much interest in limited editions, and such books as we published and tried to send to England or America were held up at the docks and in most cases we were not notified" (Quoted in Emily Wallace, *A Bibliography of WCW* [Middletown, Conn.: Wesleyan University Press, 1968], p. 20).

38. According to Linda Wagner, much of the original material of *The Descent of Winter* went unpublished: "Whether Williams himself cut the manuscript, saving the sections that dealt more specifically with Dolores Marie and other characters of the town, or whether Pound exercised his editorial prerogative, there is no way of telling" (Linda Wagner, *The Prose of WCW* [Middletown, Conn.: Wesleyan University Press, 1970], p. 95).

39. *Spring and All* has also been published in its original form by Frontier Press (California, 1970).

40. Wagner, *The Prose of WCW*, p. 46.

41. Koch, *WCW*, p. 58.

42. Wagner, *The Prose of WCW*, p. 91.

43. Koch, *WCW*, p. 58.

44. See Wagner, *The Prose of WCW*, pp. 7, 32.

45. Ibid., p. 94.

46. Quoted in Wallace, *A Bibliography of WCW*, p. 17.

47. Kenneth Burke, "The Methods of WCW," *The Dial* 82 (February 1927): 98.

48. Ezra Pound, "Dr. Williams's Position," in *WCW*, ed. Tomlinson, p. 123.

49. Munson, "WCW, a United States Poet," in *WCW*, ed. Tomlinson, p. 110.

50. Gaston Bachelard, *The Poetics of Space*, trans. Maria Jolas (New York: Orion Press, 1964), p. xxiii.

51. Breslin, *WCW*, p. 105.

52. The study of John Paul Jones, "Battle Between the Bon Homme Richard and the Serapis," is copied verbatim from the original source.

53. Donald Davie, "The Legacy of Fenimore Cooper," *Essays in Criticism* 9, no. 3 (1959): 238.

54. Ibid., pp. 230–31.

55. See Alan Holder, "*In the American Grain:* WCW on the American Past," in *WCW*, ed. Tomlinson, pp. 239–58, for a detailed discussion of Williams's manipulation of his source material.

56. Breslin, *WCW*, p. 105.

57. Cambon, *The Inclusive Flame*, p. 187.

58. See Frye's definition of an "epic tendency" in *Anatomy of Criticism* (Princeton, N.J.: Princeton University Press, 1971), p. 55.

59. Winters, *In Defense of Reason*, p. 93.

60. See Webster Schott's "Introduction" to *A Novelette* in IMAG, 271: "Williams was pursuing a synthesis of his domestic life, his personality, his profession and art, and not in an orderly fashion. The imagination of the artist and the functions of the doctor-husband had to be brought together."

61. *A Novelette and Other Prose* was brought out by TO publishers, organized by a group of objectivist poets. Williams's statements in *January, A Novelette* bear a striking similarity to the tenets of Objectivism as set forth in the preface to Louis Zukofsky's *An "Objectivist" Anthology* (Le Beausset: TO, 1932), p. 10: "An objective—rays of the object brought to a focus, An objective—nature as a creator—desire for what is objectively perfect."

62. Anon., "Local Boy," in *WCW*, ed. Tomlinson, p. 360.

63. In particular Ezra Pound, Louis Zukofsky, Charles Reznikoff, Basil Bunting, George Oppen.

64. William Carlos Williams, "*White Mule* Versus Poetry," *The Writer* 50, no. 8 (August 1937): 243.

65. Thomas R. Whitaker, "The White Mule Trilogy" in *WCW*, ed. Tomlinson, p. 355. It is precisely in this way that C. K. Stead in *The New Poetic* interprets Eliot's "escape from personality" discussed in his essay "Tradition and the Individual Talent." Stead insists that for Eliot "the 'escape' is made, not away from the self, but deeper into the self, 'below the levels of consciousness.' Once . . . [this] is understood it is not surprising to find Eliot, reviewing Ezra Pound in 1919, complaining that some of the poems fail to achieve impersonality because they were not written with sufficient spontaneity" (pp. 131–32).

66. Williams, "*White Mule* Versus Poetry," pp. 244–45. Williams also wrote numerous short stories in a similar vein. His first collection, *The Knife of the Times and Other Stories* (1932), is "all about people who were my friends" (IWW, 61). He "wrote it down, without technical tricks" (IWW, 62). In his next collection, *Life Along the Passaic River* (1938), he began, as he says, to "experiment a little," though his choice of subject matter remained much the same.

67. However, the thematic content of *In the American Grain* and *White Mule* is very similar. Williams himself comments that they both express "the idealism of America . . . the great themes of American life and aspiration in the past" ("*White Mule* Versus Poetry," p. 244). Also see Guimond, *The Art of WCW*, pp. 109–25, for an elaboration on the similarities between the two works.

68. Williams, "*White Mule* Versus Poetry," p. 245.

69. T. S. Eliot, *The Three Voices of Poetry* (New York: Cambridge University Press, 1954), pp. 6–7.

70. Ibid., pp. 12–13.

71. Quoted in Koch, *WCW*, pp. 159–60, n. 1.

72. Stanley Koehler, "The Art of Poetry VI: WCW," *Paris Review* 8, no. 32 (Summer-Fall 1964): 116.

5   Theme and Structure in *Paterson*

> The theme
> is as it may prove: asleep, unrecognized—
> all of a piece, alone
> in a wind that does not move the others—
> [I, ii, 30]

This discussion of theme and structure in *Paterson* will begin by making a distinction between what we shall call the "material" theme of the poem and its "dominant" theme.[1] *Paterson*'s material theme is a statement of divorce, of a world characterized by a variety of distinctions and separations. Several aspects of the poem's material theme were dealt with in Chapter 2 in the commentary on the concept of the city in *Paterson*. Basic to the material theme is the narrative of the poet Paterson's struggle to establish a fertile contact with his environment and achieve a living language. It is the subject matter, the "internal fiction"[2] of the poem that constitutes the material theme. The dominant theme of *Paterson* is the resolution of disunity into a complex totality by lifting the world of Paterson to expression: "The poem to me (until I go broke) is an attempt, an experiment, a failing experiment, toward assertion with broken means but an assertion, always of a new and total culture, the lifting of an environment to expression" (SL, 286). In a letter to Marianne Moore in 1951 Williams makes a distinction which will, perhaps, clarify these two areas of significance. He writes that "if I did not succeed on one level, I did cling to a living language on another. The poem, as opposed to what was accomplished in the story, came to life at moments—even when my failure was most vocal and went above that to a different sort of achievement. Or so I believe" (SL, 304).[3] This "different sort of achivement," the final impact of the poem, is its dominant theme: "I am speaking of the thing itself which surpasses, as I shall maintain, what is merely *said* in the poem; the topical matter of which it treats."[4] It is the idiom and structure of *Paterson* which discloses the dominant theme underlying the material theme of divorce and quest:

> The basic idea which underlies our art must be, for better or worse, that which Toynbee has isolated for us: abundance, that is, permission, for all. And it is in the *structure* of our works that this must show. We must embody the principle of abundance, of total availability of materials, freest association in the measure, in *that* to differ from the poem of all previous time. It will be that sort of thing, if we succeed, that shall give us our supreme distinction.[5]

One of the primary difficulties in discussing *Paterson* is that the material theme of the poem is diametrically opposed to its dominant theme of unity. Yet this fact is inevitable given what James Breslin has termed Williams's "informing myth"—"the discovery of plenty lodged, as it must be in the modern world, in barrenness."[6] As Williams writes in "Asphodel, That Greeny Flower,"

> I was cheered
> > when I came first to know
> that there were flowers also
> > in hell. [PB, 153]

This chapter's thesis confronts the critical views which assert that *Paterson*'s structure "takes the form of a 'model of confusion' that reflects the contradictions implicit in a society" and that "historical and spiritual dislocation . . . provides the poem with its theme . . . [and] suggests its shape."[7] Robert Lowell's statement that "the poem is really about . . . the divorce of modern life, of intellect and sensibility, spirit and matter"[8] is also incomplete because it encompasses only the material aspects of the poem. As we shall see, the structure of *Paterson* may be engaged on several levels which provide insight into the ways in which the poem's dominant theme of unity is articulated. All of these levels share a common dependency upon nonlinear patterning and upon a process that is open and dialectical and which occurs only with the active participation of the reader.

A

Measure

> Without invention nothing is well spaced,
> unless the mind change, unless
> the stars are new measured, according
> to their relative positions, the
> line will not change, the necessity
> will not matriculate: unless there is
> a new mind there cannot be a new
> line, the old will go on
> repeating itself with recurring
> deadliness: without invention
> nothing lies under the witch-hazel
> bush, the alder does not grow from among
> the hummocks margining the all
> but spent channel of the old swale,
> the small foot-prints
> of the mice under the overhanging
> tufts of the bunch-grass will not
> appear: without invention the line
> will never again take on its ancient
> divisions when the word, a supple word,
> lived in it, crumbled now to chalk. [II, i, 65]

Williams often asserted that the theory of relativity has a definite bearing upon the writing of poetry:

> It may seem presumptive to state that such an apparently minor activity as a movement in verse construction could be an indication

of Einstein's discoveries in the relativity of our measurements of
physical matter is drastic enough, but such is the fact [*sic*]. . . .
When Einstein promulgated the theory of relativity he could not
have foreseen its moral and intellectual implication. He could not
have foreseen for a certainty its influence on the writing of poetry.
[SL, 332, 335–36]

This observation relates to Williams's prosody as well as to the
larger, external features of *Paterson*'s structure. Before turning
to the poem's overall organization of parts, it is essential to
consider Williams's combining of the basic elements of language, for as he wrote to John Thirlwall in 1955, "If the
measurement itself is confined, every dimension of the verse
and all implications touching it suffer confinement and generate pressures within our lives which will blow it and us apart"
(SL, 332). Williams insists in a letter to Jean Starr Untermeyer
in 1948 that "until the underlying mechanism [of the poem] is
established you will never succeed in making it an organism. It
must first be regrown from the ground up—from the skeleton
out *before* the flesh, the muscles, the brain can be put upon it"
(SL, 269). And on a Yale worksheet for *Paterson* titled
"Maxims" Williams writes that "if there is no invention in the
verse, in the structure of the verse, there is no invention in the
poem" (YALE). *Paterson*'s measure is, in certain respects, a
microcosm of the poem's general organization. Williams stated
in 1948 that "only by a new measure can we break up the old
tendency toward inversion for conformity and admit new
materials."[9] Similarly in his essay "Projective Verse" Charles
Olson indicates the vital connection among prosody, content,
and the larger form of the poem:

> For I would hazard the guess that, if projective verse is practiced
> long enough, is driven ahead hard enough . . . verse again can
> carry much larger material than it has carried in our language since
> the Elizabethans. . . . The methodology of the verse in them
> [*Cantos*] points a way by which, one day, the problem of larger
> content and of larger forms may be solved.[10]

These statements made by Williams and Olson directly controvert the critical opinions (see chaps. 1, 4, and 6) which maintain that Williams's prosody, his so-called lyric talent, basically precludes him from writing a successful long poem.

Williams maintains that poets can no longer write validly in structures informed by concepts of reality made obsolete by Einstein's theories which reveal that the universe is not temporally linear or spatially continuous. Mike Weaver asserts that Williams first became aware that the theory of relativity had a bearing upon his search for a new measure as a result of his friendship and correspondence with John Riorden, a young engineer interested in writing. In 1926 Riorden sent Williams, at his request, a book on relativity by C.P. Steinmetz (*Four Lectures on Relativity and Space*), and later presented him with a copy of Whitehead's *Science and the Modern World.* Weaver suggests that Williams derives his concept of the relative length of a line of verse, the "variable foot," from illustrations of relativity in Steinmetz's book. In approaching the measurement of figures in space, Steinmetz states that we cannot measure any body "by bringing the measure to it, because the length and shape of the measure change when it is moved through space."[11] This is of obvious relevance to Williams's insistence that "order is what is discovered after the fact" (SL, 214), that the measure of the poem can only be realized during the very process of writing it:

> How can we accept Einstein's theory of relativity, affecting our very conception of the heavens about us of which poets write so much, without incorporating its essential fact—the relativity of measurements—into our own category of activity: the poem. Do we think we stand outside the universe? Or that the Church of England does? Relativity applies to everything, like love, if it applies to anything in the world. . . . What we are trying to do is not only to disengage the elements of a measure but to seek (what we believe is there) a new measure or a new way of measuring that will be commensurate with the social, economic world in which we are living as contrasted with the past. It is in many ways a different world from the past calling for a different measure.[12] [SE, 283]

Paterson is the verbal space in which Williams works to disengage the traditional elements of measure, and it is the proving ground for a new prosody, a new way of measuring. The poem is the record of a search, of "a failing experiment" (SL, 286) rather than a finished product: "I am trying in *Paterson* to work out the problems of a new prosody" (SL, 257–58). Williams clearly indicates this in the preface to *Paterson* in which he speaks of "rolling/up the sum, by defective means—" (I, p. 11) and in his reference to himself as a lame dog—standing only on three legs. The falls is perhaps the most central image in the poem, evoking a torrent of speech continually falling on the ears of the poet who strives to untangle the confusion of sound (see facsimile 5, chap. 5B).

> Caught (in mind)
> beside the water he looks down, listens!
> But discovers, still, no syllable in the confused
> uproar: missing the sense (though he tries)
> untaught but listening, shakes with the intensity
> of his listening   . [II, ii, 100]

Destruction, violence, and death permeate the pages of *Paterson*, from the ruination of "the finest pearl of modern times" (I, i, 17) in the beginning of Book I, to the hunt of the Unicorn in Book V. The human, natural, and mythic violence throughout the poem is a manifestation of energy which affirms movement, change, and life itself. So it is that Book IV concludes with the account of a hanging of a violent murderer followed by an image of birth and renewal suggested most clearly by "the final somersault" (IV, iii, 238), which is the last movement of a fetus before its emergence from the womb. Eric Mottram similarly observes that "Book Four, and the whole structure that Williams concluded here, ends with an ideogram of recurrent violence and recurrent vitality, and a theory of history which accommodates these without dehumanizing them."[13] As early as 1913 Williams wrote to Harriet Monroe that life is above all things at any moment subversive of life as it was the moment before—always new, irregular. Verse to be alive must have infused into it something of the same order, some tincture of disestablishment, something in the nature of an impalpable revolution, an ethereal reversal, let me say. I am speaking of modern verse.

   Poetry I saw accepting verse of this kind: that is, verse with perhaps nothing else in it but life—this alone, regardless of possible imperfections, for no new thing comes through perfect. In the same way the Impressionists had to be accepted for the sake of art's very life—in spite of bad drawing. [SL, 23–24]

Throughout his poetic career Williams was concerned, above all, with infusing his poems with the "subversive" energy of life. In the prose to *Spring and All* he asserts that he does not want his poems to be "like" nature but rather "transfused with the same forces which transfuse the earth" (IMAG, 121) and by that means become a reality in their own right. Williams believed that the first step toward his objective would have to be a destructive, "disjointing process" (IMAG, 285) in order to get "life" back into the writing: "Destruction . . . comes before creation. . . . We must be destructive first to free ourselves from forms accreting to themselves tyrannies we despise."[14] Williams's appreciation of the work of Walt Whitman, Gertrude Stein, Ezra Pound, and James Joyce, center on their individual contributions toward the liberation of words and forms. It is therefore significant and appropriate that they are all invoked implicitly or explicitly in *Paterson*. For instance, although Whitman's name does not appear in any of the five books of the poem, in his *Autobiography* Williams writes that at the end of Book IV

   the man rises from the sea where the river appears to have lost its identity and accompanied by his faithful bitch, obviously a Chesapeake Bay retriever, turns inland toward Camden where Walt Whitman, much traduced, lived the latter years of his life and died. He always said that his poems, which had broken the dominance of the iambic pentameter in English prosody, had only begun his theme. I agree. It is up to us, in the new dialect, to continue it by a new construction upon the syllables. [AUTO, 392]

Paterson III, which Williams indicated in his "Author's Note" would "seek a language to make them [the modern replicas in Book II] vocal," is permeated with the natural destruction of wind, fire, and flood, associated by direct statement, implication, and contrast with the breaking up of "composition," of language. It is only by virtue of a series of destructive violence in which "most things have lost their/ form" (III, iii, 167) that Book III can end with the statement that "this rhetoric/is real!" (III, iii, 173). In this book Williams makes use of the deluge symbolism of which Mircea Eliade speaks: "In water everything is 'dissolved,' every 'form' is broken up, everything that has happened ceases to exist"[15] Grammatically, the sentence is the closed space that must be broken to be opened: "Kill the explicit sentence, don't you think? and expand our meaning—by verbal sequences. Sentences, but not grammatical sentences: dead-falls set by schoolmen" (IV, iii, 222). In an essay on Gertrude Stein in 1935 Williams asserts that "everything we know and do is tied up with words, with the phrases words make, with the grammar which stultifies, the prose or poetical rhythms which bind us to our pet indolences and medievalisms. . . . This is a moral question at base, surely but a technical one also and first" (SE, 163). On a worksheet for *Paterson* Williams writes that

anything which will break up cliché of sound is an advantage. Therefore write the poem on the page as it strikes your fancy, especially if the appearance of it break up stodgy (therefore lying, and only because they lyingly defeat the imagination) sound tracks. [BUFFALO]

The most obvious and extreme example of this occurs in the third section of Book III, where phrases concerned with measurement, time, and death are slanted indiscrimately on the page: "Let the words/fall any way at all—that they may/hit

love aslant" (III, iii, 169). In this section he salutes Antonin
Artaud "pour les/lignes trés pures: et d'évocations plastiques
d'élements de" (III, iii, 164), and in a letter to Parker Tyler he
asserts that Artaud was involved "in breaking down . . .
fixations toward the metrical traditions of yesterday" (SL,
242).[16]

The rules of grammar are allegedly rooted in an outmoded
concept of reality which assumes the smooth continuities of
time and space. Marshall McLuhan points out that the "artistic
discovery for achieving rich implication by withholding the
syntactical connection is stated as a principle of modern physics
by A.N. Whitehead in *Science and the Modern World*."[17]
Paratactic and nonlinear constructions are, of course, hardly
confined to our modern world informed by the theory of
relativity. Yet it is likely that the *rediscovery* and increasing use
of parataxis has grown out of new facts which have been
revealed about the nature of time and space and a desire to
imitate the structure of contemporary reality. Erich Auerbach
in *Mimesis* talks of a similar early movement from syntactic
arrangement to parataxis when the Judaeo-Christian tradition
introduced a new conception of history:

> This conception of history [that occurrences are vertically linked
> to Divine Providence] is magnificent in its homogeneity, but it was
> completely alien to the mentality of classical antiquity, it annihi-
> lated that mentality down to the very structure of its language, at
> least of its literary language, which—with all its ingenious and
> nicely shaded conjunctions, its wealth of devices for syntactic
> arrangement, its carefully elaborated system of tenses—became
> wholly superfluous as soon as earthly relations of place, time, and
> cause had ceased to matter, as soon as a vertical connection,
> ascending from all that happens, converging in God, alone became
> significant.[18]

This statement provides further evidence that changing con-
ceptions of reality do eventually affect language. In both
instances, in the early Judaeo-Christian period and the modern

period, paratactic constructions developed because temporal and causal sequences were largely deemphasized, although for quite different reasons. It is also significant, in the light of Williams's insistence on the use of the spoken language as the basis of his measure, that, according to Auerbach, "in the classical languages paratactic constructions belong to the low style; they are oral rather than written, comic and realistic rather than elevated."[19] Despite his insistence on the relationship between the new physics and his new measure, Williams gradually became conscious of belonging to a poetic tradition that certainly extended beyond Whitman. The final proof of this is recorded in a letter which he wrote to Louis Martz in 1951: "The 'new measure' is much more particular, much more related to the remote past than I, for one, believed" (SL, 299). In a definition of free verse which he wrote for the *Encyclopedia of Poetry and Poetics*, Williams mentions "Gr. and L. 'art prose,' " "medieval tropes and sequences," "alliterative verse," "Hebrew cadences" as some of the antecedents of free verse.[20] On an unpublished worksheet for an essay titled "Free Verse" he lists a number of other precursors among which are included the King James version of the *Song of Songs*, Thomas Campion, Milton in *Comus* and "Lycidas," Dryden in *Absalom and Achitophel,* and Gerard Manley Hopkins (YALE).

Notwithstanding the emphasis Williams places on destruction and liberation, he knew well the necessity of achieving some kind of order and discipline "*to free* [*us*] from the vagaries of mere chance and to teach us to rule ourselves again" (SL, 336). He told Edith Heal that from the beginning "the orderliness of verse appealed to me . . . but even more I wanted a new order. I was positively repelled by the old order which, to me, amounted to restriction" (IWW, 29). He found himself faced with the difficult problem of how to make the transference from the "actual" to the formal and at the same time retain a sense of life and energy. In a letter to Kenneth Burke, Williams writes:

My whole intent, in my life, has been, as with you, to find a basis (in poetry, in my case) for the actual. It isn't a difficult problem to solve theoretically. All one has to do is to discover new laws of the metric and use them. That's objective enough and little different from the practical deductions of an Edison. The difficulty lies in the practice. [SL, 257]

Williams's search for a new measure which culminated in his concept of the variable foot involved a process of listening to and writing down the language as he heard it spoken about him every day, for he maintains that poetry "deals with reality, the actuality of every day, by virtue of its use of language" (SL, 131). Through such a process he hoped to discover what "formal elements"[21] in the language might serve as the ordering principles of his poems: "In some of my work all I have to do is to transcribe the language when hot and feelingly spoken. For when it is charged with emotion it has a tendency to be rhythmic, low-down, inherent in the place where it is being used. And that is, to me, the origin of form, the origin of measure. The rhythmic beat of charged language."[22] In 1932 Williams confided to Kay Boyle that he had not been writing much poetry because of his sense of the need for form coupled with his rejection of orthodox forms. "Instead," he writes,

I have been watching speech in my own environment from which I continually expect to discover whatever of new is being reflected about the world. . . . I have been actively at work . . . in the flesh, watching how words match the act, especially how they come together. The result has been a few patches of metrical coherence which I don't as yet see how to use—but they seem to run to groups of lines. Occasionally they give me the feel of authenticity. [SL, 129–30]

Williams came to realize that despite a lack of a satisfactory form, he must continue to write poetry rather than "logic," in order "to work out the problems of a new prosody" (SL, 257–58). *Paterson* is the result of this realization: "The Falls let out a roar as it crashed upon the rocks at its base. In the imagination this roar is a speech or a voice, a speech in particular; it is the poem itself that is the answer" (AUTO, 392).

From the very beginning Williams was disturbed as to how he would put *Paterson* on the page. Eventually he decided to "let form take care of itself; the colloquial language, my own language, set the pace" (IWW, 83). Williams fully recognized that the American language of everyday speech on which he pinned such hopes, was debased and "defective" (I, p. 11)— pervaded with lying habits, clichés, evasive chatter. Yet he persisted in its study and use, maintaining that the only way to capture and retain the fullness of immediate experience in words is through contact with, and a use of, "live speech" (SL, 134): "For it is in that, that it [*Paterson*] be particular to its own idiom, that it lives" (AUTO, 392). He wrote to John Holmes in 1952:

> What shall we say more of the verse that is to be left behind by the age we live in if it does not have some of the marks the age has made upon us, its poets? . . . They should be horrible things, those poems. To the classic muse their bodies should appear to be covered with sores. They should be hunchbacked, limping. And yet our poems must show how we have struggled with them to measure and control them. And we must SUCCEED even while we succumb. [SL, 315–16]

Williams wrote to Ralph Nash in 1954, in reference to an article Nash had written on prose in *Paterson*, that a man must "fight his way to a world which breaks through to the actual. . . . In my reference to Hipponax, the Greek in *Paterson*, you can again see it breaking out" (SL, 324). Williams places his reference to Hipponax after the end of Book I, thereby giving the impression that the passage is a footnote, an explanation, or perhaps even an *apologia* for what has gone before and what is to come. In addition, by including this reference to Greek poetry within *Paterson* Williams indicates a unity, which he often insisted upon, between classical literature and the literature of today (see chap. 6). It is certainly true that the passage

does serve as a commentary on Williams's recourse to the
language of common speech in his search for a new measure:

> N.B. "In order apparently to bring the meter still more within
> the sphere of prose and common speech, Hipponax ended his
> iambics with a spondee or a trochee instead of an iambus, doing
> thus the utmost violence to the rhythmical structure. These
> deformed and mutilated verse were called   χωλίαμβοι   or
> ίαμβοι σκάζοντες (lame or limping iambics). They com-
> municated a curious crustiness to the style. The choliambi are in
> poetry what the dwarf or cripple is in human nature. Here again,
> by their acceptance of this halting meter, the Greeks displayed
> their acute aesthetic sense of propriety, recognizing the harmony
> which subsists between crabbed verses and the distorted subjects
> with which they dealt—the vices and perversions of humanity—as
> well as their agreement with the snarling spirit of the satirist.
> Deformed verse was suited to deformed morality."
> —*Studies of the Greek Poets,* John Addington Symonds
> Vol. I, p. 284 [I, iii, 53]

To say that Williams listened for and eventually discovered
his new measure in the spoken language is not, of course,
simply to say that he found it in the rhythms of prose, for the
structure of speech differs from that of spoken or written prose
as Northrop Frye aptly indicates by relating that "if we are lost
in a strange town and ask someone for directions, we do not get
prose: we get pure Gertrude Stein, a speech rhythm that is
prolix and repetitive, and in which the verbal unit is no more a
prose sentence than it is a villanelle."[23] Poetry establishes
contact with reality through its use of the spoken language by
virtue of the personal as well as the social nature of speech:

> The melody and measure of speech are very much a *personal,* as
> well as a social thing. There are established patterns, in rhythm and
> intonation, for each language or dialect, as much a *part* of that
> language as its articulate sounds or its grammar. But within these
> patterns, or "norms," there is room for great individual variation,
> variation which expresses our personality and our feelings and
> emotions of the moment. Through these features spoken language

is always *tied* closely to its immediate occasion, to the situation and to the persons participating.[24]

Since the character of an area is inevitably reflected in its idiom, its living speech, the poet concerned with penetrating and capturing the life of his world best serves his objective by paying close attention to "the spontaneous . . . conformations of language as it is *heard*" (BUFFALO). Williams states he "knew that the American language must shape the pattern" of his verse but that later he "rejected the word language and spoke of the American idiom" because idiom "was a better word than language, less academic, more identified with speech" (IWW, 76).[25] He told Stanley Koehler that his poems "had to be modified by the conversation about me . . . language modified by *our* environment; the American environment."[26] In his *Autobiography* Williams relates that in the process of his patients' struggling to articulate themselves, a "rare element" would manifest itself so that "some secret twist of a whole community's pathetic way of thought" (AUTO, 359) would be revealed in the words:

> For under that language to which we have been listening all our lives a new, a more profound language . . . offers itself. It is what they call poetry. . . . It is actually there, in the life before us, every minute that we are listening, a rarest element—not in our imaginations but there, there in fact. . . . By listening to the minutest variations of the speech we begin to detect that today, as always, the essence is also to be found, hidden under the verbiage, seeking to be realized. . . . The poem springs from the half-spoken words of such patients as the physician sees from day to day. He observes it in the peculiar, actual conformations in which its life is hid. Humbly he presents himself before it and by long practice he strives as best he can to interpret the manner of its speech. In that the secret lies. [AUTO, 361–62]

Because speech is also dependent upon the breathing of the speaker, it is, as Abercrombie points out, linked to each particular moment.[27] In his introduction to "The Wedge" (1944)

Williams defines the poem as a "machine made of words" and continues, "As in all machines its movement is intrinsic, undulant, a physical more than a literary character. In a poem this movement is distinguished in each case by the character of the speech from which it arises" (CLP, 4). Williams later asserts to Koehler that the measure "must be transcribed to the page from the lips of the poet, as it was with such a master as Sappho."[28] In the beginning of Book V, ii of *Paterson*, there is a quotation from A. P. (Arnold Post according to unpublished notes) which emphasizes the importance of the poet's physical voice:

> "I am no authority on Sappho and do not read her
> poetry particularly well. She wrote for a clear
> gentle tinkling voice. She avoided all roughness.
> 'The silence that is in the starry sky,' gives
> something of her tone,   ." [V, ii, 253]

Charles Olson appropriately begins his essay on projective verse by referring to its physical nature:

> Verse now, 1950, if it is to go ahead, if it is to be of *essential* use, must, I take it, catch up and put into itself certain laws and possibilities of the breath, of the breathing of the man who writes as well as of his listenings.[29]

He goes on to say that "verse will only do in which a poet manages to register both the acquisitions of his ear *and* the pressures of his breath"[30]—that is to say, the cultural idiom as well as the poet's personal speech. In Book I of *Paterson* Williams writes,

> Only of late, late! begun to know, to
> know clearly (as through clear ice) whence
> I draw my breath or how to employ it
> clearly—if not well: [I, ii, 31]

In *The Great American Novel* Williams asserts that "in the

moment exists all the past and the future" (IMAG, 214). A poem which is closely tied to its immediate occasion through its unique structure thereby embodies an element of timeliness and timelessness: "A life that is here and now is timeless. That is the universal I am seeking: to embody that in a work of art, a new world that is always 'real' " (SE, 196). And so in *Paterson*, "the roar of the present, a speech—/is, of necessity, my sole concern" (III, iii, 172).

On several occasions Williams acknowledges Gerard Manley Hopkins as a pioneer in the reestablishment of contact with the living language and in the break with the pentameter.[31] On a *Paterson* worksheet he writes that "the lecture on uranium (Curie) the splitting of the atom . . . has a *literary* meaning—in the splitting of the foot—(sprung meter of Hopkins)" (YALE). There is, in fact, a marked resemblance between the prosodic theory and practice of the two poets. Hopkins's conviction that "a perfect style must be of its age"[32] and Williams's search for a new measure to "include the age" (SL, 135) led both poets to the use of speech and prose rhythms. According to Hopkins, "sprung rhythm," because it is based on the number of stresses in a line rather than of syllables, reflects "the rhythm of common speech and of written prose, when rhythm is perceived in them."[33] Hopkins's avoidance of inversions of the language in his poetry "because they weaken and because they destroy the earnestness or in-earnestness of the utterance," as well as his statement that "the poetical language of an age shd. be the current language heightened"[34] aptly defines Williams's position in regard to language used in poetry. Hopkins also was convinced that a poem should not have its form brought to it but that the form should grow out of the interpretive stress of language with which both poets experimented and which led Hopkins to his "sprung rhythm" and Williams to his concept of the "variable foot." Williams states that he discovered the variable foot in what he had himself previously written (specifically "The descent beckons" passage in II, iii, 96), and then he began to notice its presence elsewhere in what others had written. He maintains that Shakespeare's use of prose rhythms "gives him [Shakespeare] some of his most impressive effects which may be interpreted as presaging the advent of the variable foot."[35] He also told Walter Sutton that even "Whitman's verse could be counted as spaced, let us say, spaced long or short, but variable."[36] Hopkins discovered his "sprung rhythm" in a similar manner. He writes that "I had long had haunting my ear the echo of a new rhythm which now I realised on paper."[37] He then proceeded to come across his new rhythm in such varied places as Anglo-Saxon verse, Milton's prosody, and nursery rhymes. In an essay on Hopkins's sprung rhythm Walter J. Ong, S.J., similarly observes that Hopkins did not derive his rhythm from any one place but that

> he noticed *what* it was when it was already in his own possession, after he had already picked it up. . . . This much is certain: the real sources of a rhythm which makes such a radical claim on a language as that of being the rhythm of the language's prose can hardly be narrowed to one or two authors or to nursery rhymes, though these may provide quite valid instances of the rhythm's appearance. . . . If Hopkins' claims for his rhythm are acceptable, he must have been, consciously or unconsciously, hearing it everywhere.[38]

Both poets were sensitively attuned to the rhythms of natural and emotive speech and they both attempted to develop a way in which to use consciously what they heard in the measuring of their poems to produce a poetry "simple as speech itself and subtle as the subtlest brain could desire on the basis of the measure."[39] As Hopkins wrote to his friend Robert Bridges, "I do not of course claim to have invented *sprung rhythms* but only *sprung rhythm*"[40] The affinity between Hopkins and Williams is further evidenced by the similar equivocal opinions which they held in regard to Walt Whitman. Although Hopkins describes Whitman's verse as "an irregular rhythmic prose" and his style as "savage," he also writes in the same letter,

> I always knew in my heart Walt Whitman's mind to be more like

my own than any other man's living. As he is a very great scoundrel this is not a pleasant confession.[41]

Paterson includes an astonishing range of speech and prose rhythms which run the entire gamut from the "low" demotic to the "middle" hieratic.[42] The prose letters vary in style from DJB's colloquial slang to the consciously literary quality of Cress's letters. In a chapter on "Conversation and Spoken Prose" in his collection of essays *Studies in Phonetics and Linguistics*, David Abercrombie discusses the difficulty of recording conversation in writing:

> To write conversation adequately, we must be able to include the intonation in the text, whereas there is no need at all to do so in writing prose.
> We ought to be able to write down other things too—variations in tempo, in voice quality, in loudness; pauses, coughs, stammers, interjections.[43]

Williams's transcriptions of individual speech rhythms in lines of poetry, which range from Klaus Ehren's oratorical harangue to Corydon's self-conscious attempts at sophistication in Book IV, are in effect, experiments with the transposition of speech intonation—pitch, tempo, and even volume. Francis Berry points out in *Poetry and the Physical Voice* that there are a number of ways in which a poet can indicate voice:

> Each voice defines itself by its choice of themes and imagery, by its choice of phonic elements to provide the equivalents in sound of such themes and imagery, and by the choice of those grammatical forms and constructions requiring an appropriate vocal inflexion.[44]

Williams told Stanley Koehler that "an American is forced to try to give the intonation. Either it *is* important or it is not important. It must have occurred to an American that the question of the line *was* important. The American idiom has much to offer us that the English language has never heard of."[45] In a review of H.L. Mencken's *The American Language*,

Williams criticizes Mencken for failing to point out that the new American poetry bears witness to the unique character of the American language. Williams writes,

> The inner spirit of the new language is original. Its difference from standard English is not merely a difference in vocabulary to be disposed of in an alphabetical list, it is above all a difference in pronunciation, in intonation, in conjugation, in metaphor and idiom, in the whole fashion of using words.[46]

An American poet, therefore, has to be concerned with finding a way to indicate these differences. In addition, Williams includes prose within the body of *Paterson* partly, as he says, to emphasize "a metrical continuity between all word use" (SL, 263) because he maintains that both prose and verse rest "on the same time base, the same measure" (SL, 265). Although Williams does not elaborate on this statement, except to say that prose came after verse, not before it,[47] he must have been aware, consciously or unconsciously, that the "stress-timed rhythm of English" is the basis of verse as well as prose.[48] Williams further experimented with the forms of written language by putting prose into lines of verse. The longest example of this occurs in Book IV, where a prose description of "old Paterson," partly paraphrased but primarily taken verbatim from Longwell's *A Little Story of Old Paterson,* is printed as verse.[49] The worksheets for the poem reveal that Williams originally attempted to arrange many of the prose pieces of the poem as poetry, such as the Sam Patch story in Book I, Cress's letters, and many of the prose sections in III, iii. All of these experimentations with the spoken as well as the written language were directed toward a discovery of the unit of the new measure which Williams predicted would replace the English foot: "And I would have you understand all the irregularities that you find in modern verse—bizarre and puzzling—are attempts or related initiatives toward the discovery (and use) of a new measure."[50]

On a worksheet for *Paterson* in 1944 Williams wrote that the poem "is fast becoming, as it inevitably must, a restudy of the poetic line—following Whitman's first effects—on a new sensual (auditory) basis using the local dialect as heard: Counted as heard. This is its chief value as a work of art—the conscious objective" (YALE). It must have gratified Williams, therefore, that he was able to write to Marianne Moore in 1951 in reference to *Paterson*, "I say even that the language is even more sensuous, more convenient to the line, more fits the line in the last book than in the first" (SL, 305). In fact, Williams focused a considerable amount of attention on developing a new integrity for the poetic line which he held to be "the seat of . . . stasis"[51] and where "the battle lodges."[52] He wrote to Denise Levertov that "the test of how the poet is going to divide her lines is the test of what she or he is."[53]

In his study *Ezra Pound: Poet as Sculptor*, Donald Davie writes:

> It was only when the line was considered as the unit of composition, as it was by Pound in *Cathay*, that there emerged the possibility of "breaking" the line, of disrupting it from within, by throwing weight upon smaller units within the line. . . . Only when the line was isolated as a rhythmical unit did it become possible for the line to be rhythmically disrupted or dismembered from within.[54]

In *Paterson* Williams experiments with separating the line into its rhythmical members as in the following verse paragraph from Book I whose lines are divided by punctuation and line division into units of from 1 to 4:

> And there, against him, stretches the low mountain.
> The Park's her head, carved, above the Falls, by the quiet
> river; Colored crystals the secret of those rocks;
> farms and ponds, laurel and the temperate wild cactus,
> yellow flowered   .   .   facing him, his
> arm supporting her, by the *Valley of the Rocks*, asleep.
> Pearls at her ankles, her monstrous hair

spangled with apple-blossoms is scattered about into
the back country, waking their dreams—where the deer run
and the wood-duck nests protecting his gallant plumage. [I, i, 17]

Such dismemberment of the line from within was only one short step away from Williams's concept of the variable foot. Williams wrote to Thirlwall in 1955 that "The descent beckons" passage in Book II, iii, 96 of *Paterson* is where "the implications of the variable foot first struck" him and "prompted . . . his solution of the problem of modern verse" (SL, 334). The following is Williams's revised version of the beginning of this important passage (with the addition of numerals), which was published in *The Desert Music and Other Poems* (1954):

   (1) The descent beckons
         (2) as the ascent beckoned.
                (3) Memory is a kind
   (4) of accomplishment,
         (5) a sort of renewal
                (6) even
   (7) an initiation, since the spaces it opens are new places
         (8) inhabited by hordes
                (9) heretofore unrealized,
  (10) of new kinds
         (11) since their movements
                (12) are toward new objectives
  (13) (even though formerly they were abandoned). [PB, 73]

Williams offers an explanation of his variable foot in a letter to Richard Eberhart. He writes, referring to poems written in a similar pattern as seen above, "Count a single beat to each numeral. You may not agree with my ear, but that is the way I count the line. Over the whole poem it gives a pattern to the meter that can be felt as a new measure. It gives resources to the ear which result in a language which we hear spoken about us every day" (SL, 327).[55] In a letter to Mary Ellen Solt in 1958 Williams refers to these beats as "stops" or "qualitative" stresses.[56] Williams's triadic line consists therefore, of three short lines each of which is a variable foot or a qualitative stress. In Williams's variable-foot poems he primarily uses the space of the page rather than punctuation to indicate the rhythmical members, allowing him to move farther away from grammatical constructions, toward an open, "projective" form, more consonant with speech.[57] Williams also refers to his new measure, in the letter to Eberhart, as "musical pace," suggesting that the words in each variable foot are analogous to musical notes, each measure, of course, taking up the same amount of time. Thus the sixth foot, "even," should occupy approximately the same time as the fifth foot, "a sort of renewal." This implies the existence of moments of silence, similar to "rests" as in music. These "rests" are also analogous to the pauses in spoken language which Abercrombie notes: "In spoken prose these [pauses] are closely related to the grammatical structure of the sentences, but in conversation pauses seem to play a different kind of role—they frequently come at places which, in the present state of our knowledge, are unpredictable."[58]

A remarkable correspondence between Williams's triadic line, measured by the variable foot, and the structure of John Cage's "Lecture on Nothing" (1949) confirms a close association among poetry, music, and everyday speech. Using a typographical spacing similar to Williams's triadic line, Cage states that the "Lecture on Nothing" was written in the same rhythmic structure which he was using in his musical compositions at that time. He introduces this lecture in *Silence* by explaining that there are four measures in each line:

> The text is printed in four columns to facilitate a rhythmic reading. . . . This should not be done in an artificial manner (which might result from an attempt to be too strictly faithful to the position of the words on the page), but with the *rubato* which one uses in everyday speech.[59]

These instructions closely parallel a statement made by Hopkins in reference to the oral delivery of "Spelt from Sibyl's Leaves:"

Of this long sonnet above all remember what applies to all my verse, that it is, as living art should be, made for performance and that its performance is not reading with the eye but loud, leisurely, poetical (not rhetorical) recitation, with long rests, long dwells on the rhyme and other marked syllables, and so on. This sonnet shd. be almost sung: it is most carefully timed in *tempo rubato*.[60]

The similarities in the terminology employed here by both poet and musician (most notably their use of the word "rubato"),[61] coupled with correspondences with Williams's theory of the variable foot, further emphasize the roles played by music, speech rhythms, and their intervening moments of silence, in the structuring of their work. Cage writes that in his "new music nothing takes place but sounds: those that are notated and those that are not. Those that are not notated appear in the written music as silences, opening the doors of the music to the sounds that happen to be in the environment."[62] The silences which Williams's new measure necessitates or invites also function, to a certain extent, on this level where "silence becomes something else—not silence at all, but sounds, the ambient sounds."[63] Letting silence back into poetry is another, structural way of permeating the poem with the immediate energy of life. In *The Incarnate Word* Cary Nelson asserts that "space, words, and punctuation are dramatic events in the poem [*Paterson*]. They sustain the page as a field of force, making even a period a tangible function of the structure. A period is immense; yet it is the waste of absolute finitude."[64] Jonathan Raban similarly maintains that one of the main features of the "New Verse" is "that the silence in which a poem occurs has as great a semantic value as the words which are imposed on that silence."[65]

In all of his statements in reference to the variable foot Williams gives the impression that the term is his own invention.[66] Yet he must have been acquainted with Edgar Allan Poe's coinage of "variable foot" in "The Rationale of Verse." The only indication that Williams did indeed read the essay is provided by Solt, who interviewed him in 1960 and writes that "he [Williams] did not object to the suggestion that many of his views on prosody are developments of principles set forth by Poe in his essay 'The Rationale of Verse.' "[67] It is, in fact, surprising that the correspondence between Poe's term and Williams's subsequent use of it has never been emphasized or even pointed out, except briefly by Solt. Poe's variable foot refers to the caesura, which, he maintains, "is a perfect foot, the most important in all verse, and consists of a single long syllable; but the length of this syllable varies."[68] Poe writes,

> We pause on it [the caesura], by a seeming necessity, just as long as it has taken us to pronounce the preceding feet, whether iambuses, trochees, dactyls, or anapests. It is thus a variable foot, and, with some care, may be well introduced into the body of a line, as in a little poem of great beauty by Mrs. Welby:
> I have / a lit / tle step / ¯son¯/ of on / ly three / years old.
> Here we dwell on the caesura, "son," just as long as it requires us to pronounce either of the preceding or succeeding iambuses. Its value, therefore, in this line, is that of three short syllables. In the following dactylic line its value is that of four short syllables:
> Pale as a / lily was / Emily / Gray
> I have accentuated the caesura with a dotted line (----) by way of expressing this variability of value.[69]

In an essay on Pound in 1947 Williams writes that the caesura offers him [Williams] "the greatest hope I have discovered so far for a study of the modern line. The cesura [*sic*] is to take the place of Greek quantity."[70] Although in this essay Williams states that it is Pound's use of the caesura that influenced his thoughts concerning a "modern meter," it is quite possible that Williams was also influenced by Poe's identification of the classical caesura as a variable foot. Not only did Williams apparently adopt Poe's phrase "variable foot," he also converted to his own purposes Poe's general concept of a foot whose length varies according to its rhythmical context. There are, of course, a number of crucial differences between the two writers' uses of the term. Poe, for instance, defines length in terms relating to Greek quantity, and his variable foot derives its length from the traditional feet with which it is surrounded. Williams, on the other hand, determines length qualitatively rather than quantitatively:

> Its [the variable foot's] characteristic, where it differs from the fixed foot with which we are familiar, is that it ignores the counting of the number of syllables in the line, which is the mark of the usual scansion, for a measure more of the ear, a more sensory counting.[71]

Williams appears to have adapted and generalized Poe's term to refer to his own poetic units, each of which is relative and variable and adjusts its length according to "the demands of the language."[72] Despite these differences, there is a degree of similarity between Poe's and Williams's use of the term. This fact, coupled with the duplication of the exact phrase itself, does indeed confirm that "The Rationale of Verse" strongly influenced Williams's thoughts concerning his new measure.

The general inadequacy of Williams's attempted explanations of his variable foot has been widely noted.[73] These explanations were further confused by the inconsistency of Williams's oral readings of poems he claims are measured by the variable foot. Stanley Koehler in the *Paris Review* interview with Williams comments on the fact that he does pause in the middle of his lines and then asks, "Then what is the integrity of the line?" Williams replies, "If I was consistent in myself it would be very much more effective than it is now. I would have followed much closer to the indicated divisions of the line than I did. It's too haphazard."[74] In addition, Williams admits that confusion arose among the critics because of his retention of the concept of feet in his verse while it was clear that his new theory of measure did not relate in any way to classical quantitative meter or English syllable and stress meter. No doubt Williams continued to use the word "foot" partly in order to emphasize the relationship between his new measure and traditional prosody: "Be assured that measure in

mathematics as in verse is inescapable; so in reply to the fixed
foot of the ancient line, including the Elizabethans, we must
have a reply [*sic*]: it is the variable foot which we are beginning
to discover after Whitman's advent."[75] Furthermore, it is quite
likely that Williams wanted to retain, through terminology, the
association between poetry and dance: "Poetry began with
measure, it began with the dance, whose divisions we have all
but forgotten but are still known as measures. Measures they
were and we still speak of their minuter elements as feet" (SL,
331). Williams ends the fifth book of *Paterson* with the lines, "to
dance to a measure/contrapuntally/satyrically, the tragic foot"
(V, iii, 278). Koehler asked Williams, "Is anything implied, in
'contrapuntally,' about the nature of the foot?"; Williams
replied, "It means 'musically'—it's a musical image. The
Indians had a beat in their own music, which they beat with
their feet."[76] We are thus reminded that "foot" also means, "To
move the foot, step, or tread to measure or music; to dance"
(*OED*).

Despite the inconsistency and inadequacy of Williams's
explanations of his new measure and despite the confusions
which result from his choice of terminology, it is possible to
isolate aspects of the variable foot, however tenuous they may
be, that contribute to Williams's conviction that it forms a
"measured" rather than a "free" verse. As Williams wrote to
Eberhart, "Not that I ever count when writing but, at best, the
lines must be capable of being counted, that is to say,
measured—(believe it or not).—At that I may, half consciously,
even count the measure under my breath as I write—" (SL,
326).

Winifred Nowottny maintains that

> when items from the common vocabulary enter into a complex
> structure they partake of the power of the structure and function in
> an arresting way. . . . The difficulty for the critic, especially when
> there is no conspicuous innovation at the level of vocabulary, is to
> arrive at an understanding of those processes in the poem which

enable familiar words to convey unique quality. It is obvious
enough that in order to make them do this the poet has done
something specific to overcome both the generalizing quality and
the great range of indeterminacy of words in very frequent and
varied use.[77]

Common speech is the basis of Williams's poetry, but he
attempts to go beyond commonality through an "intimate
form" which will "constitute a revelation in the speech that he
uses" (CLP, 5). Francis Berry writes, "*What* any person says is
almost always too common and too commonplace, a denial of
individuality, but *how* he says it . . . *will* have an individuality."[78] Olson similarly insists that "*all* parts of speech suddenly,
in composition by field, are fresh for both sound and percussive
use, spring up like unknown, unnamed vegetables in the
patch, when you work it, come spring."[79] It is the revelation of
his private time and rhythm to the reader, his unique voice,
that is the most vital and "measured" aspect of Williams's
variable foot and it is also the aspect which has been most
disregarded.

Williams describes his early poetry to Edith Heal as a "lyrical
outburst," and an "excited pace"—"I was discovering, pressed
by some violent mood. The lines were short, *not* studied"
(IWW, 27). However, during the process of arriving at his
variable foot he found that "the verse must be coldly, intellec-
tually considered. Not the emotion, the heat of life dominating,
but the intellectual concept of the thing itself" (IWW, 86). In an
essay "On Measure—Statement for Cid Corman" Williams
writes that "instinctively we have continued to count as always
but it has become not a conscious process and being unconscious has descended to a low level of the invention" (SE, 340).
Through listening to the spoken language, Williams recognized that ordinary speech consists of rhythmic units determined by the stress-timed rhythm of the language in combination with the emphasis which sense, interpretation, or emotion
of the speaker demands. These sense-stress units or "speech
impulses"[80] with their tendency toward isochronism, became

the basis of his poetic "feet": "Thus, as in speech, the prosodic pattern is evaluated by criteria of effectiveness and expressiveness rather than mechanical syllable counts."[81] The very nature of the "relativistic or variable foot" (SL, 335) requires that each foot be represented typographically in a separate line. Thus in Williams's new measure, a variable foot and a line are identical. In this simple way, Williams avoids the difficulty which readers sometimes encounter when they try to identify the feet which measure Hopkins's sprung rhythm. Hopkins himself was aware that his rhythm was not invariably clear and he attempted to indicate his metrical intentions in certain instances by the use of diacritics, which he found to be "always offensive."[82] The effectiveness of the variable foot is, however, dependent upon the reader's acceptance of each line (each variable foot) as a rhythmic unit and as equal in duration regardless of its length. In a letter to Kay Boyle in 1932 Williams asserts that "speech for poetry is nothing but time—I mean time in the musical sense. That is where the real battle has been going on" (SL, 136). Williams credits Pound with the discovery "that *time* is the real matter of measure and not stress."[83] Since Williams's poetry is neither accentual, syllabic, nor quantitative, he had to devise ways in which to persuade the reader of the equality of the lines. Donald Davie writes that "the ear permits itself to be thus persuaded [that two cadences of unequal length are metrically equal] only in specially favorable circumstances."[84] Williams, for example, in some of his poems, exploits the tendency for an established rhythm to be conserved by the reader and thus the impact of the poem is cumulative. In "The descent beckons" passage, the regular pulsing rhythm set up by the first five short lines carries over into the sixth line "even" and also encourages the reader to voice the nine words in the seventh line rather rapidly. Father Ong points out in an essay on Hopkins that sense stress units "are intimately connected with interpretation: increase in feeling tends to heighten and draw out the stress and countenances hurrying over unimportant syllables so that otherwise disparate units come to be equivalent to one another."[85] In addition, Williams often arranges his words on the page (as in his triadic line) in order to induce further a sense of regularity and of line equality through the eye. Williams wrote to Denise Levertov that "a certain regularity in the actual putting of the words on the page does wonders for the poem in making it acceptable to the eye and to the mind but if at the cost to the interior arrangement of the words themselves . . . it is fatal."[86] With a pattern of equal line duration established, through whatever means, Williams can then demonstrate to the reader how he wants his poems to be read, how the rhythmic adjustment works out according to his unique articulation of the occasion. In other words, he can, to a certain degree, embody his intonation by indicating the presence and length of pauses, the words and phrases to be emphasized and drawn out and those to be passed over quickly. Williams became increasingly conscious of how the careful manipulation of terminal junctures can draw out the meaning, indicate to an extent the required vocal inflection, and also, when desirable, produce subtle and equivocal effects.

Williams, of course, experimented with lineation throughout his poetic career. Winifred Nowottny observes in relation to "The Red Wheelbarrow,"

> If the line and stanza endings were nullified by reading out the poem, to someone who had never seen it on the page, as though it were continuous prose, the poem would lose its point. . . . The conflict between the lineation and our tendency to read continuously, automatically, practising grammatical subordination, and abstraction, as we go, has to be decided by a very strong stress on the peculiarity of the lineation—a stress achieved by keeping out of the poem other relations which might interfere with it.[87]

Williams composed almost exclusively with the use of a typewriter, which undoubtedly proved a valuable tool in the creation of a visual patterning on the page. Charles Olson discusses the importance of the typewriter to the modern poet in "Projective Verse:"

> It is the advantage of the typewriter that, due to its rigidity and its space precisions, it can, for a poet, indicate exactly the breath, the pauses, the suspensions even of syllables, the juxtapositions even of parts of phrases, which he intends. For the first time the poet has the stave and the bar a musician has had. For the first time he can, without the conventions of rime and meter, record the listening he has done to his own speech and by that one act indicate how he would want any reader, silently or otherwise, to voice his work.[88]

Williams told Koehler that "I would gladly have traded what I have tried to say, for what came off my tongue, naturally. . . . I wanted to say something in a certain tone of my voice which would be exactly how I wanted to say it, to measure it in a certain way."[89] He also stated in reference to "The descent beckons" that "I was attempting to imitate myself."[90] It was during the writing of that passage that he discovered his answer to the question which Francis Berry poses in *Poetry and the Physical Voice:*

> How does the poet create . . . [an] awareness of his personal voice in the mind of the reader, a voice which the reader must—presumably—imitate, or attempt to imitate, when he renders the poem, or the passages of poetry, aloud?[91]

Williams maintains that by means of the variable foot he is able to reveal, and in a sense to transfer, his private time and rhythm to the reader, forcing him "into a new and special frame of mind favorable to the receipt of his disclosure" (SE, 28). It must, however, be acknowledged that Williams's new measure does rely heavily for its effectiveness on what Berry terms "aural empathy"[92] and what Abercrombie calls "phonetic empathy."[93] Abercrombie defines his term as "an intuitive reaction of the hearer to be aware of the movements of the

various organs of speech which the speaker is making. . . .
Speech rhythm, and therefore the rhythm of verse, is *in* the
speaker, and it is in the hearer in so far as he identifies himself
with the speaker."[94] In the course of a discussion of Williams's
idiom, Hugh Kenner writes:

> We tell which sentence is British, which American, by the
> cadence, and know accordingly what scope of feeling to accord the
> words, and do this so well we do not know we do it, do not even
> know, until someone makes us see, how much of what we suppose a
> dictionary can sort out (it cannot) is controlled by our sense of the
> voices cadence imitates. Dr. Williams' concern for "the American
> idiom" and his shaping of a metric that can flatten lilt . . . are
> interdependent functions in his poetic.[95]

Williams's new measure is criticized by Conrad Aiken as

> a prescription for anarchy, for formlessness, for a complete indi-
> vidualist "let-go"? For one man's breath is by no means another's;
> there will be no common measure here, and therefore no identi-
> fiable line; without a norm, comparison and value become chimeri-
> cal: the doctor has thrown out the baby with the placenta.[96]

Similarly, John Malcolm Brinnin writes that "the way in which
one hears naturally determines the way one writes, but the
enormous variability in the capacity to hear, plus all the
intricacies of selection that set one hearer apart from another,
gives Williams' theory so much latitude that it becomes all but
useless for analysis or for emulation."[97] It is typical that the
reasons for which Aiken and Brinnin choose to criticize Williams's variable foot summarize the very situation which
Williams felt argued for the need of some kind of new measure
to replace the pentameter. It is, for example, precisely because
"one man's breath is by no means another's," because it has
now been proposed that we live in a pluralistic rather than an
absolutist world, that in a Williams poem there is no rhythmical
unit or pattern, no "norm," or frame of reference which can be
defined outside of the poem under hand; each poem estab-

lishes its own rhythmical context and tensions. Williams told Edith Heal that he had

> always wanted a verse that was ordered, so it came to me that the concept of the foot itself would have to be altered in our new relativistic world. . . . The foot not being fixed is only to be described as variable. If the foot itself is variable it allows order in so-called free verse. Thus the verse becomes not free at all but just simply variable, as all things in life properly are. [IWW, 86]

Williams recognizes that the measurement of time has to be relative, variable, and private rather than absolute and universal as Newton's cosmology required. He told Solt that the following statement from Edward Sapir's *Language* clarifies his position:

> It is strange how long it has taken the European literatures to learn that style is not an absolute . . . but merely the language itself, running in its natural grooves, and with enough of an individual accent to allow the artist's personality to be felt as a presence. [98]

Williams sought for an "ordered" verse because he became increasingly conscious of an audience and of the necessity of transferring the private life and energy of the occasion, through the poem, over to the reader. Olson calls this process "the kinetics of the thing:"

> A poem is energy transferred from where the poet got it . . . by way of the poem itself to, all the way over to, the reader. Okay. Then the poem itself must, at all points, be a high-energy construct and, at all points, an energy-discharge. [99]

Robert Creeley points out that there is no "unity of view . . . in the more classical sense" in a Williams poem: "Williams makes us aware of all the emotional conflicts involved in the act of thinking, so that you get apparent juxtapositions of feeling in a Williams poem that would not be understandable unless one

were to take it literally as the context in which the mind has
shifted to another point of contact in the very writing."[100] As
Jerome Mazzaro points out, Williams's world is "the cubist
world . . . the world of a new physics," of a reality "that . . . can
have no absolute contours but varies with the angle from which
one sees it."[101] Williams, in fact, even began to shy away from
some of his own later compositions in *Pictures from Brueghel*
which he found to be "too regular."[102] This statement is
reminiscent of Williams's complaint regarding the figure taken
from a design on a pebble which was on the cover of *Al Que
Quiere*, his 1917 book of poems. He states that

> To me the design looked like a dancer, and the effect of the dancer
> was very important—a natural, completely individual pattern. The
> artist made the outline around the design too geometrical; it should
> have been irregular, as the pebble was. [IWW, 30]

Out of "juxtapositions of feelings," and "twist[s] of the
imagination" (KORA, 82), there emerges in Williams's poetry a
new kind of unity more consonant with the workings of the
imagination, the bodily experience,[103] and of our universe
which Einstein has revealed to be "an amorphous continuum,
without any fixed architecture, plastic and variable constantly
subject to change and distortion."[104] It is not surprising,
therefore, that in *Paterson*, his poem which was to embody the
whole knowable world about him, Williams's measure is
continually searching, changing, destroying, and striving always to be linked to the fullness of immediate experience
through its use of "live" speech. In a passage from "Pages from
a Notebook" Robert Duncan, in writing of his own work, also
encapsulates Williams's position in regard to the language and
the intimate form of the poem:

> In one way or another to live in the swarm of human speech. This
> is not to seek perfection but to draw honey or poetry out of all
> things. After Freud, we are aware that unwittingly we achieve our
> form. It is, whatever our mastery, the inevitable use we make of

the speech that betrays to ourselves and to our hunters (our readers) the spore of what we are becoming. . . . A longing grows to return to the open composition in which the accidents and imperfections of speech might awake intimations of human being.[105]

B
Structure

1

The longer I lived in my place, among the details of my life, I realized that these isolated observations and experiences needed pulling together to gain "profundity." [AUTO, 391]

> —of this, make it of *this*, this
> this, this, this, this   . [III, iii, 168]

> Have you left something out:
> Negative, says my Gunslinger
> no *thing* is omitted.[1]

In a review of John Hargrave's novel *Summer Time Ends* Williams expresses admiration for Hargrave's "encyclopedic consciousness" and "comprehensive scope."[2] He similarly admired David Lyle's[3] democratic interest in all the disparate facts of his environment. Both Linda Wagner and Mike Weaver have pointed out the influence which Lyle's correspondence with Williams exerted on the wide-ranging materials of *Paterson:* "Economics, cybernetics, social ills, the price of bread, the motives for murder—every subject was relevant in Lyle's picture of the world."[4] According to Weaver, Lyle was the original Noah Faitoute Paterson: "Faitoute was a man through whom the whole contemporary scene disclosed itself; contained in the one individual was the social experience of a community."[5] In fact, Williams had originally intended to dedicate Book IV to David Lyle "for his studies of the tracks by which the various categories of knowledge are interrelated" (YALE) and to include Lyle's letters in the body of the poem and in an "appendix" to *Paterson*. The catalogue which precedes the preface to *Paterson* lists the phrases "a basket," "a column," "a gathering up," "by multiplication a reduction to one." Throughout the body of the poem are interspersed such lines as "To make a start/out of particulars" (I, p. 11), "a mass of detail/to interrelate on a new ground" (I, ii, 30), and "an elucidation by multiplicity" (II, i, 77). These phrases and statements coupled with Williams's assertion in the "Author's Note" that "all the details [of the city] . . . may be made to voice his most intimate convictions," clearly indicate that Williams intended *Paterson* to be encyclopedic in scope, to embrace "everything we are" (SL, 286). His inclusions in *Paterson* range from "THE FANTASTIC" (BUFFALO), typified by Peter the Dwarf, to the very ordinary people in the park, to the "irrational," which, according to Williams, "enters the poem in those letters, included in the text, which do not seem to refer to anything in the 'story' yet do belong somehow to the poem—how, it is not easy to say" (SL, 309). Williams's attempt at comprehensiveness also extended to his own literary output as is indicated on a manuscript sheet for the poem: "(Put everything I've written—pieces—bits revisions into it etc)" (BUFFALO). The preface to *Paterson* concludes with an image of accumulation and of evolution in which a whole issues out of division and multiplicity:

> divided as the dew,
> floating mists, to be rained down and
> regathered into a river that flows
> and encircles:
>
> shells and animalcules
> generally and so to man,
>
> to Paterson. [I, p. 13]

In the survey (Chapter 4) of Williams's experiments with extended patterns, it was observed that Williams became increasingly conscious of a moral obligation to synthesize the pieces of his environment, maintaining that it is the poet's duty to create a "culture" by making a shape out of the things of his place. In "The American Background" Williams writes:

> It [culture] is the realization of the qualities of a place in relation to the life which occupies it; embracing everything involved, climate, geographic position, relative size, history, other cultures—as well as the character of its sands, flowers, minerals and the condition of knowledge within its borders. It is the act of lifting these things into an ordered and utilized whole which is culture. [SE, 157]

Williams wrote to Henry Wells in 1950 that "the poem to me . . . is . . . an assertion, always, of a new and total culture, the lifting of an environment to expression" (SL, 286).

It was proposed in Chapter 3 that Williams's "metaphysical conception" of a man identified with a city was a highly appropriate image for his long poem. In *A World on the Wane* Claude Lévi-Strauss observes:

> Cities have often been likened to symphonies and poems, and the comparison seems to me a perfectly natural one: they are, in fact, objects of the same kind. The city may even be rated higher, since it stands at the point where Nature and artifice meet. A city is a congregation of animals whose biological history is enclosed within its boundaries and yet every conscious and rational act on the part of these creatures helps to shape the city's eventual character. By its form, as by the manner of its birth, the city has elements at once of biological procreation, organic evolution, and aesthetic creation. It is both natural object and a thing to be cultivated; individual and group; something lived and something dreamed; it is *the* human invention *parexcellence*. [6]

Williams similarly conceived of the city as a body through which the mind of man expresses itself. Paterson is a poem, a city, and a man. Paterson is also a giant body, which is not only a symbol of Williams's apprehension of a lost unity, but also a symbol of the structure of *Paterson*—a whole whose parts are interrelated. Yet, as Williams acknowledges in *I Wanted to Write a Poem*, the discovery of the form in which to embody the city, his protagonist, his collection of disparate details, "came gradually" (IWW, 81). In a letter to Pound in 1936 Williams refers to "that magnum opus I've always wanted to do: the poem *PATERSON*. . . . I've been sounding myself out in these years working toward a form of some sort" (SL, 163). In 1945 he confided to Horace Gregory that "just yesterday I learned one of the causes of my inability to proceed [with *Paterson*]: I MUST BEGIN COMPOSING again. I thought all I had to do was to arrange the material but that's ridiculous" (SL, 234). As late as 1948, after his completion of two books of *Paterson*, Williams wrote to David Ignatow:

> We are all caught in an era which has overtaken the world and which will "come out" into an unexpected shape fairly soon. We are all trying to get our hands and our arms *around* this total shape. No one has the answer to everything in the grand shape of the modern which we all look forward to. But there is enough which many of us have in common to begin to see that it will be an astonishingly new *thing* which is shaping itself, a newly designed appearance—to which each of us is contributing a part. [SL, 267]

Williams states in his *Autobiography* that *Paterson* "called for a poetry such as I did not know, it was my duty to discover or make such a context on the 'thought,' " (AUTO, 392). The key word in this statement is "context," which according to the *OED* derives from the Latin *contextus*, meaning "connection," and from *contexere*, "to weave together, connect." "Context" is defined as

> the whole structure of a connected passage regarded in its bearing upon any of the parts which constitute it; the parts which immediately precede or follow any particular passage or "text" and determine its meaning.

A number of Williams's shorter city poems examined in Chapter 2 are composed of one element—a catalogue of things—and thus have a basically linear or one-dimensional structure.[7] This indicates, in part, why the discussion of them ran mainly along thematic lines. However, Williams became increasingly dissatisfied with the nonrelated lyrics formed by his "isolated observations and experiences" (AUTO, 391). As he stated in a 1935 essay on the *Cantos*, "There is a flatness to most poetic form which needs enlargement in our day" (SE, 169). In *Paterson* "things" are no longer merely catalogued, they are given a context, but not, as Williams indicated to Norman Macleod, a "neo-classic *recognizable* context" (SL, 239).

2

Formal patterns of all sorts represent arrests of the truth in some particular phase of its mutations, and immediately thereafter, unless they change, become mutilations. [SE, 205–206]

Plot is like God: the less we formulate it the closer we are to the truth. [SL, 146]

Meaning is new, or not at all; a new creation, or not at all; poetry or not at all.[8]

Williams's *Paterson* notes bear witness to his industrious search for the form in which to embody his environment. He initially conceived of the poem as a "lyric-drama":

The conception of a lyric (or tragic) drama demands lyrics! Studies in language should precede that, the spontaneous (not natural) conformations of language as it is *heard*. Attempt to feel and then transcribe these lyrical language patterns. The drama, the lyric drama (Lope de Vega) should be one expanded metaphor. [BUFFALO][9]

He also experimented with structuring the poem as "imagi-

nary conversations" between "Doc" and "Willie" with the
history of the area and its inhabitants revealed in the course of
their conversation and interaction with each other. On another
manuscript sheet he writes that the poem is to be

> a design on the general structure of Chaucer's *Canterbury Tales*—
> at least in Parts such as The Dream of the Beautiful Women
>   (to be the dreams of N.F. Paterson—stirred by Mrs. Paterson)
> but not to be (unless desired) stated as dreams. They are not
> "dreams" but more than ever the actuality—the "actuality" by
> being dreams.) [BUFFALO]

After James Laughlin suggested that he reread his book of short
stories *Life Along the Passaic River,* Williams began to con-
template structuring his long poem along similar lines. He
writes that "the form looks as if it is what I have been looking for
for the poem *Paterson*" (BUFFALO). However, *Paterson*'s
larger organization is not based upon any one of the frameworks
which Williams originally considered. Nevertheless, Williams
did utilize aspects of these early ideas, with their variety of
structures, styles, and conventions, in the course of *Paterson,*
where they contribute to the encyclopedic range of the poem
and become, in effect, stylistic materials.[10] In fact, the
catalogue preceding the poem originally included the phrase "a
summary of poetic devices" (BUFFALO). For example, the
"idyl" in Book IV is basically a "lyric-drama" structured by the
conversation between Phyllis and Corydon and Phyllis and
Paterson. The dream framework convention is established in
the beginning of the poem where Paterson is introduced as a
sleeping landscape giant dreaming the inhabitants of the city:
"Eternally asleep,/his dreams walk about the city where he
persists/incognito" (I, i, 14). In the course of the five books of
Paterson the stories of a number of people are told but, except
for those briefly narrated in the prose fragments, not in the
narrative style found in some of the *Canterbury Tales* or in *Life
Along the Passaic River.* For example, we gradually learn about

Cress by reading her letters, which appear sporadically throughout the first two books.

The early stages of *Paterson,* which are documented by Williams's unpublished notes, indicate that he initially found it difficult not to think in terms of narrative plots and linear frameworks. It can be safely conjectured, however, that Williams rejected his early ideas regarding structure because he recognized that they would circumscribe and perhaps even trap his material within an Aristotelian beginning, middle, and end, whereas his thoughts regarding the function of his long poem were more closely allied with D.H. Lawrence's assertions in "Morality and the Novel":

> The business of art is to reveal the relation between man and his circumambient universe, at the living moment. . . . The relation between all things changes from day to day, in a subtle stealth of change. Hence art, which reveals or attains to another perfect relationship, will be for ever new. . . . If a novel reveals true and vivid relationships, it is a moral work, no matter what the relationships may consist in. If the novelist *honours* the relationship in itself, it will be a great novel.[11]

According to Williams, Book IV of *Paterson* was criticized by Randall Jarrell because he "couldn't take the identification of the filthy river with the perversion of the characters." Williams comments that "it was typical of him that he lost track of the poem as a poem and became identified with the characters. . . . What in the world is an artist to do? He is not a moralist. He *sees* things, reacts to them, must take them into consideration. . . . To have a moral reaction to this section of the poem because I have seen what I have seen is just too bad" (IWW, 91–92). Here Williams is asserting that art has nothing to do with conventional morality. Rather, the artist is most moral when he, in Lawrence's words, "reveals true and vivid relationships." Elsewhere Williams states that "of all moral hells that of the faithless artist is the worst since his responsibility is the greatest."[12] Williams came to the realization that "a work of art is important only as evidence, in its structure, of a new world which it has been created to affirm" (SE, 196).

It was observed in the previous section on "Measure" that Williams's first step in his search for a new prosody was, by necessity, destructive. To a certain extent, *Paterson*'s overall structure also reflects the process of liberating form. Williams instructs himself to "write the poem on the page as it strikes your fancy" (BUFFALO) and to "write carelessly so that nothing that is not green will survive" (III, iii, 155). As late as Book III, after the destruction of the tornado, fire, and flood, Williams asks the basic question

> How to begin to find a shape—to begin to begin again,
> turning the inside out   :   to find one phrase that will
> lie married beside another for delight   .   ?
> —seems beyond attainment   . [III, iii, 167]

In fact, "The liberation of the form" is a phrase found on a prescription blank among Williams's manuscripts for the poem in Buffalo. There are thirteen of these blanks, which together form one of his loose outlines for the poem. A draft of the poem's preface includes the lines "chaos the mother/of knowledge and knowledge/chaotic" (BUFFALO). These lines became "rolling up out of chaos, a nine months' wonder, the city/the man, an identity" (I, p. 12). Mircea Eliade defines chaos as "the ultimate disappearance of limits," an interval in which "all forms merge together."[13] The preface to *Paterson* describes a *coincidentia oppositorum* which, according to Eliade, effects "the dissolution of the world—of which the community is a copy—and restore[s] the primeval *illud tempus* which is obviously the mythical moment of the *beginning* (chaos) and the end (flood or *ekpyrosis*, apocalypse)"[14]:

> For the beginning is assuredly
> the end. . . .

        obverse, reverse;
        the drunk the sober; the illustrious
        the gross; one [I, pp. 11–12]

Chaos abolishes the past and is always followed by a new creation of the cosmos, the community. Similarly, Williams believed that out of a chaotic liberation of form, a new and vital form would be generated. In his notes he describes *Paterson* as "a fragmentary sort of poem strung together, with notes and comments, for what may come of it" (BUFFALO). Williams told Edith Heal in reference to *Paterson* that

> I knew I had what I wanted to way. I knew that I wanted to say it in *my* form. I was aware that it wasn't a finished form, yet I knew it was not formless. I had to invent my form, if form it was. I was writing in a modern occidental world; I knew the rules of poetry even though I knew nothing of actual Greek; I respected the rules but I decided I must define the traditional in terms of my own world. [IWW, 83–84]

While he was in the process of writing *Paterson II* in 1947 Williams confided to Kenneth Burke: "For myself I reject almost all poetry as at present written, including my own. I see tendencies, nodes of activity, here and there but no clear synthesis" (SL, 257).

    Williams's initial search for a structure for *Paterson* culminated in a rejection of traditional, linear frameworks because of his apprehension that such frameworks are rooted in a philosophy which maintains that the poem copies nature which is itself temporally linear and spatially continuous. In the first place, Williams repudiated the concept that the poem "copies" nature. He progressed beyond his symbolic experience in "The Wanderer" as he gradually came to the firm conclusion that his function, as a maker of poems, is not to be a "mirror to this modernity" (CEP, 3), not to hold a "mirror up to nature but with his imagination . . . [to rival] nature's composition with his own" (IMAG, 121). Williams wrote to Frank L. Moore in 1951 that

> to copy nature is a spineless activity; it gives us a sense of our mere existence but hardly more than that. But to imitate nature involves the verb: we then ourselves become nature, and so invent an object which is an extension of the process. The *Iliad* is a pure invention; the *Odyssey* is another. [SL, 297]

Furthermore, as we discussed in the previous section on "Measure," Williams discerned that Einstein's theories regarding the relativity of time and space demanded a revaluation of our concepts of reality which, in turn, must exert an influence upon the formal structures of art. Certainly it is no longer possible to think of our personal or collective existence simply in terms of a chronological continuum. In the *Irrational Man* William Barrett writes:

> The formal dictates of the well-made play or the well-made novel, which were the logical outcome of thoroughly rational preconceptions about reality, we can no longer hold to when we become attentive "to the things themselves," to the facts, to existence in the mode in which we do exist.[15]

Williams came to recognize the futility and immorality of bringing a preconceived, inflexible pattern to a poem which was to encompass and move the world, not tamper with it:

> I look for a direct expression of the turmoils of today in the arts. Not *about* today in classical forms but in forms generated, invented, today direct from the turmoil itself—or the quietude or whatever it might be so long as it is generated in *form* directly from the form society itself takes in its struggles.[16]

Williams continued his search for a context within which his material could interact; a context which would create a simultaneous, complex impression rather than a linear effect, maintaining that "everything in the social, economic complex of the world at any time-sector ties in together—" (SE, 283).

3

I enter the poem as I entered my own life, moving between an initiation and a terminus I cannot name.[17]

It is a popular superstition that a house is somehow the possession of the man who lives in it. But a house has no relation whatever to anything but itself. The architect feels the rhythm of the house drawing his mind into opaque partitions in which doors appear, then windows and so on until out of the vague or clearcut mind of the architect the ill-built or deftly-built house has been empowered to draw stone and timbers into a foreappointed focus. If one shut the door of a house he is to that extent a carpenter. [KORA, 68]

"Everything speaks in its own way."[18]

It is, of course, true that the majority of Williams's oral as well as written statements in reference to *Paterson* convey a basically linear impression. In his "Author's Note," which originally appeared in the beginning of the first edition of Book I in 1946, he writes that "a man in himself is a city, beginning, seeking, achieving and concluding his life." He continues by revealing that Part One will introduce the place's "elemental character," Part Two comprise its "modern replicas," Part Three seek a "language to make them vocal," and Part Four will be "reminiscent of episodes—all that any one man may achieve in a lifetime." The catalogue prefacing the poem, which is composed of a number of phrases descriptive of *Paterson*, includes the progression "spring, summer, fall and the sea." In 1955 Williams wrote to Henry Wells that "I found myself always conceiving my abstract designs as possessing four sides. That was natural enough with spring, summer, autumn and winter always before me" (SL, 333). In a publisher's release in 1949 he disclosed:

From the beginning I decided that there would be four books following the course of the river whose life seemed more and more to resemble my own life as I more and more thought of it: the river above the Falls, the catastrophe of the Falls itself, the river below the Falls, and the entrance at the end into the great sea.[19]

Williams wrote a poem in 1943 entitled "Paterson: The Falls," which appears to be outlining the structure of his long poem: "This is my plan. 4 sections: First,/the archaic persons of the drama." He then introduces the Evangelist who appears in Book II and continues by revealing that the third book is to be the "old town," and the fourth book the "modern town" (CLP, 10–11). Despite the fact that critics have accepted this poem for what it purports to be and probably what Williams originally intended it to be (Thirlwall, for example, categorically states that "Williams himself has summarized the poem [*Paterson*] in 'Paterson: the Falls',"[20]) it does not, by any means, encompass the structure of the finished *Paterson*.[21] In the first place, Williams rarely worked strictly according to plan and he also felt uncomfortable with the thought that any creative writer did. In 1947 Kenneth Burke sent Williams a projected summary of Vergil's plan for the *Aeneid*. It is not clear whether this summary was written by Burke or someone else. However, Williams wrote to Burke after his receipt of the summary that

> I do not believe you think Vergil formulated any such preliminary plan as this before beginning composition on the *Aeneid*. . . . He may, at an outside guess, have indulged in a bit of logical philandering—if he found the time for it in a dull moment! But that he set down a primary scheme and followed it I can't for a moment believe. [SL, 251]

As Williams observed, "Nobody will attempt to think, once a convenient peg to hang his critical opinion on without thinking is found" (SL, 265). It is therefore not surprising that many of *Paterson*'s critics are either willing to accept unequivocally Williams's four-part plan[22] (so much so that some of them cannot accept Book V as part of the poem) or else they inveigh against him for not adhering to his own schemes thereby creating a "chaotic" poem.[23]

Williams indicates through a variety of statements that his plans for *Paterson* and even his *ex post facto* descriptions of the poem's movement, are not intended to be taken literally or considered to be definitive summaries. In a 1951 press release Williams stated that "there were a hundred modifications of this general plan ['four books following the course of the river'] as, following the theme rather than the river itself, I allowed myself to be drawn on."[24] Williams wrote to Henry Wells in 1955, after reading an essay on *Paterson* which Wells had written and sent to him, that "I did not theorize directly when I was writing but went wherever the design forced me to go" (SL, 333). This is not to say that linear rhythms are excluded from the context created by *Paterson*, but rather that all the materials, events, and things of the poem are not, by any means, subordinated to a coherently developed, preconceived theme or scheme. During a 1953 dialogue with Thirlwall, Williams made the important and revealing statement:

> In telling the incidents that occurred to people, the story of the lives of the people naturally unfolds. Without didactically telling what happened, you make things happen on the page, and from that you see what kind of people they were—what they suffered and what they aspired to. And that's what I hoped to do. I couldn't write—well, I really didn't want to write a didactic account of this that happened to that and that to another. I made the thing insofar as possible happen on the page. The imagistic method comes in there. You can't tell what a particular thing signified, but if you see the thing happening before you, you infer that that is the kind of thing that happens in the area. This is the imagistic method.[25]

Perhaps the most straight-forward example of the "imagistic method" occurs in the "idyl" in Book IV. Williams told Robert Lowell that he began by writing of the lesbian Corydon in a "satiric mood," but she won him over: "I ended by feeling admiration for her and real regret at her defeat" (SL, 302).

In the last chapter we saw that Williams became increasingly aware of the necessity of removing his ego from what he had to say. Yet the fact remains that a great deal of *Paterson* criticism lays stress on what is considered to be the personal nature of the poem. The poem has been variously described as a "Personal Epic,"[26] a "lyric-epic,"[27] a "Whitmanesque celebration of the Self,"[28] and as an autobiographical epic in the "Romantic" tradition (see Chap. 1). Robert Lowell maintains that "taken together, Paterson is Williams' life, and Williams is what makes Paterson alive"[29] and Eric Mottram observes that "*Paterson* is Williams."[30] Such statements, coupled with Williams's own admissions—such as "I never remember anything about the men. They were always there, but they became inevitably me: Paterson, once I had solved the problem of differentiating"[31]—appear on the surface to indicate that the function of *Paterson* is primarily self-expression. Yet this is certainly not the case and the key to an accurate understanding of this issue lies in a statement Williams made in the course of comparing his own long poem to Hart Crane's *The Bridge:* "I suppose the thing was that he [Crane] was searching for something inside, while I was all for a sharp use of the materials" (SL, 186).[32] Williams intended his life and the events of that life to be no more than materials he uses to make his poem, as objectively as he uses the materials with which the city of Paterson present him: "to objectify the man himself as we know him and love him and hate him."[33]

The creation of the man Paterson provided Williams with the means of "objectifying" himself—of observing himself in the process of interaction with his environment. This was in agreement with Alfred North Whitehead's "objectivist" philosophy set forth in *Science and the Modern World.* After Williams read this work in 1927, he wrote, "A milestone surely in my career, should I have the force & imagination to go on with my work."[34] According to Whitehead's objectivist point of view,

> the things experienced are to be distinguished from our knowledge of them. So far as there is dependence, the *things* pave the way for

the *cognition*, rather than *vice versa*. . . . The objectivist holds
that the things experienced and the cognisant subject enter into
the common world on equal terms. . . . We seem to be ourselves
elements of this world in the same sense as are the other things
which we perceive.[35]

Here we can recognize a philosophic basis for Williams's credo
"no ideas but in things" as well as his statement that a man's
"life is a thing at any moment absolute and perfect as a tree or a
stone. And the sooner he regards it objectively as such with
composure and assurance (not with blind conceit) the sooner he
will be of use to himself and his world."[36] Charles Olson's
coinage of the term "objectism" to indicate such a relationship
between the poet and his own life bears a marked similarity to
Whitehead's theories as well as to the above statement which
was made by Williams in 1930. According to Olson,

> objectism is the getting rid of the lyrical interference of the
> individual as ego, of the "subject" and his soul. . . . For a man is
> himself an object, whatever he may take to be his advantages, the
> more likely to recognize himself as such the greater his advantages,
> particularly at that moment that he achieves an humilitas sufficient
> to make him of use.[37]

The following quotation from *Paterson I* reveals Williams's
awareness that reality, "the rose," is not an attribute of his
personality and does not depend for its existence on his
cognizance of it:

> How strange you are, you idiot!
> So you think because the rose
> is red that you shall have the mastery?
> The rose is green and will bloom,
> overtopping you, green, livid
> green when you shall no more speak, or
> taste, or even be. My whole life
> has hung too long upon a partial victory. [I, iii, 41]

In the section on "Measure" it was observed that Williams

discovered the variable foot in what he had himself previously written. It was only after writing "The descent beckons" passage that he became tangibly aware of the principles upon which his new measure could rest. Similarly, Williams's discovery and understanding of the method which would create *Paterson*'s larger organization occurred during the process of "The liberation of the form" (BUFFALO). The basic principle of the method is to allow the "things" of the poem, insofar as possible, to speak for themselves. This principle developed out of Williams's growing realization that the poem has a life of its own, that its materials can create their own motivation and discover their own center, regardless of any preconceived plans the poet brings to it. Glauco Cambon observes in *The Inclusive Flame* that "relativity replaces any binding absolutes within this expanding universe. Any given moment or theme can be the *center;* moreover, each motif is perennially redefined, and therefore changed, by its relation to others."[38] In his introduction to Charles Olson's *Selected Writings*, Robert Creeley points out the parallel between Jackson Pollock's comments on his painting and what was happening to poetry during the 1950s. Pollock writes,

> When I am in my painting, I'm not aware of what I'm doing. It is only after a sort of "get acquainted" period that I see what I have been about. I have no fears about making changes, destroying the image, etc., because the painting has a life of its own. I try to let it come through. It is only when I lose contact with the painting that the result is a mess. Otherwise there is pure harmony, an easy give and take, and the painting comes out well.[39]

It is thus significant that Pollock is one of the artists whom Williams invokes in *Paterson V:*

> Pollock's blobs of paint squeezed out
> with design!
> pure from the tube. Nothing else
> is real   . . [V, i, 248–49]

Along with Pollock, Williams recognized the necessity of maintaining close contact with his material. He writes in his *Autobiography* that

> I wanted, if I was to write in a larger way than of the birds and flowers, to write about the people close about me: to know in detail, minutely what I was talking about—to the whites of their eyes, to their very smells. [AUTO, 391]

The concept that it is necessary for the artist to be intimately acquainted with his material in order for it to be free to speak for itself is, in a sense, paradoxical. As Denise Levertov maintains, "I believe content determines form, and yet that content is discovered only *in* form. Like everything living, it is a mystery."[40] Throughout *Paterson* Williams strives to let reality speak, to reveal a complex situation, rather than to impose a subjective unity upon the diversity of his world: "As poets all we can do is to say what we see and let the rest speak for itself" (SL, 305). Williams maintains that in the writing of his long poem he was "not driven by the search for personal distinction" (SL, 313) or the need for self-expression; he wanted above all to make Paterson live, to make his poem "an astonishingly new *thing*" (SL, 267): "Maybe I'm just an engineer of some sort—of the written poem on the page. To be sentimental about the poem or mystical is just an ignorant joke. You have to keep your senses clear to write a good poem and alert to what is going on in the world, structurally—and live as Pasteur has warned us always with a theory of what is new in the world."[41]

4

Meaning is not in things but in between; in the iridescence, the interplay; in the interconnections; at the intersections, at the crossroads. Meaning is transitional as it is transitory; in the puns or bridges, the correspondence.[42]

Signatures of all things I am here to read, seaspawn and seawrack, the nearing tide, that rusty boot.[43]

Of the many traits peculiar to process, one of the most vital—and problematical—is the radical alteration in the relation between writer and reader. . . . He [the reader] must learn to discover and invent through his own immersion in a work from which he can no longer remain detached if any meaning at all is to emerge.[44]

The doctrine of contact and an accompanying respect for the life in "things" remained with Williams throughout his poetic career. However, the writing of a large structure demanded that contact, in some measure, be accompanied and trans-cended by synthesis. The "meaning" of *Paterson* does not reside in explanations, observations, or general statements on the significance of what happens or an elucidation of the material; neither does it reside simply in the things of the poem, but rather in the relations between, and amplification of, the matter itself. He writes in "An Approach to the Poem," "WE must take the elements, the particulars (which exist today as they existed then) and combine them *today* in a manner similar to the work of the past—but completely different in form—we must make anew! of old particulars."[45] Williams wrote to the editor of *A Year Magazine* in 1934:

"Simply physical or external realism" has an important place in America still. We know far less, racially, than we should about our localities and ourselves. But it is quite true that the photographic camera will not help us. We can though, if we are able to *see* general relationships in local setting, set them down verbatim with a view to penetration. And there is a cleanliness about this method which if it can be well handled makes a fascinating project in which every bit of subtlety and experience one is possessed of may be utilized. [SL, 146]

In 1961 Williams told Walter Sutton that he

was tremendously involved in an appreciation of Cezanne. He was a designer. He put it down on the canvas so that there would be a meaning without saying anything at all. Jus the relation of the parts to themselves. In considering a poem, I don't care whether it's finished or not; if it's put down with a good relation to the parts, it becomes a poem. And the meaning of the poem can be grasped by attention to the design.[46]

According to Williams, therefore, the poet's responsibility is to compose the material which is available in such a way that it shows forth its own significance. It is the poet who "sees, links together and discloses in the symmetry of his work this bastardy of all ages" (SE, 167). His function is to lead the race "by a magnificent organization of those materials his age has placed before him for his employment" (SE, 103). As Marshall McLuhan observes in the course of an interpretation of Stéphane Mallarmé's stance on writing,

> The job of the artist is not to sign but to read signatures. Existence must speak for itself. It is already richly and radiantly signed. The artist has merely to reveal, not to forge the signatures of existence. But he can only put these in order by discovering the orchestral analogies in things themselves.[47]

In light of the fact that Williams's writing of *Paterson* was influenced by his reading of Joyce's *Ulysses*, it is significant that Joyce also thought of the artist as

> a composer who takes the facts which experience offers and harmonizes them in such a way that, without losing their vitality and integrity, they yet fit together and form a concordant whole.[48]

A skilful poet is in tune with the available material and knows how to organize it and what to include and exclude: "The better artist he is, the better he's able to recognize what is good and *why* it's good—and how to organize it into a satisfactory poem."[49] Throughout *Paterson* Williams uses the words "discover" and "invent" to indicate the process through which the poet goes first to determine the meaning implicit in the matter and then to structure the poem so that the meaning is revealed.

James Guimond points out that in the passage beginning "Without invention nothing is well spaced" (II, i, 65), Williams "seems to use 'invent' in all three of its meanings: the modern word meaning to construct newly, the archaic usage meaning to discover, and the Latin root *inventus* which means to 'come upon' or 'come into,' i.e., impregnate."[50]

In the course of the discussion of Williams's creation of larger structures in Chapter 4 it was observed that Williams became increasingly conscious of an audience and a desire to make himself understood. It was suggested in the previous section on prosody that Williams's new measure relies heavily for its effectiveness on the reader's "aural empathy" or "phonetic empathy" (see Chap. 5A.). *Paterson* represents a further development of the poet/audience relationship in that its larger organization invites and actually requires the *active* participation of the reader. This is described by Donald M. Kartiganer as part of the "process style" which assumes "that literature really occurs somewhere *between* author and reader, depending on both for its existence."[51] In a work whose connections, actions, and motivations are not necessarily rational or linear, the "bond of writer and reader is not a shared awe at the remorselessly closing lines of an action, but rather the quest for the very nature of the action, the structure which both book and reader are struggling to demonstrate."[52]

5

Von der Sirenen Listigkeit
Tun die Poeten dichten.[53]

The owners of media always endeavor to give the public what it wants, because they sense that their power is in the *medium* and not in the *message* or the program.[54]

My heart rouses
     thinking to bring you news
        of something

```
that concerns you
            and concerns many men. Look at
                        what passes for the new.
You will not find it there but in
            despised poems.
                        It is difficult
to get the news from poems
            yet men die miserably every day
                        for lack
of what is found there.
            Hear me out
                        for I too am concerned
and every man
            who wants to die at peace in his bed
                        besides. [PB, 161–62]
```

In these lines from "Asphodel, that Greeny Flower" Williams creates an image of the poem as news. This is an image or an analogy which became increasingly meaningful to Williams and as such it is not surprising to come across it, charged with a lifetime of growing conviction and understanding, in his late love poem to his wife. Mike Weaver suggests that David Lyle first "turned Williams' attention to the news, and the conception of a poem as the truth of contemporary events."[55] The information and facts discovered in newspapers figure prominently in Lyle's letters in which he attempted to correlate all the disparate facts and happenings which came his way.

Williams also may have been influenced by a claim made by John Dewey in *The Dial:*

> The newspaper is the only genuinely popular form of literature we have achieved. The newspaper hasn't been ashamed of localism. It has revelled in it, perhaps wallowed is the word. I am not arguing that it is highclass literature, or for the most part good literature, even from its own standpoint. But it is permanently successful romance and drama, and that much can hardly be said for anything else in our literary lines.

Dewey goes on to maintain that "we are discovering that the

locality is the only universal,"[56] which suggests that Williams had indeed read this particular article, for in his *Autobiography* he writes that "John Dewey had said (I discovered it quite by chance), 'The local is the only universal, upon that all art builds' " (AUTO, 391).

Williams's sense of a connection between the daily newspaper and what he maintains the new, modern poem should be involves three interrelated convictions which reach their culmination in *Paterson:*

> The truth is that news offers the precise incentive to epic poetry, the poetry of events; and now is precisely the time for it since never by any chance is the character of a single fact ever truthfully represented today. If ever we are to have any understanding of what is going on about us we shall need some other means for discovering it.
>
> The epic poem would be our "newspaper."[57]

In the first place Williams insists that a poem should use "the same materials as newsprint, the same dregs" (SE, 295). The poem must consist of "Facts, facts, facts, tearing into us to blast away our stinking flesh of news. Bullets."[58] There is ample evidence that Williams considers the poet to be a type of reporter who gathers and then relays the news of his world: "In a word you got to go and be where the news is happening and then dish it."[59] Williams describes his preparation for the writing of *Paterson* in similar terms:

> I started to make trips to the area. I walked around the streets; I went on Sundays in summer when the people were using the park, and I listened to their conversation as much as I could. I saw whatever they did, and made it part of the poem.[60]

Not only did Williams go to where the news was happening in the present, he also read about what had been news in the past as recorded in historical documents as well as in actual newspapers. A letter to Horace Gregory in 1945 indicates that he had originally thought of putting at least some of the material he had gathered into footnotes: "Sometimes a chance hint, such as that about avoiding footnotes in the 'Paterson' thing, completely resolves my nerves, and I do docilely what you have suggested with absolute assurance that it is the correct answer" (SL, 236).

One of Williams's technical problems was to find a material occasion, an inciting circumstance to allow for the inclusion of parts of the real world within the body of the poem. On a worksheet for *Paterson* he directs himself to "Make it factual (as the Life is factual—almost casual—always sensual—usually visual: related to thought)" (BUFFALO). The loose narrative element involving the poet Paterson's movement through the multiple facets of his environment in his search for a "redeeming language" provides Williams with the occasion for incorporating actual facts in the poem in the form of letters, observations, and direct transcriptions or summaries of newspaper items and historical accounts. For example, many of the letters interlaced throughout the poem are ostensibly received by Dr. Paterson. Similarly the dispersion of historical accounts and newspaper items throughout the poem is accounted for, within the poem itself, by Paterson's visit to the library in Book III: "It is to the library Faitoute went for reference and a cloudy head—to discover news of the tightrope walkers" (YALE).[61] A plan for the "idyl" in Book IV reveals that Phyllis's "internal comments" are to take the "form of letters to her father" (YALE).

Ralph Nash points out in his article "The Use of Prose in 'Paterson' " that the presentation of actual fragments of the world "contributes to a sense of immediacy . . . while at the same time it gives a sense of distance and objectivity."[62] This is exactly the dual effect which ideally a newspaper reporter aims to produce. Williams states in *I Wanted to Write a Poem* that it was very important to him to make *Paterson* "topical" and interesting to the reader: "I knew the reader, any reader, would be interested in scandal so scandal went in. The documentary notations were carefully chosen for their live interest, their verisimilitude" (IWW, 83).

The fact that Williams was reading *Ulysses* at the time of his conception of *Paterson* (IWW, 82) suggests the possibility that he was influenced by Joyce's use of newspaper material. In the course of writing *Ulysses* Joyce copied passages verbatim from the newspapers of the day as well as paraphrased and manipulated news articles to his own purposes. In addition, many of Joyce's characters discuss topics which are alluded to in contemporary newspapers.[63]

Another aspect of the poem as news is illuminated by Ezra Pound's statement that "literature is news which stays news."[64] Which is to say that the poet is not merely a reporter but the maker of news, the maker of "a new thing, unlike any thing else in nature, a thing advanced and apart from it" (AUTO, 241). According to Williams, writing should not be "a conscious recording of the day's experiences 'freshly and with the appearance of reality' " (IMAG, 120). The poet has a duty to raise the material of the newspaper, the "dregs" from which he must start, to a new level of distinction. In his *Autobiography* Williams writes that "the common news of the day" has no "light" in it, it is "trivial fill-gap." "But," he continues, "the hunted news I get from some obscure patients' eyes is not trivial." This news is "a glimpse, an intimation of all that which the daily print misses or deliberately hides" (AUTO, 359–60). Williams maintains that the newspapers "reveal nothing whatever, for they only tell you what you already know—you wouldn't recognize it otherwise" (SE, 269).

A number of newspaper clippings interspersed throughout *Paterson* report violence, death, or murder.[65] Yet this "convincing strewing of corpses" does not possess the impact or the "light" to "move the mind" in any way (IV, iii, 233). This is vividly emphasized by the scene he presents in Book IV of New Yorkers on their lunch hour "pressed together / talking excitedly . of the next sandwich . / reading, from one hand, of some student, come / waterlogged to the surface following / last night's thunderstorm" (IV, i, 196). On a worksheet Williams writes, "Quite as a matter of course (the newspapers) thoroughly detached (carefully slected [sic], carefully excluded) No revealed emotion, no emotion whatever, the gravest scandals" (YALE). It is the poet who must make "the jump between fact and the imaginative reality" (IMAG, 135), thereby bringing the real news of his world into permanent existence. In an introduction to Byron Vazakas's *Transfigured Night* Williams praises the fact that

> Vazakas doesn't *select* his material. What is there to select? It *is*. Like the newspaper that takes things as it finds them,—mutilated and deformed, but drops what it finds as it was, unchanged in all its deformity and mutilation—the poet, challenging the event, re-creates it as of whence it sprang from among men and women, and makes a new world of it.[66]

It is interesting to note that both Williams and Joyce, despite their mutual aversion to the press, heavily utilize both its materials and its forms.

Williams's conviction that it is structure rather than content or subject matter which puts us into direct contact with reality underlies a third aspect of the relationship between *Paterson* and the modern newspaper, for the layout of items in a newspaper can be seen as an analogical technique for the structure of the poem. In an unpublished essay on "The Present Relationship of Prose to Verse" Williams writes:

> If there is nothing to be discovered by the scrutiny of particulars [in the daily newspaper] should we not take a broader view? If we take the front page as a whole or even the sometimes all but undecipherable headlines from which all but the barest punch words have been cut. What have we then? In the case of headlines it's an expedient [which] may very well be used in a lyric and might go, if the interest could be maintained. But headlines die in less than twenty four hours and become meaningless. It's too short lived a mode for serious thought.
>
> The page as a whole in its divisions is where I think the secret lies. [YALE]

Accordingly, Eric Mottram observes that "in the true explicit sense, made familiar through the ideas of Mallarmé, Joyce and, today, Marshall McLuhan, *Paterson* is news, a living newspaper with a newspaper's curiously brilliant unity in disparity."[67] Marshall McLuhan discusses the implications of the fact that the French Symbolists, followed by Joyce, recognized a model for a new art form in the technical layout of the newspaper:

> The newspaper, from its beginnings, has tended, not to the book form, but to the mosaic or participational form. With the speed-up of printing and news-gathering, this mosaic form has become a dominant aspect of human association; for the mosaic form means, not a detached "point of view," but participation in process. . . . The press is a daily action and fiction or thing made, and it is made out of just about everything in the community. By the mosaic means, it is made into a communal image or cross-section.[68]

When the structure of *Paterson* is perceived to be in certain respects a "newspaper landscape," then the meaning and design of the poem begins to emerge.

The multiple implications of Marshall McLuhan's term "newspaper landscape" encompass a very crucial aspect of the context which Williams created in the writing of his long poem. McLuhan first employed the phrase "newspaper landscape" in reference to the structure of *Ulysses*,[69] and the fact that Williams was a great admirer of Joyce and openly acknowledged a debt to *Ulysses* in relation to *Paterson* further supports the relevance of this concept to the structure of *Paterson*.

The paratactic constructions used by Williams in his prosody have their counterpart in the larger structural elements of his long poem.[70] At any given moment, *Paterson*'s organization resembles the format of the modern daily press, which is simply the presentation of heterogeneous items in juxtaposition. Eugène Vinaver's distinction made in *The Rise of Romance* between "contrived" and "genuine" parataxis has considerable relevance to Williams's juxtaposition of material in *Paterson*. In a discussion of *Paterson* as a "newspaper landscape," it is necessary to be concerned only with the kind of juxtaposition in the poem which is the counterpart of genuine parataxis. The juxtaposition of the poem's material which is the counterpart of contrived parataxis will play a part in the following discussion of the interlace structure of the poem. According to Vinaver, genuine parataxis

> invites simple acceptance, not elaboration; it does not conceal continuity and cohesion in silent intervals, but dispenses with such things, and any exegesis that attempts to supply them results in a distortion of the linguistic and poetic pattern of the work.[71]

A seemingly abrupt or irrational juxtaposition of material which corresponds to "genuine parataxis" is prevalent throughout *Paterson*, and any reader of the poem who attempts rationally and temporally to connect every piece of writing to every other piece does indeed succeed in destroying the "poetic pattern of the work." For example, the letter from T. in Book I, that from DJB in Book III, and the letters from A.G. in Books IV and V are not related in an immediately specific manner to what comes before or after, nor are the various newspaper and historical accounts of violent and murderous acts which are interspersed throughout the poem. On a worksheet Williams instructs himself to "(—interrupt the course of the poem whenever the occasion present[s], items to separate the course of the stream—THE STREAM: carcasses of horses floating in the river that SURROUNDS THEM without making them a part of itself)" (YALE). Such interpolation is related to what Williams calls the "irrational" in the poem:

> One fault in modern compositions . . . is that the irrational has no place. Yet in life (you show it by your tolerance of things which you feel no loss at not understanding) there is much that men exclude because they do not understand. The truly great heart *includes* what it does not at once grasp, just as the great artist includes things which go beyond him. . . . The irrational enters

the poem in those letters, included in the text, which do not seem to refer to anything in the "story" yet do belong somehow to the poem—how, it is not easy to say. [SL, 309]

Williams firmly held that "from the unselected nature of the material, just as it comes in over the phone or at the office door . . . there is no better way to get an intimation of what is going on in the world" (AUTO, 360). On a manuscript sheet he writes that there is to be "no over selection but plenty of cutting for effect" (YALE). On a note for II, ii, he explicitly instructs himself to include "a few *unrelated* bits" (BUFFALO), and on a "GENERAL NOTE" for the whole poem he writes:

> There are to be completely worked up parts in *each* section—as completely formal as possible: in each part well displayed.
>
> BUT—juxtaposed to them are unfinished pieces—put in without fuss—for their very immediacy of expression—as they have been written under stress, under LACK of a satisfactory form
>
> —or for their need to be just there, the information. [YALE]

To a certain, if limited degree, Williams is more interested in the simple putting down of what exists than in always providing a coherent motivation or explanation for its existence: "sometimes when I write I don't want to say anything. I just want to present it. Not a didactic meaning."[72] As we briefly explore the implications of a "newspaper landscape" format, we shall see that this fact does not contradict his desire to synthesize his material and to create a context, as might first be supposed.

McLuhan writes:

> It was Mallarmé who formulated the lessons of the press as a guide for the new impersonal poetry of suggestion and implication. He saw that the scale of modern reportage and of the mechanical multiplication of messages made personal rhetoric impossible. Now was the time for the artist to intervene in a new way and to manipulate the new media of communication by a precise and

delicate adjustment of the relations of words, things, and events. His task had become not self-expression but the release of the life in things.[73]

As a consequence of modern technology, particularly the telegraph, the press no longer has a definite point of view: "As the book page yields the inside story of the author's mental adventures, so the press page yields the inside story of the community in action and interaction."[74] The press is "a daily cross-section of the activities and impulses of the race."[75] It is a microcosm, "an X-ray drama,"[76] a "minature cameo of the world we live in."[77] Through the juxtaposition of diverse and unconnected materials in *Paterson* which represent a variety of points of view, Williams similarly creates the impression of a "community in action and interaction" and a world in miniature. Williams's use of a series of newspaper headlines in an outline of Book II ("FLASH! Middle Aged Romeo Confesses Strange Practice! Prominent Banker Rescues Convicted Defaulter! Wealthy Churchwoman Revealed As Long Sought Swindler! Mrs. Switchback, etc." [YALE]has structural as well as material significance. This aspect of *Paterson*'s organization can be loosely described as montage, an "artistic composite of juxtaposed more or less heterogeneous elements."[78]

McLuhan observes:

> Montage has to be arranged forwards or backwards. Forwards it yields narrative. Backwards it is reconstruction of events. Arrested it consists of the static landscape of the press, the co-existence of all aspects of community life. This is the image of the city presented in *Ulysses*.[79]

This is also the image of the city which Williams attempts to create in *Paterson* through the juxtaposition of multifarious items.

Within each book of *Paterson*, the old and the modern coexist, supplementing the linearity which characterizes Williams's original four part plans. As Williams wrote in reference to John Hargrave's novel *Summer Time Ends,* "The effect is to link the past with the present into a whole."[80] The "newspaper landscape" of *Paterson* is more a horizontal than a vertical extension since beginnings and ends, past and present, here and there, are flattened out upon one plane. This horizontal extension allows for expansion and growth and indicates why Williams came to the realization that *Paterson* would always be a work-in-progress and could end only with his death: "I have been forced to recognize that there can be no end to such a story I have envisioned with the terms which I had laid down for myself" (Author's Note).

A mosaic literary form presents a variety of points of view whose meaning emerges only through the participation of the reader, whose mind perceives and contemplates the interplay between the various items of the mosaic: "To the alerted eye, the front page of a newspaper is a superficial chaos which can lead the mind to attend to cosmic harmonies of a very high order. Yet when these harmonies are more sharply stylized by a Picasso or a Joyce, they seem to give offense to the very people who should appreciate them most."[81]

In *The Exile of James Joyce* Hélène Cixous makes the observation that in *Portrait of the Artist as a Young Man* and in *Ulysses,* "Joyce attains . . . formal order by making division the instrument of reconstruction instead of merely another symptom of fragmentation."[82] It would be dificult to find a statement which expresses more accurately the intent of Williams's mosaic method in *Paterson. Paterson* is a superficial rather than a literal chaos. It is an acentric composition which is nevertheless a complex totality—city, man, and poem: "by multiplication a reduction to one." In "Reply to a Young Scientist" Williams writes that "you poor fishes haven't yet understood that one plus one plus one plus one plus one equals not five but one. A thing every artist has known from the beginning of time, so thoroughly inescapable that even science is beginning at last to catch on to it."[83] McLuhan maintains that

it is on its technical and mechanical side that the front page is linked
to the techniques of modern science and art. Discontinuity is in
different ways a basic concept of quantum and relativity
physics. . . . They have provided new facts about the world, new
intelligibility, new insights into the universal fabric. Practically
speaking, they mean that henceforth this planet is a single city.[84]

The nature of the unity which the juxtaposition of heterogeneous items in newspaper fashion contributes to *Paterson* is
symbolic rather than literal, taking its cues from modern
physics, which has implied that "there can be symbolic unity
among the most diverse and externally unconnected facts or
situations."[85]

6

        .   .   a mass of detail
to interrelate on a new ground, difficultly;
an assonance, a homologue
                        triple piled
pulling the disparate together to clarify
and compress [I, ii, 30]

Jostled as are the waters approaching
the brink, his thoughts
interlace, repel and cut under,
rise rock-thwarted and turn aside
but forever strain forward—or strike
an eddy and whirl, marked by a
leaf or curdy spume, seeming
to forget   . [I, i, 16]

                —to refresh himself
at the sight direct from the 12th[86]
century what the old women or the young
or men or boys wielding their needles
to put in her green thread correctly
beside the purple, myrtle beside
holly and the brown threads beside:
together as the cartoon has plotted it

for them. All together, working together—
all the birds together. The birds
and leaves are designed to be woven
in his mind eating and
all together for his purposes [V, iii, 269–70]

The meaning of *Paterson* emerges out of the relationships
and the interpenetrations between various pieces of seemingly
amorphous matter. By examining the implications of McLuhan's term "newspaper landscape," the previous section emphasizes one way in which Williams's materials interrelate.
Although at any given moment the mosaic concept is valid, by
its very nature it is nontemporal and static and does not, by
itself, encompass the complexity of *Paterson*'s larger organization. This section will examine another aspect of the structure
of the poem by discussing the interlacing and "contrived"
juxtaposition of *Paterson*'s material.

In the section on "Measure" it was observed that the turn to
paratactic and nonlinear constructions is not unique to the
modern period informed by the theory of relativity, and that
Williams came to recognize that, rather than inventing something new, he was involved in the rediscovery of certain
principles of poetic form which had become obscured. Similarly, *Paterson*'s larger organization has a number of counter-
parts in the literary and artistic forms of an earlier period. The
early sixteenth-century French or Flemish Unicorn tapestries
which now hang in the Cloisters at Fort Tryon Park in New
York City contribute to the subject matter of Book V and
provide a symbolic depth which the poem had previously
lacked. In his essay "The Unicorn in *Paterson:* Williams Carlos
Williams," Louis Martz maintains that in Book V "Williams is
defending and explaining his own technique by suggesting an
analogy with the mode of the tapestries." Martz is referring
specifically to the subject matter of the tapestries, which he
describes as "a peculiar combination of the local and the
mythical."[87] The analogy is, however, of even deeper

significance. In his essay "The Interlace Structure of *Beowulf*," John Leyerle writes:

> The past participle of *texere*, "to weave, braid, interlace," is *textus*, the etymon of our words text and textile. The connection is so obvious that no one thinks of it. In basic meaning, then, a poetic text is a weaving of words to form, in effect, a verbal carpet page. . . .
> At a structural level, literary interlace has a counterpart in tapestries where positional patterning of threads establishes the shape and design of the fabric, whether the medium is thread in textile or words in a text.[88]

Similarly, the Unicorn tapestries provide an analogy for understanding Williams's arrangement of the material in *Paterson*. That is to say, the weaver's interlacing of colored threads to form a design is analogous to the ways in which Williams develops his material themes by the interlacing and juxtaposition of events, images, phrases, and other "things" which he had amassed for his long poem.[89] In his essay "Caviar and Bread Again" Williams describes the poet's function in terms of weaving: "he [the poet] has been the fortunate one who has gathered all the threads together that have been spun for many centuries before him and woven them into his design" (SE, 103). On a manuscript sheet for *Paterson III*, i he writes that "through the over-all wind theme—a wind of books—run threads: 3 themes: 1. the woman disclad—2. conspiracy 3. the flower" (YALE). A manuscript sheet for *Paterson V* reveals that Williams also thought of the poem in terms of a fugue, which is basically an interlace structure defined as "a polyphonic musical composition in which one or two themes are repeated or imitated by successively entering voices and contrapuntally developed in a continuous interweaving of the voice parts."[90] Accordingly, a note for Book III instructs that "the colored—girls and preacher" are to be "the same as Bppk [*sic*] II in a different key" (YALE).

Eugène Vinaver offers an explanation for the fact that discoveries made in relation to the structure of medieval

literary works provide a key to an understanding of a
twentieth-century poem. He writes:

> There is no need to think . . . of a possible revival of the
> medieval view of the art of composition. What some art historians
> and literary critics have taken to be a return to the medieval
> concept of analogy is in reality a recurrence of one of the
> constants—actual or potential—of poetic structure, occasionally
> obscured by certain conventions imported from outside.[91]

Vinaver maintains that the modern reader has difficulty understanding, explaining, or describing what it is that gives life and
meaning to medieval literary art or to much of the literature of
his own time because of his classical expectations of organic
unity:

> And when, in a thrust against the functional, the rational, and
> the straightforward, poetic form in our modern age proclaims its
> own autonomous value, when it discards those other, much
> heavier, chains known as simplicity, brevity, and singleness, who
> can say that the discoveries of the past have been lost, or that the
> meeting-point between the Middle Ages and ourselves has not at
> long last been reached?[92]

According to Vinaver in "contrived" parataxis

> the absence of causal connectives may be merely apparent; they
> may be there even though they are not expressed; our mind then
> rushes into the artificially created verbal vacuum to supply by its
> own cogitations all that the poet has deliberately left unsaid. In
> such cases parataxis is a mere device, productive of comic or
> sublime effects as the case may be—sometimes, as in the great
> examples of biblical narrative, creating a sense of depth and
> expectancy, the feeling that the unfathomable is there for us to
> discover, or at least to apprehend.[93]

In *Paterson* Williams makes use of a kind of juxtaposition which
is the counterpart of contrived parataxis to produce the whole
gamut of effects from the comic to the serious. An example of a

comic effect occurs in Book I where Williams berates "the university" and describes the academics as

> clerks
> got out of hand forgetting for the most part
> to whom they are beholden.
>
> spitted on fixed concepts like
> roasting hogs [I, iii, 44]

This is directly followed by a prose account in which Williams describes a doctor, no doubt representative of himself, who is

> more concerned, much more concerned with detaching the label from a discarded mayonnaise jar, the glass jar in which some patient had brought a specimen for examination, than to examine and treat the twenty and more infants taking their turn from the outer office. [I, iii, 44]

By means of this juxtaposition Williams equates the fixed concepts of the university "clerks" with the label of a jar containing urine. The majority of the comic effects have serious overtones and by making himself the subject of the prose piece Williams acknowledges his own inadequacy and narrowmindedness, his own lack of commitment both as poet and as doctor to those who depend upon him. Another comic juxtaposition occurs in Book II where a letter from Pound written in an exaggerated American dialect (intended, perhaps, to ape Williams)[94] informs Williams what he should read—"*all* the Gk tragedies in / Loeb.—plus Frobenius, plus / Gesell plus Brooks Adams /. . . . Then Golding 'Ovid' " (III, iii, 165). This letter is followed by the "Substratum" of an "Artesian Well at the Passaic Rolling Mill, Paterson." This "Substratum" concludes with the statement that "the fact that the rock salt of England, and of some of the other salt mines of Europe, is found in rocks of the same age as this, raises the question whether it may not also be found here" (III, iii, 166). This juxtaposition functions as a critical commentary upon Pound's expatriation, his academic and foreign interests and affirms the validity of American sources and materials.[95]

"Contrived" juxtapositions of a more serious nature are prevalent throughout *Paterson*. In Book I Williams presents a "romantic" description of Paterson's landscape and environs— "Pearls at her ankles, her monstrous hair/spangled with appleblossoms is scattered about into/the back country" (I, i, 17). This description is succeeded by a historical prose account of a search for pearls which resulted in the destroying of millions of mussels and of the pearls themselves—"the finest pearl of modern times, was ruined by boiling open the shell" (I, i, 17). The romantic landscape account is thus immediately undercut by a historical excerpt which suggests the beginnings of usury, destruction, violence, and greed. Another example occurs in Book III where Williams writes about Marie Curie's discovery of radium—"a stain at the bottom of the retort/ without weight, a failure, a/nothing. And then, returning in the/night, to find it ./LUMINOUS!" (III, ii, 209). These lines are followed by an excerpt from Christopher Columbus's journal written at the time of his discovery of the New World—"During that time I walked among the trees which was the most beautiful thing which I had ever known" (III, ii, 209). In this manner Curie's discovery of radium is associated with Columbus's discovery of the New World.[96]

Williams also counterbalances *Paterson*'s linear structure by presenting his material themes, insofar as possible, simultaneously, so that they "alternate like threads in a woven fabric, one theme interrupting another and again another, and yet all remaining constantly present in the author's and the reader's mind."[97] On a manuscript sheet for *Paterson* entitled "OVER-ALL PLOT AND STRUCTURAL SCHEME: hint for the nature of a poem .," Williams states that "there are two interchanging themes through whatever else, alternating, interrupted as may be desired, in sequences but always returning" (YALE). The interlacing of his material permits

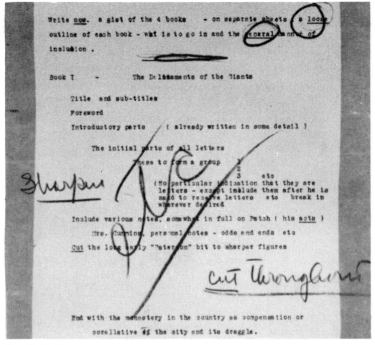

Facsimile 3

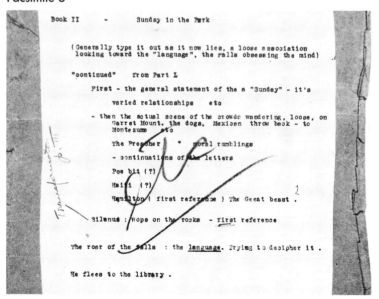

Facsimile 4

The Language

[He seeks an interpretation of the Falls - that obsesses him -
in reading, in books   - but finds it not in the books but in
his mind that wanders as he reads :]

Thinking over the sermon in the park.

The enigma posed .   Riddle in the Greek or Joycian sense.
    The language, the language : the Falls

The history of SUM -
    begin, also, the history of the place.

The Curie : radium lecture

Psycho- somatic : the mind and body as it listens for the
    language - the search goes on and becomes more confused.

First mention of the 2 murders - Van Winkle (for money)
                                     Adrianne   etc

    give notes, first notes, of both - fairly full (but not
    the outside of either

    Continuation of the various letters : and some of them.

The mind.   Variation of the sermon ; letters of the
                                             colored girls.

The search : where to search ?

    The solving of the riddle.

Facsimile 5

    - the river also of blood (which is the actual of that
      symbol (?)

    [Love] - the singular outcome of the language .

        Statement of the. - confession, the peculiarity that
        is the personal : the individual : Restrice -
        the humiliating (intrinsic) truth.

        The flow of the factual history   - alongside

        The consolation of the river (below the falls)

    The letters concluded.

    Praise of the river ; short appearances of it through the
        other texts.

    What of Paterson himself, that solitary man - ?

    The river of blood (escape or attempted escape to the N.Y.
        his return "home"

    The river as a WOMAN.

    Murder and blood. The crowd gathered to witness.

Facsimile 6

Williams "to achieve juxtapositions impossible in a linear narrative":[98] "Unless a poem be beyond thought new, full of amazing juxtapositions, a new pace a new and unsuspected order—it is not worthy" (YALE). The interlacement throughout the poem allows for the events, things, phrases, and prose material to be introduced again at a later point or points where they will, perhaps, be more fully understood or be seen in a new perspective in the light of what has since transpired in the poem and of the new material with which they are juxtaposed. That is to say that "the recurrence of a theme can confer fresh significance upon it, whether the theme is a statement of fact, or a description of an object, or an expression of feeling."[99] Even Williams's sketchy outlines for Books I–IV (see facsimiles 3, 4, 5, 6) reveal his concern with the placement of his blocks of material and his use of the technique of interlace to unify the poem (see the chart based on facsimiles 3, 4, 5, 6).[100]

There are basically two kinds of interlace in *Paterson*. The first can be described generally as the interweaving of originally or logically continuous, or of basically homogeneous material (such as newspaper items or historical excerpts) throughout a section or sections of the poem. The effect of this type of interlace will perhaps be best understood by first considering a fairly straightforward and compact example. In II, ii, Williams presents a sermon delivered by Klaus Ehrens in which the evangelist tells the story of his giving away of his money in favor of the "treasures of our Blessed Lord" (II, ii, 90). Williams had instructed himself in his unpublished notes for the section to

—divide the minister's exhortation into four parts:

His desire for riches and getting them
His unhappiness and divination as to cause
Getting rid of his money and return of happiness
Divine mission to preach [BUFFALO]

In *Paterson* these four general sections can be discerned and

The Interlace Elements in
Facsimiles 3, 4, 5 and 6.

I	II	III	IV
The initial parts of all letters	—continuations of the letters	Continuation of the various letters: end some of them.	The letters concluded.
Cut the long early "Paterson" bit to sharper figures		begin, also, the history of the place.	The flow of the factual history
	The roar of the falls: the *language*. Trying to decipher it.	He seeks an interpretation of the Falls	The consolation of the river (below the falls)
	The Preacher moral rumblings	Thinking over the sermon in the park.	
	Hamilton (first reference)	The history of SUM	
		First mention of the 2 murders. . . . give notes, first notes, of both—fairly full (but *not* the outcome of either).	Murder and blood. The crowd gathered to witness.

they are interlaced primarily with quotations from a mimeographed sheet put out by Alfredo and Clara Studer and a pamphlet entitled "Tom Edison on the Money Subject," dealing critically with Alexander Hamilton and the Federal Reserve System.[101] The technique of interlace allows for the subjects of these narratives, widely separated in time, to be presented simultaneously to the reader. The juxtaposition of this material reveals the underlying pathos and tragedy of the inhabitants of Paterson, who have not only suffered from the completion of Hamilton's plans but who also lack any viable contemporary leadership or hope: "And it all came to me then—that those poor souls had nothing else in the world, save that church, between them and the eternal stony, ungrateful and unpromising dirt they lived by" (II, ii, 78).

The interweaving of excerpts from Cress's letters throughout the first two books of *Paterson* provides another example of this type of interlace. The seven excerpts are taken from actual letters which Williams received from the poet Marcia Nardi. The first fragment in which Cress, obviously distressed, politely solicits Paterson's attention and consideration, occurs early in Book I immediately following the lines

> A man like a city and a woman like a flower
> —who are in love. Two women. Three women.
> Innumerable women, each like a flower.
>
> But
>
> only one man—like a city. [I, i, 15]

These lines are undermined by the letter introducing the theme of divorce which continues throughout the poem. James Breslin similarly observes that "this dream [a man like a city etc.] is interrupted by the first letter from the poetess Cress, by the voice of an actual woman in distress accusing him of personal remoteness."[102] Because of the letter's placement Cress is associated with one of the "Innumerable women" whom Williams identifies with "a flower." This association takes on a discomforting and prophetic significance a few pages later where

> The flower spreads its colored petals
> wide in the sun
> But the tongue of the bee
> misses them [I, i, 20]

The remaining six letters are interlaced throughout Paterson's walk in the park in Book II. On a manuscript sheet for this section Williams wrote

                            external
                            walking
                       internal [BUFFALO]

suggesting that Paterson's walk through the park encompasses
not only his external, physical movement from place to place
among the people, but also an internal walking as his
"thoughts/interlace, repel and cut under" (I, i, 16). Williams
places the second letter after a description of walking taken
from an article on "Dynamic Posture."[103] In this letter Cress
holds Paterson responsible for the "damming up" of her
"creative capacities" because of his ignoring of the "real
contents" of her letters to him. She speaks of "blockage"—
"exiling one's self from one's self—have you ever experienced
it? I dare say you have, at moments" (II, ii, 59–60). Williams
begins the very next section of the poem with the word
"Blocked," indicating that he is, in fact, experiencing difficulty
moving through the poem, a damming up of his own "creative
capacities." The fact that Williams uses a form of the same word
as Cress suggests that his blockage is also a product of his failure
to relate meaningfully to the realities of his human and physical
environment. Because of the context which has been gradually
developing around the theme of divorce throughout Books I
and II—the alienation of man from woman, the lack of communication, the loss of roots—the accusations and the
psychological condition described in this letter can be better
understood. The third fragment interrupts a section in which
Paterson imaginatively recaptures the presence of a red stone
grasshopper. The letter is preceded by the line "He is led
forward by their announcing wings" (II, i, 63) and succeeded by

           —his mind a red stone carved to be
           endless flight   .
           Love that is a stone endlessly in flight,
           so long as stone shall last bearing
           the chisel's stroke   . [II, i, 63]

Once again, Cress's letter tends to undermine or at least to counterbalance Paterson's imaginative achievement by reminding the reader of his failure in another area. The next two letters are interlaced with the section dealing with Klaus Ehrens and they function not only as criticism of his naïve message but also of the way in which it is presented. The excerpt which concludes section ii and substantially ends the evangelist section is concerned primarily with Cress's need to communicate with Paterson and thus serves to pinpoint one of the major difficulties with Klaus—his inadequate language and his consequent inability to relate to his following: "Minister: He does not have it (the language) though his leap is just" (BUFFALO). In the sixth letter Cress finally articulates the statement which her letters have been leading up to:

> You might as well take all your own literature and everyone else's and toss it into one of those big garbage trucks of the Sanitation Department, so long as the people with the top-cream minds and the "finer" sensibilities use those minds and sensibilities not to make themselves more humane human beings than the average person, but merely as means of ducking responsibility toward a better understanding of their fellow men, except theoretically—which doesn't mean a God damned thing. [II, iii, 10]

This fragment is strategically placed at one of the turning points of the poem, which suggests that Cress's letters along with the other "complex voices" (II, i, 76) of the park have had a cumulative effect upon Paterson. Before the interpolation of Cress's letter, Paterson listens to the falls

> But discovers, still, no syllable in the confused
> uproar: missing the sense (though he tries)
> untaught but listening, shakes with the intensity
> of his listening   . [II, iii, 100]

After the letter he flees (to the library) "pursued by the roar"

(II, iii, 104). Book II concludes with the last of Cress's letters, which brings together all of the themes which have been interlaced throughout the first two books—divorce, economics, and the moral obligation that a writer has to "embrace the foulness" (III, i, 126) and "life in the raw" (II, iii, 106). In reference to this letter, Williams wrote to Robert D. Pepper in 1951:

> I did not compose it. It is, as you see, an attack, a personal attack upon me by a woman. It seemed a legitimate one. It had besides a certain literary quality which was authentic, that made it a thing in itself worth recording. . . .
> The five or six friends to who[m] I then showed it, men and women, were divided in their opinions but, watching their reactions, I decided that [there] were more reasons for putting the letter in than there were for leaving it out: In the first place it was a reply from the female side to many of my male pretensions. It was a strong reply, a reply which sought to destroy me. If it could destroy me I should be destroyed. It was just that it should have its opportunity to destroy. If I hid the reply it would be a confession of weakness on my part.[104]

The interlacing of fragments from Cress's letters accomplishes basically three things. In the first place, Williams is able to sustain a linear rhythm throughout the first two books as the reader gradually learns what is on Cress's mind. Secondly, the technique of interlace also creates an acentric, simultaneous effect as beginnings, endings, and incongruent materials are juxtaposed. Finally, the juxtapositions which are created confer new significance upon the letters and also upon the material with which the letter interacts upon the page.

The second and most dominant type of interlace in *Paterson* is the continual process of cross-referencing which occurs throughout the poem. It is based primarily on a number of narrative sequences, events, or images, initially related in full, elements of which are later used to amplify and illuminate certain aspects of the poem. The later references bring to mind the original event and as a result that event, as well as the context in which the new reference occurs, acquires an added dimension and must be continuously reevaluated. For example, in Book I a prose excerpt taken from Barber and Howe's *Historical Collections*[105] relates in detail the story of Mrs. Cumming's fall into the Passaic River. This account is juxtaposed with the narration of Sam Patch's career as a jumper copied out of *A Little Story of Old Paterson* by Charles Pitman Longwell.[106] Williams associates the deaths of both Mrs. Cumming and Patch with the failure of language and communication. Following the prose description of Mrs. Cumming's fall are the lines:

> A false language. A true. A false language pouring—a
> language (misunderstood) pouring (misinterpreted) without
> dignity, without minister, crashing upon a stone ear. [I, i, 24]

Williams purposefully omits from his transcription of the prose account the fact that Mrs. Cumming had been dizzy earlier that morning which might have accounted for her fall. His interpretation of her "accident" is made very obvious in an earlier draft for this section:

> What was that cry? What was that fall?
> Nobody saw her. It was, or was it?
> the laughter of the waterfall—a true
> language she could understand [BUFFALO]

Williams actually interpolates the theme of failed speech into the prose account dealing with Patch: "But instead of descending with a plummet-like fall his body wavered in the air— Speech had failed him. He was confused. The word had been drained of its meaning" (I, i, 27). To appreciate fully the function of these two prose accounts it is necessary to be aware of the range of meaning which the Passaic falls encompasses in the poem. Throughout *Paterson* the falls represents a chaotic power to which people are attracted as a relief from their meaningless and sterile existence. The falls is also associated with a "common language" which the poet has to "unravel" (I, i, 15) and which is "hard to interpret" (I, i, 26). In Book II the waterfall is referred to as a "confused uproar" in which Paterson cannot discover a "syllable" (II, iii, 100). In Book III it is described as "the roar of the present, a speech" (III, iii, 172). The cumulative impression suggests that the falls represents the unformed language of the present which the poet has to control, measure, and organize: "The roar of the falls: the *language*. Trying to decipher it" (BUFFALO; see facsimile 4). Williams had originally thought of including David Lyle's letters in the body of the poem to impersonate the torrent of the falls. He also instructed himself to use the falls "as background to everything else, to heighten everything else and to stitch together every other thing" (YALE). Therefore, as we shall see, the premature deaths of Cumming and Patch, which are intermittently referred to or subtly evoked throughout the first four books of *Paterson*, contribute to the elucidation and development of the poem's most important material theme which Williams delineates in a note for the publication of *Paterson III*:

> *Paterson* is a man (since I am a man) who dives from cliffs and the edges of waterfalls, to his death—finally. But for all that he is a woman (since I am not a woman) who *is* the cliff and the waterfall. She spreads protecting fingers about him as he plummets to his conclusions to keep the winds from blowing him out of his path. But he escapes, in the end, as I have said. . . .
>
> The brunt of the four books of *Paterson* . . . is a search for the redeeming language by which a man's premature death, like the death of Mrs. Cumming in Book I, and the woman's (the man's) failure to hold him (her) might have been prevented.
>
> Book IV will show the perverse confusions that come of a failure to untangle the language and make it our own as both man and woman are carried helplessly toward the sea (of blood) which, by their failure of speech, awaits them. The poet alone in this world holds the key to their final rescue.[107]

Paterson is clearly and initially associated with Patch by the fact that the prose passage in Book I is introduced by the lines

> THE GRRRREAT HISTORY of that
> old time Jersey Patriot
> N. F. P A T E R S O N ! [I, i, 25]

Throughout the first four books of the poem Paterson is drawn toward the idea of jumping into the falls. The references to Sam Patch and Mrs. Cumming provide explicit reminders of Paterson's possible fate. In Book I Paterson wonders "Why have I not/but for imagined beauty where there is none/or none available, long since/put myself deliberately in the way of death?" (I, ii, 30–31). Immediately thereafter Patch and Cumming are reintroduced reminding Paterson as well as the reader of their accomplished fate in Book I and his imminent fate:

> :a body found next spring
> frozen in an ice-cake; or a body
> fished next day from the muddy swirl—[I, ii, 31]

Similarly in Book II, "Only the thought of the stream comforts him,/its terrifying plunge" (II, iii, 100) and "He all but falls" (II, iii, 102). At this crucial point the memory of Mrs. Cumming is vividly evoked:

> and leaped (or fell) without a
> language, tongue-tied
>   the language worn out   . [II, iii, 103]

Discouraged after his sojourn in the library in Book III, Paterson decides to go "to the river for/an answer/for relief from 'meaning' " (III, i, 135). Once again the spectre of Patch intervenes:

> and the poor cotton-
> spinner, over the roofs, preparing to dive
> looks down [III, i, 136]

Near the end of Book I there is a passage which encapsulates this tension which Paterson labors under throughout the poem:

> Moveless
> he envies the men that ran
> and could run off
> toward the peripheries—
> to other centers, direct—
> for clarity (if
> they found it)
>   loveliness and
> authority in the world—
>
> a sort of springtime
> towards which their minds aspired
> but which he saw,
> within himself—ice bound
>
> and leaped, "the body, not until
> the following spring, frozen in
> an ice cake" [I, iii, 48]

On the one hand, Paterson hopes to resist the solution represented by the expatriates Eliot and Pound. On the other hand, he does not want to submit to the attraction which the power of the cataract holds for him and to immerse himself irresponsibly in the "roar of the present." Paterson and Cumming "plunged, they fell in a swoon" into the falls, but ideally Paterson desires to find "a place/apart from it" (III, iii, 172–73):

> I must
> find my meaning and lay it, white,
> beside the sliding water: myself—
> comb out the language—or succumb [III, iii, 173]

In light of the numerous drownings throughout the poem, it is significant that at the end of Book IV a man walks out of the water, indicating that at least a key to a redeeming language has been found through the enactment of the four books of Paterson: "But he escapes, in the end, as I have said."[108]

The interlacing of references to Cumming and Patch throughout the poem induces in the reader not only a continuous reappraisal of these two episodes but also a recognition of the poem's development. As we have seen, the implications of Paterson's thoughts or actions are often revealed without the necessity of authorial commentary by juxtaposing them with references to Cumming and Patch. Williams expects his readers to keep the poem's events in mind so that even a slight reference to a previous occurrence interlaces it with the present event, thereby creating the larger design of the poem. This continual process of cross-referencing also contributes further to the creation of a simultaneous effect and at the same time suggests the circularity of time. As John Leyerle observes: "This design reveals the meaning of coincidence, the recurrence of human behaviour, and the circularity of time, partly through the coincidence, recurrence, and circularity of the medium itself—the interlace structure."[109]

On a manuscript sheet outlining Book I Williams specifically instructs himself to "include various notes, somewhat in full on Patch (his *acts*)" (BUFFALO, see facsimile 3). It is significant that Williams particularly stresses Patch's "*acts*," for the expression of meaning in *Paterson* is primarily developed through the interpenetration of actions and factors, of what has happened and what is happening, of what has existed and what now exists. As Leyerle remarks of the *Beowulf* poet, "The relations between events are more significant than their temporal sequence and he used a structure that gave him great freedom to manipulate time and concentrate on the complex interconnections of events."[110] A worknote for Book IV states, "*Starts* with reminiscence—is *interrupted* fitfully by occurrances [sic] & thoughts" (YALE). In *Allegorical Imagery* Rosemond Tuve observes:

Web-structure has special possibilities of gradually discernible meaning as the woven pattern shows it *is* a pattern and *takes* shape. Hence it was a superbly invented instrument for conveying not only what we called the polyphonic nature of what is happening, but that which interested Spenser supremely, the fact that to human minds what happens "means" something, is significant.[111]

Paterson's structure is not simply one of theme and variation wherein a theme is stated and then examples are presented to support the theme, although the poem has often been described as primarily operating in this manner. Rather, the poem is a "field of action" in which meanings and themes arise and gradually emerge through the complex interaction of its materials—through the process and enactment of the poem: "that which exists through itself is what is called meaning."[112] John Leyerle points out that the interlace technique

> is an organizing principle closer to the workings of the human imagination proceeding in its atemporal way from one associative idea to the next than to the Aristotelian order of parts belonging to a temporal sequence with a beginning, middle, and end. . . . The human imagination moves in atemporal, associative patterns like the literary interlace.[113]

In his "Prologue to Kora in Hell" Williams writes that "the imagination goes from one thing to another" (SE, 11). Olson defines this movement as "the *process* of the thing" whose principle is that "ONE PERCEPTION MUST IMMEDIATELY AND DIRECTLY LEAD TO A FURTHER PERCEPTION."[114] Williams similarly affirms that "one thing *leads* to another which is thereby activated."[115] On his worksheets for *Paterson* Williams constantly stresses the presentation of Paterson's stream of consciousness. A note for Book III states: "(He seeks an interpretation of the Falls—that obsesses him—in reading, in books—but finds it not in the books but in his mind that wanders as he reads:)" (YALE; see facsimile 5). In fact, all of the varied incidents which occur in Book II take place in Paterson's wandering mind. As Josephine Herbst (Josie) writes in a letter to Williams in Book V, "A place is made up of memories as well as the world around it" (V, i, 245). Another relevant analogy to this aspect of *Paterson*'s structure is provided by David Jones in his preface to *The Anathemata* in reference to the plan and the shape of his own poem: "Rather as in a longish conversation between two friends, where one thing leads to another; but should a third party hear fragments of it, he might not know how the talk had passed from the cultivation of cabbages to Melchizedek, king of Salem."[116] *Paterson* was originally to be structured as imaginary conversations between "Doc" and "Willie" and as it now stands the poem still retains elements of the associational patterns of discourse. In an interview with Robert Creeley, Charles Tomlinson observes that if "one taps Williams on that level [of discourse], one can really take the localism."[117]

Although "thought," whether expressed by Paterson or Williams, is a part of the poem's material and therefore interlaced and juxtaposed throughout the poem, there is a distinction between the interior monologue of Paterson's mind and Williams's own lyrical interpolations into the poem's movement. In a letter to Norman Macleod in 1945 Williams writes in reference to the structure of *Paterson* that "Dewey might do something for me, but I am not worth his notice" (SL, 239). Jerome Mazzaro maintains:

> The reference is undoubtedly to John Dewey's extension of the Jamesian "streams of consciousness" into "contexts of experience." These "contexts" saw the continuity of life as a gradation of qualitative fusions, here and there broken into by articulated analyses and discriminations. Unity in art became a system of fusions.[118]

This point of view suggests that Williams's intermittent lyrical exclamations contribute directly in another way to the unity of the poem, as through poetic expression he uncovers another dimension of the material which he has joined together. As Gaston Bachelard observes in *The Poetics of Space*, "By means of poetic language, waves of newness flow over the surface of being. And language bears within itself the dialectics of open and closed. Through *meaning* it encloses, while through poetic expression, it opens up."[119] These intermittent lyric "fusions" contribute primarily an emotional rather than an explanatory dimension to the poem and are referred to by Williams as "short poems that separate themselves out by their intense feeling—let them" (BUFFALO). These "short poems" are the most direct communication in *Paterson* between Williams and the reader.

The use and presentation of material in *Paterson* contributes to the creation of the world of Paterson, just as our apprehension of any city or person is only arrived at through the selection, arrangement, and recollection of information which comes our way in a nonrational, often random sequence.[120] As we read *Paterson,* we gradually inhabit the area of a city. Episodes, fragments, ideas, and images appear, disappear, and recur in constantly shifting patterns. The interlacing and juxtaposition of these things, punctuated by lyric "fusions," reveal the relevance of the separate elements while simultaneously creating a complex totality whose parts are interrelated—city, man, and poem.

NOTES TO CHAPTER 5

1. "Material theme" is a phrase which Williams himself uses in reference to *Paterson*: "The noise of the Falls seemed to me to be a language which we were and are seeking, and my search, as I looked about, became the struggle to interpret and use this language. This is the substance of the poem. But the poem is also the search of the poet after his language, his own language which I, quite apart from the material theme, had to use to write at all" (quoted in John Thirlwall, "WCW's *Paterson*," in *New Directions in Prose and Poetry 17* (Norfolk, Conn.: New Directions, 1961), p. 263). Although the term "dominant theme" is not used specifically by Williams, he does indicate on several occasions his awareness of a theme in his poetry other than the material theme: "The broad general theme is the one that has most impressed me in my life. The problem is to be both local (all art is local) and at the same time to surmount

that restriction by climbing to the universal in all art. . . . What I am trying to get over is that there is a theme which is greater than any poem or any poet worthy of following—or if not, there's not much use bothering about what a poem 'means' " (SL, 286).

2. Northrop Frye uses this phrase to refer to the relationship between the hero and his society. Frye's distinction between plot or narrative and *dianoia* or poetic thought has certain similarities to the distinction we are making here between material and dominant theme. See *Anatomy of Criticism* (Princeton, N.J.: Princeton University Press, 1971), pp. 52–53.

3. Williams is referring specifically here to the "idyl" in Book IV.

4. William Carlos Williams, "An Approach to the Poem," *English Institute Essays, 1947* (New York: Columbia University Press, 1948), p. 51.

5. Quoted in Mike Weaver, *WCW: The American Background* (Cambridge: Cambridge University Press, 1971). p. 114.

6. James Breslin, "WCW and the Whitman Tradition," *Literary Criticism and Historical Understanding*, ed. Phillip Damon (New York: Columbia University Press, 1967), p. 161.

7. John Malcolm Brinnin, "WCW," in *Seven Modern American Poets*, ed. Leonard Unger (Minneapolis: University of Minnesota Press, 1967), p. 110.

8. Robert Lowell, "Paterson I," *Sewanee Review* 4 (Summer 1947): 503.

9. Quoted in Thirlwall, "WCW's *Paterson*," p. 279.

10. Charles Olson, "Projective Verse," in *The New American Poetry*, ed. Donald Allen (New York: Grove Press, 1960), p. 396.

11. Quoted in Weaver, *WCW*, p. 49.

12. On an unpublished worksheet for an essay titled "The American Language Again" Williams concedes that "it seems unnecessary to bring mathematics to mediate in a purely literary controversy but when pressed for an answer we grasp what comes to hand. Mathematics has long been an ally of the poets. In scanning a line they count syllables, do they not? What can be wrong with counting them in a new fashion?" (YALE).

13. Eric Mottram, "The Making of *Paterson*," *Stand* 7, no. 3 (1964), p. 24.

14. William Carlos Williams, "Letter to an Australian Editor," *Briarcliff Quarterly* 3, no. 2 (October 1946), p. 207.

15. Mircea Eliade, *Patterns in Comparative Religion*, trans. Rosemary Sheed (Cleveland: World, 1963), p. 194.

16. See Bram Dijkstra, *The Hieroglyphics of a New Speech* (Princeton, N.J.: Princeton University Press, 1969), p. 29, where Dijkstra states that in the second issue of *291* (1915) there was "a page on which thought flashes, in what amounts to a stream of consciousness technique, were interspersed with advertising slogans and disjointed comments of what would seem to be passers-by. Written by Katherine N. Rhoades, the piece was called 'Mental Reactions.' De Zayas had interconnected the words, or broken them up, by means of drawings and line structures of angular shapes; some words seemed to be falling off the page, and whole lines of type stood at odd angles to each other: the result was *les mots en liberté* with a vengeance." It is more than likely that Williams was acquainted with this issue, not only because of his interest in painting at that time but also because of his friendship with Charles Demuth, Alfred

Kreymborg, and Alfred Stieglitz. Certainly one cannot fail to notice the striking similarity between the page from *Paterson* III, iii, 169 and the page from 291.

17. Marshall McLuhan, *The Mechanical Bride* (New York: Vanguard, 1951), p. 80.

18. Erich Auerbach, *Mimesis* (Princeton, N.J.; Princeton University Press, 1973), p. 74.

19. Ibid., pp. 109–10.

20. Williams, "Free Verse," *Princeton Encyclopedia of Poetry and Poetics*, ed. Alex Preminger (Princeton, N.J.: Princeton University Press, 1974), p. 289.

21. Williams, "An Approach to the Poem," p. 73.

22. Quoted in Brinnin, "WCW," p. 109.

23. Northrop Frye, *The Well-Tempered Critic* (Bloomington: Indiana University Press, 1963), p. 19.

24. David Abercrombie, *Studies in Phonetics and Linguistics* (London: Oxford University Press, 1971), p. 43. Also see pp. 5–7, where Abercrombie isolates a number of the noticeable differences between "spoken prose" and "genuine conversation."

25. Richard Eberhart in "General Points," *Agenda* 11, nos. 2–3 (Spring–Summer, 1973), claims that he "gave" the idea of the "American idiom" to Williams in 1950 during the course of a conversation with him concerning his triadic line: "He grasped this idea with enthusiasm and used it subsequently" (p. 41).

26. Stanley Koehler, "The Art of Poetry VI: WCW," *Paris Review* 8, no. 32 (Summer–Fall 1964): 117.

27. See Abercrombie, *Studies in Phonetics and Linguistics*, pp. 16–17, where he briefly discusses the bodily movements which produce sound.

28. Koehler, "The Art of Poetry VI: WCW," pp. 118–19.

29. Olson, "Projective Verse," in *The New American Poetry*, ed. Allen, p. 386.

30. Ibid., p. 388. Cf. Antonin Artaud, *The Theater and Its Double*, trans. Mary Caroline Richards (New York: Grove Press, 1958), p. 134: "The question of breath is in fact primary; it is in inverse proportion to the strength of the external expression. The more sober and restrained the expression, the deeper and heavier the breathing, the more substantial and full of resonances. Similarly an expression that is broad and full and externalized has a corresponding breath in short and broken waves. It is certain that for every feeling, every mental action, every leap of human emotion there is a corresponding breath which is appropriate to it."

31. SL, 321, 335; Williams, "Free Verse," p. 289.

32. Gerard Manley Hopkins, 1 December 1881, *The Correspondence of Gerard Manley Hopkins and Richard Watson Dixon*, ed. Claude Colleer Abbott (London: Oxford University Press, 1935), p. 99.

33. Gerard Manley Hopkins, *The Poems of Gerard Manley Hopkins*, ed. W. H. Gardner and N. H. MacKenzie (London: Oxford University Press, 1967), pp. 48–49.

34. Gerard Manley Hopkins, 14 August 1879, *The Letters of Gerard Manley Hopkins to Robert Bridges*, ed. Claude Colleer Abbot (London: Oxford University Press, 1935), p. 89.

35. William Carlos Williams, "Poetry and the Making of Language," *The New Republic* 133, no. 18 (31 October 1955): 17.

36. Walter Sutton, "A Visit with WCW," *Minnesota Review* 1 (Spring 1961): 309.

37. Hopkins, 5 October 1878, *Correspondence with Richard Watson Dixon*, p. 14.

38. Walter J. Ong, S.J., "Hopkins' Sprung Rhythm and the Life of English Poetry," in *Immortal Diamond*, ed. Normand Weyand, S.J. (New York: Sheed & Ward, 1949), pp. 100–101. See Geoffrey Hill, "Redeeming the Time," *Agenda* 10, no. 4–11, no. 1 (Autumn–Winter 1972–73): 87–111, where Hill argues for "Hopkins's vital perception of the underlying ambiguities in nineteenth century speech rhythms" (p. 105), questions "the premiss of 'rooted' speech rhythms" (p. 108), and asserts that "one answer to Father Ong's question 'what was this thing [Hopkins] was discovering all around him?' could be 'increasing tempo'; another answer could be 'the ambivalent power of the "short words" ' " (p. 108).

39. Quoted in Linda Wagner, *The Poems of WCW*, (Middletown, Conn.: Wesleyan University Press, 1964), p. 111.

40. Hopkins, 21 August 1877, *Letters to Robert Bridges*, p. 45.

41. Hopkins, 18 October 1882, ibid., pp. 155–57.

42. See Northrop Frye's definitions for these terms in *The Well-Tempered Critic*, pp. 95–104.

43. Abercrombie, *Studies in Phonetics and Linguistics*, pp. 6–7.

44. Francis Berry, *Poetry and the Physical Voice* (London: Routledge and Kegan Paul, 1962), p. 82.

45. Koehler, "The Art of Poetry VI: WCW," p. 148. In *Agenda* II, nos. 2–3 (Spring–Summer, 1973), Donald Hall writes that "it is true that there are typical American noises, which an Englishmen [sic] cannot make, and cannot even hear. This accounts for the obtuseness of most Englishmen to the ear of William Carlos Williams" (p. 45). Mike Weaver similarly acknowledges that "as an Englishman there was much in his [Williams's] idiom which, for lack of his viewpoint, I could not 'hear.' " (*WCW*, p. ix).

46. Quoted in Weaver, *WCW*, pp. 79–80.

47. Frye provides a brief explanation for this fact. He writes that "we have verse when the arrangement of words is dominated by recurrent rhythm and sound, prose when it is dominated by the syntactical relation of subject and predicate. Of the two, verse is much the simpler and more primitive type, which accounts for its being historically earlier than prose" (*The Well-Tempered Critic*, p. 21). Cf. Percy Bysshe Shelley, "A Defense of Poetry," *English Literary Criticism* (New York: Scribner's, 1896), where Shelley asserts that "the popular division into prose and verse is inadmissible in accurate philosophy" (p. 166). He also writes that "in the infancy of society every author is necessarily a poet, because language itself is poetry. . . . Every original language near to its source is in itself the chaos of a cyclic poem: the copiousness of lexicography and the distinctions of grammar are the works of a later age, and are merely the catalogue and the form of the creations of poetry" (p. 164).

48. Abercrombie, *Studies in Phonetics and Linguistics*, p. 18: "The rhythmic basis of verse is thus the same as that of prose (and, it should be added, of conversation too)—as far, at any rate, as English is concerned. . . . I do not believe their rhythmical features to be different *in kind* from each other."

49. In *Poetry and the Age*, Randall Jarrell criticizes this section as "flatter than the flattest blank verse I have ever read" (p. 232), betraying his ignorance not only of the experimental nature of the section, but also of the relationship between prose and poetry in the poem.

50. Williams, "An Approach to the Poem," p. 74.

51. Ibid., p. 65.

52. Williams, "Letter to an Australian Editor," p. 207.

53. William Carlos Williams, "Letters to Denise Levertov," *Stony Brook* 1/2 (Fall 1968): 168.

54. Donald Davie, *Ezra Pound: Poet as Sculptor* (New York: Oxford University Press, 1964), p. 45.

55. Despite the fact that Williams's letter to Eberhart is the most succinct recorded explanation of his new measure, Eberhart felt that "he never made it clear. You cannot make a physiological explanation satisfactorily scientific" ("General Points," p. 41).

56. Mary Ellen Solt, "WCW: Poems in the American Idiom," *Folio* 25, no. 1 (1960): 20.

57. Hugh Kenner in *The Pound Era* (Berkeley: University of California Press, 1971), p. 541, maintains that after Williams's strokes, "his eyes followed a line of type with ease but had trouble finding the start of the next line; the three-step indentation he came to favor was in part a way of making a page he could reread."

58. Abercrombie, *Studies in Phonetics and Linguistics*, p. 7.

59. John Cage, *Silence* (Cambridge, Mass.: M.I.T. Press, 1969), p. 109.

60. Hopkins, *Poems of Gerard Manley Hopkins*, p. 284.

61. See Percy A. Scholes, *The Oxford Companion to Music*, ed. John Owen Ward (London: Oxford University Press, 1970), p. 894, for a discussion of "rubato": "This term should be reserved as the name of that type of flexibility which consists of a '*give and take*' *within a limited unit of the time scheme*. In performance that is both deeply felt and sanely controlled this latter type of flexibility does undoubtedly constantly occur within the phrases of the music, the 'give and take' principle operating to bring the phrase back to the beat as it ends. Keenly analytical performers and listeners are . . . aware that the prhase, as the unit in music, has its own elasticity and that a stretching out is compensated by a drawing in and vice versa, with a consequent 'return to the beat.' . . . A good deal of the charm of rubato seems to come from this 'return to the beat,' which over a longer stretch than a phrase would probably not be felt at all. A suggestion is communicated of free time' but not 'bad time'; 'bent but not broken,' as Matthay has put it, and thus, paradoxically, only a very good time-keeper can be a very good 'rubatist.' "

62. Cage, *Silence*, pp. 7–8.

63. Ibid., p. 22.

64. Cary Nelson, *The Incarnate Word: Literature as Verbal Space* (Urbana: University of Illinois Press, 1973), p. 202.

65. Jonathan Raban, "Chance, Time and Silence: The New American Verse," *Journal of American Studies* 3, no. 1 (July 1969): 89. In reference to Phyllis's conversation in IV, i, 185–86, Raban writes that "the effect of this sequence is rather like listening to silence made real in a theatre by introducing a minimal noise—a twitter of birdsong, or the sound of rain falling. Or at a level of more self-conscious artistic activity, one could compare it with John Cage's composition 4'33", in which a pianist sits at a piano for four and a half minutes without touching the keys. One is made aware of the *possibility* of language and sound by being brought oppressively face to face with silence" (p. 93). Leslie Fiedler presents the opposite point of view in "Some

Uses and Failures of Feeling," where he criticizes Williams for pursuing "the seen poem: speech that rejects the illusion of being heard; lines broken on the page regardless of cadence to make the eye's pattern or emulate plastic form; at last, the absurd periods set off by chaste white space   .   .   as if they were the poem ultimately reduced and framed by a respectful silence" (p. 929).

66. According to Emily Wallace, Williams did not begin to use the phrase "variable foot" until 1954 or 1955 (*A Bibliography of WCW*, Middletown, Conn.: Wesleyan University Press, 1968), p. xvii.

67. Mary Ellen Solt, "WCW: Poems in the American Idiom," *Folio* 25, no. 1 (1960), p. 4.

68. Edgar Allen Poe, *Complete Works of Edgar Allen Poe* (New York: Fred De Fau & Co., 1902), 1:207.

69. Ibid., pp. 236–37.

70. William Carlos Williams, "A Study of Ezra Pound's Present Position," *The Massachusetts Review* 14, no. 1 (Winter 1973): 122.

71. Williams, "Poetry and the Making of Language," p. 17.

72. Ibid., p. 17.

73. See Paul Ramsey, "WCW as Metrist: Theory and Practice," *Journal of Modern Literature* 1, no. 4 (May 1971): 579; Brinnin, "WCW," pp. 108–09; A. Kingsley Weatherhead, "WCW: Prose, Form, and Measure," *Journal of English Literary History* 33 (March 1966): 119, 121–23; Paul Fussell, "Some Critical Implications of Metrical Analysis," in *WCW*, ed. Tomlinson, p. 316; Benjamin Sankey, *A Companion to WCWs's Paterson* (Berkeley: University of California Press, 1971), p. 22; Mottram, "The Making of *Paterson*," p. 26; Meinke, "WCW: Traditional Rebel," in *Profile of WCW*, comp. Jerome Mazzaro (Columbus, Ohio: Charles E. Merrill, 1971), p. 108; Donald Davie, "Answer to Question 1 on American Rhythm Questionnaire," *Agenda* 11, nos. 2–3 (Spring–Summer 1973): 40.

74. Koehler, "The Art of Poetry VI: WCW," p. 126.

75. Williams, "The American Idiom," *New Directions 17*, ed. J. Laughlin (New York: New Directions, 1967), p. 251. Jonathan Raban in "Chance, Time and Silence" suggests that "perhaps he wanted to retain the word 'foot' in order to remind us that his own verse works as a kind of metrical critique of traditional poetic practice" (p. 91).

76. Koehler, "The Art of Poetry VI: WCW," pp. 130–31.

77. Winifred Nowottny, *The Language Poets Use* (New York: Oxford University Press, 1962), pp. 99, 105–06.

78. Berry, *Poetry and the Physical Voice*, p. 36.

79. Olson, "Projective Verse," in *The New American Poetry*, ed. Allen, p. 392.

80. Koehler, "The Art of Poetry VI," p. 126.

81. Williams, "Free Verse," p. 289.

82. Hopkins, 24 October 1883, *Letters to Robert Bridges*, p. 189.

83. Williams, "The Later Pound," *The Massachusetts Review* 14, no. 1 (Winter 1973): 125, n. 2. Note also Hopkins's statement on time in poetry in a letter dated 26 May 1879 to Bridges: "Since the syllables in sprung rhythm are not counted, time or equality in strength is of more importance than in common counted rhythm, and your times or strengths do not seem to me equal enough" (*Letters to Robert Bridges*, pp. 81–82).

84. Davie, *Poet as Sculptor*, p. 44.

85. Ong, "Hopkins' Sprung Rhythm," p. 113.

86. Williams, "Letters to Denise Levertov," p. 163.

87. Nowottny, *The Language Poets Use*, p. 120. Also see Ramsey, "WCW as Metrist: Theory and Practice," p. 583: "The strain of . . . focused lines against more normal speech movement is, I venture, the chief metrical principle of such verse."

88. Olson, "Projective Verse," in *The New American Poetry*, ed. Allen, p. 393. In an essay on Williams, Leslie Fiedler objects to the use to which the typewriter is put: "In our world where not the brush, intimate with the hand, but a remote machine composes the poem on the page, there is an inevitable air of nostalgia, or even parody about the attempt to unify the seen and heard forms of the poem—and in the end what is involved is a kind of betrayal, a surrender to typography of music and resonance" ("Some Uses and Failures of Feeling," *Partisan Review*, 15, no. 8 [August 1948]: 929).

89. Koehler, "The Art of Poetry VI: WCW," p. 117.

90. Ibid., p. 119.

91. Berry, *Poetry and the Physical Voice*, p. 3.

92. Ibid., p. 3.

93. Abercrombie, *Studies in Phonetics and Linguistics*, p. 19.

94. Ibid., p. 19.

95. Kenner, *The Pound Era*, p. 98.

96. Conrad Aiken, *A Reviewer's ABC* (New York: Meridian Books, 1958), p. 385.

97. Brinnin, "WCW," p. 109.

98. Edward Sapir, *Language* (New York: Harcourt Brace and Co., 1921), p. 242.

99. Olson, "Projective Verse," in *The New American Poetry*, ed. Allen, p. 387.

100. "Robert Creeley in Conversation with Charles Tomlinson," *The Review* 10 (January 1964): 26–27.

101. Jerome Mazzaro, *WCW: The Later Poems* (Ithaca, N.Y.: Cornell University Press, 1973), p. 40. This is a quote from Wylie Sypher in *Rococo to Cubism in Art and Literature*.

102. Koehler, "The Art of Poetry VI: WCW," p. 145.

103. See Alfred North Whitehead, *Science and the Modern World* (New York: Macmillan, 1947), p. 133: "In being aware of the bodily experience, we must thereby be aware of aspects of the whole spatio-temporal world as mirrored within the bodily life. . . . My theory involves the entire abandonment of the notion that simple location is the primary way in which things are involved in space-time."

104. Lincoln Barnett, *The Universe and Dr. Einstein* (New York: Bantam Books, 1972), p. 85.

105. Robert Duncan, "Pages from a Notebook," in *The New American Poetry*, ed. Allen, pp. 400–401.

NOTES TO CHAPTER 5 SECTION B

1. Edward Dorn, *Gunslinger 1* (London: Fulcrum Press, 1970), p. 8.

2. Williams, "New Direction in the Novel," *New Democracy* 5 (1 November 1935): 81–82.

3. David Lyle was a resident of Paterson with whom Williams began corresponding in 1938.

4. Linda Wagner, *The Prose of WCW* (Middletown, Conn.: Wesleyan University Press, 1970), p. 155.

5. Mike Weaver, *WCW* (Cambridge: Cambridge University Press, 1971), p. 127.

6. Claude Lévi-Strauss, *A World on the Wane*, trans. John Russell (London: Hutchinson, 1961), p. 127.

7. See discussion of "Young Love," "Perpetuum Mobile: The City," "January Morning," "A Marriage Ritual," "The Forgotten City," "Franklin Square," "A Place (Any Place) to Transcend All Places," and "Approach to the City" in Chapter 2.

8. Norman Brown, *Love's Body* (New York: Random House, 1966), p. 248.

9. It is possible that Williams derived the idea of the poem as "lyric-drama" from Ezra Pound. See Monroe K. Spears, *Dionysus and the City* (New York: Oxford University Press, 1970), p. 26: "The basic notion of the poem as drama (rather than statement) and as gaining intensity by ellipsis was clearly defined by Pound as early as 1908, in a letter to W. C. Williams: To me the short so-called dramatic lyric . . . is the poetic part of a drama the rest of which (to me the prose part) is left to the reader's imagination or implied or set in a short note. I catch the character I happen to be interested in at the moment he interests me. . . . And the rest of the play would bore me and presumably the audience.' " I am indebted to Geoffrey Hill for pointing out that G. Wilson Knight in *The Wheel of Fire* (New York: Meridian Books, 1957), originally published in 1930, uses and perhaps originated the term *expanded metaphor:* "We should not look for perfect verisimilitude to life, but see each [Shakespeare] play as an expanded metaphor" (p. 15).

10. See John C. Thirlwall, "WCW's *Paterson*," *New Directions in Prose and Poetry 17* (Norfolk, Conn.: New Directions, 1961), pp. 266–67, where Thirlwall attempts to establish the relationship of the early *Paterson* material to the finished poem as well as to Williams's other works. He suggests, for example, that Williams used much of the material originally intended for *Paterson* in his novel *White Mule* and in *Many Loves and Other Plays.*

11. D. H. Lawrence, "Morality and the Novel," *Phoenix*, ed. Edward D. McDonald (New York: The Viking Press, 1936), pp. 527, 530.

12. Quoted in M. E. Solt, "WCW: Idiom and Structure, *The Massachusetts Review* 3, no. 2 (Winter 1962): 308.

13. Mircea Eliade, *Patterns in Comparative Religion*, trans. Rosemary Sheed (Cleveland: World, 1963), p. 399.

14. Ibid., p. 400.

15. William Barrett, *Irrational Man* (New York: Doubleday & Co., 1958), p. 45.

16. William Carlos Williams, "Letter to an Australian Editor," *Briarcliff Quarterly* 3, no. 2 (October 1946), p. 207.

17. Robert Duncan, *Bending the Bow* (New York: New Directions, 1968), p. v.

18. James Joyce, *Ulysses* (New York: The Modern Library, 1942), p. 120.

19. Quoted in Thirlwall, "WCW's *Paterson*," p. 254.

20. Ibid., p. 299.

21. See Louis Martz "*Paterson*: A Plan for Action," *Journal of Modern Literature* 1, no. 4 (May 1971): 512–22, where Martz advocates forgetting "all about Williams'

original plan for composing a poem in four parts, even though he has stated that plan vehemently many times" (p. 512). Also see Gordon Grigsby, "The Genesis of *Paterson*," *College English* 23, no. 4 (January 1962): 281.

22. See James Guimond, *The Art of WCW* (Chicago: University of Illinois Press, 1968), pp. 177–89; Benjamin Sankey, *A Companion to WCWs's Paterson* (Berkeley: University of California Press, 1971), p. 213; and Thirlwall, "WCW's *Paterson*," p. 299.

23. See Randall Jarrell, *Poetry and the Age* (London: Faber & Faber, 1955), pp. 231–32; Joseph Bennett, "The Lyre and the Sledgehammer," *Hudson Review* 5, no. 2 (Summer 1952): 303; John Malcolm Brinnin, "WCW," in *Seven Modern American Poets*, ed. Leonard Unger (Minneapolis: University of Minnesota Press, 1967), pp. 115–16; Edward Honig, "The Paterson *Impasse*," *Poetry* 74 (April 1949): 39.

24. Quoted in Martz, *"Paterson:* A Plan for Action," p. 515.

25. Quoted in Thirlwall, "WCW's *Paterson*," p. 309.

26. Thirlwall, p. 252.

27. Jerome Mazzaro, "Dimensionality in Dr. Williams' 'Paterson'," *Modern Poetry Series* 1, no. 3 (1970): 116.

28. Bennett, "The Lyre and the Sledgehammer," p. 300.

29. Robert Lowell, "*Paterson I*," *Sewanee Review* 4 (Summer 1947): 501.

30. Eric Mottram, "The Making of *Paterson*," *Stand* 7, no. 3 (1964): 34.

31. Quoted in Thirlwall, p. 269.

32. Crane, however, writes in an essay on "General Aims and Theories," in *Prose Keys to Modern Poetry*, ed. Karl Shapiro (New York: Harper & Row, 1962), that "I would like to establish it [the poem] as free from my own personality as from any chance evaluation on the reader's part" (p. 224).

33. Quoted in Thirlwall, "WCW's *Paterson*," p. 254. In Book III Williams does confess to some confusion over this intent: "What more clear than that of all things / nothing is so unclear, between man and / his writing, as to which is the man and / which the thing and of them both which / is the more to be valued" (III, ii, 140).

34. Quoted in Weaver, *WCW*, p. 48, n. 2.

35. Alfred North Whitehead, *Science and the Modern World* (New York: Macmillan, 1947), pp. 124–25.

36. Quoted in Weaver, *WCW*, p. 52.

37. Charles Olson, "Projective Verse," in *The New American Poetry*, ed. Donald Allen (New York: Grove Press, 1960), p. 235.

38. Glauco Cambon, *The Inclusive Flame* (Bloomington: Indiana University Press, 1963), p. 129.

39. Robert Creeley, "Introduction," *Selected Writings of Charles Olson* (New York: New Directions, 1966), p. 7.

40. Denise Levertov, "Statements on Poetics," in *The New American Poetry*, ed. Allen, p. 412.

41. John C. Thirlwall, "WCW as Correspondent," *The Literary Review* 1 (Autumn 1957): 26.

42. Brown, *Love's Body*, p. 247.

43. Joyce, *Ulysses*, p. 38.

44. Donald M. Kartiganer, "Process and Product," *The Massachusetts Review* 12, no. 2 (Spring 1971): 304–305.

45. William Carlos Williams, "An Approach to the Poem," *English Institute Essays, 1947* (New York: Columbia University Press, 1948), p. 54.

46. Walter Sutton, "A Visit with WCW," *Minnesota Review* 1 (Spring 1961): 322.

47. Marshall McLuhan, "Joyce, Mallarmé, and the Press," *The Interior Landscape* (New York: McGraw Hill, 1969), p. 15.

48. Stuart Gilbert, *James Joyce's Ulysses* (Harmondsworth, Middlesex: Penguin Books, 1963), p. 21.

49. Quoted in Guimond, *The Art of WCW*, p. 28.

50. Ibid., p. 182.

51. Kartiganer, "Process and Product," p. 307.

52. Ibid., p. 306.

53. Joyce, *Ulysses*, p. 647. The following section, in a slightly altered form, was published under the name, Margaret Lloyd Bollard, "The 'Newspaper Landscape' of Williams' *Paterson*," *Contemporary Literature* 16, no. 3 (summer 1975): 317–27.

54. Marshall McLuhan, *Understanding Media* (New York: New American Library, 1964), p. 193.

55. Weaver, *WCW*, p. 126.

56. John Dewey, "Americanism and Localism," *The Dial* 68, no. 6 (June 1920): 686, 687.

57. Quoted in Weaver, *WCW*, p. 120.

58. Quoted in ibid., p. 120.

59. William Carlos Williams, "Four Unpublished Letters by WCW," *Massachusetts Review* 3, no. 2 (Winter 1962): 293.

60. Quoted in Thirlwall, "WCW's *Paterson*," p. 308.

61. According to Weaver, *WCW*, p. 120, Williams obtained the copies of *The Prospector*, from which he lifted his newspaper items, in a sale during the summer of 1944 of the Passaic County Historical Society.

62. Ralph Nash, "The Use of Prose in *Paterson*," *Perspective* 6, no. 4 (Autumn 1953), p. 198.

63. See Robert Martin Adams, *Surface and Symbol* (New York: Oxford University Press), pp. 226–33.

64. Ezra Pound, *ABC of Reading* (New York: New Directions, 1960), p. 29.

65. See *Paterson* I, iii, 46–47; I, iii, 48; II, i, 61; III, i, 120; IV, iii, 229; IV, iii, 232–33; IV, iii, 238.

66. Byron Vazakas, *Transfigured Night* (New York: Macmillan, 1946), pp. xi–xii.

67. Mottram, "The Making of *Paterson*," p. 28.

68. McLuhan, *Understanding Media*, pp. 188–89.

69. McLuhan, "Joyce, Mallarmé, and the Press," *The Interior Landscape*, p. 16.

70. Cf. Matthew Corrigan, "Malcolm Lowry, New York Publishing, & the 'New Literarcy'," *Encounter* 35, no. 1 (July 1970): 93, where Corrigan similarly observes that the modern-day newspaper is characterized by parataxis, although his use of the term is pejorative: "One has only to pick up a newspaper in any American city to see the extent of the damage. . . . The syntax is of another order altogether. It is not syntax in the truest sense; nothing 'holds together.' It is mere *parataxis*, telegraphy."

71. Eugéne Vinaver, *The Rise of Romance* (Oxford: Oxford University Press, 1971), p. 6.

72. Sutton, "A Visit with WCW," p. 321.

73. McLuhan, "Joyce, Mallarmé, and the Press," *The Interior Landscape*, p. 11.

74. McLuhan, *Understanding Media*, p. 183.

75. McLuhan, "Joyce, Mallarmé, and the Press," *The Interior Landscape*, p. 17.

76. Marshall McLuhan, *The Mechanical Bride* (New York: Vanguard, 1951), p. 5.

77. Joyce, *Ulysses*, p. 631.

78. *Webster's New Collegiate Dictionary* (Springfield, Mass.: G. & C. Merrian, 1973).

79. McLuhan, "Joyce, Mallarmé, and the Press," *The Interior Landscape*, p. 21.

80. Williams, "New Direction in the Novel," p. 82.

81. McLuhan, *The Mechanical Bride*, p. 4. Cf. Roland Barthes in "The Death of the Author": "A text consists of multiple writings . . . but there is one place where this multiplicity is collected, united, and this place is not the author . . . but the reader: the reader is the very space in which are inscribed, without any being lost, all the citations a writing consists of; the unity of a text is not in its origin, it is in its destination" (quoted in Nelson, *The Incarnate Word*, p. 205).

82. Hélène Cixous, *The Exile of James Joyce*, trans. Sally A. J. Purcell (New York: David Lewis, 1972), p. 636.

83. Quoted in Sister M. Bernetta Quinn, *The Metamorphic Tradition in Modern Poetry* (New Brunswick, N.J.: Rutgers University Press, 1966), p. 104.

84. McLuhan, *The Mechanical Bride*, p. 3. See also Monroe Spears's observation in *Dionysus and the City:* "We recognize the perception of discontinuity, specific or generalized, as descriptive of our age and of ourselves. . . . The exploration of discontinuity is as characteristic of the twentieth century as the elaboration of continuity was of the nineteenth." He goes on to say, however, that Einstein's theory of relativity posits "a new kind of continuity to subsume discontinuities" (p. 21).

85. Ibid., p. 80.

86. Williams is in error here. The Unicorn tapestries are early sixteenth century, not twelfth century. The following section, in a slightly altered form, was published under the name Margaret Lloyd Bollard, "The Interlace Element in *Paterson*," *Twentieth Century Literature* 21, no. 3 (October 1975): 288–304.

87. Louis Martz, "The Unicorn in *Paterson:* WCW," in *WCW: A Collection of Critical Essays*, ed. J. Hillis Miller (Englewood Cliffs, N.J.: Prentice-Hall, 1966), p. 72.

88. John Leyerle, "The Interlace Structure of *Beowulf*," *University of Toronto Quarterly* 37 (1967–68): 4, 5.

89. At one point in "The Unicorn in *Paterson*," Martz does briefly touch upon this idea that "Book V suggests that we might regard *Paterson* as a kind of tapestry woven out of memories and observations, composed by one man's imagination, but written in part by his friends, his patients, and all the milling populace of Paterson, past and present" (p. 75).

90. *Webster's New Collegiate Dictionary*.

91. Vinaver, *The Rise of Romance*, pp. 121–22.

92. Ibid., p. 98. Also see McLuhan, "Joyce, Mallarmé, and the Press," *The Interior Landscape*, pp. 17–18, where McLuhan relates the medieval "grotesque" as defined

by Ruskin to contemporary art and to the work of Joyce. Similarly, Jerome Mazzaro in *WCW*, pp. 48–49, points out that Georges Lemaître in *From Cubism to Surrealism in French Literature* (1947) relates Cubist art to medieval multiple depictions of saints' lives.

93. Vinaver, *The Rise of Romance*, p. 6.

94. See Sutton, "A Visit with WCW," p. 34, where Williams asserts that "I think it [Pound's use of an exaggerated American dialect] was personally directed toward making fun of me, as an American."

95. For further examples of comic juxtapositions, see I, iii, 51; III, iii, 160; IV, ii, 208.

96. For further examples of serious juxtapositions, see I, iii, 45; I, iii, 48; III, i, 122.

97. Vinaver, *The Rise of Romance*, p. 76.

98. Leyerle, "The Interlace Structure of *Beowulf*," p. 7.

99. Vinaver, *The Rise of Romance*, p. 83.

100. The facsimile pages of outlines for Books I and II are in Buffalo, while those for Books III and IV are in Yale. Nevertheless, their obvious consistency of content and presentation, quite apart from the fact that they are all similarly pasted to manila envelopes and that "etc." is written over each outline, clearly indicates that these four pages belong together forming the most comprehensive outline of *Paterson* which can be found among his manuscripts.

101. Weaver, *WCW*, p. 208.

102. Breslin, *WCW*, p. 177.

103. Weaver, *WCW*, p. 206.

104. Ibid., pp. 208–209.

105. Ibid., p. 202.

106. Ibid., p. 203.

107. William Carlos Williams, "A Note on Paterson: Book III," *Paterson* (Book Three) (Norfolk, Conn.: New Directions, 1949), back flap of dust jacket.

108. Williams, "A Note on Paterson: Book III."

109. Leyerle, "The Interlace Structure of *Beowulf*," p. 8. Further examples of this type of interlace would be the "*Geographic* picture" on pp. 22–23 and 32; the "Two half-grown girls" on pp. 29 and 32; John Johnson on pp. 89, 232, and 238; and "Peter the Dwarf" on pp. 18–19, 225–26. Sometimes just the repetition of a phrase is enough to interlace the material together such as the phrase "Beautiful Thing" on pp. 119, 123, 125, 127, 129, 141, 145, 148, 150 and 153; "a great beast" on pp. 61, 70, 84 and 98; "So be it" on pp. 120, 142 and 156.

110. Ibid., p. 13.

111. Rosemond Tuve, *Allegorical Imagery* (Princeton, N.J.: Princeton University Press, 1966), p. 364.

112. Charles Olson, *Causal Mythology* (San Francisco: Four Seas Foundation, 1969), p. 2.

113. Leyerle, "The Interlace Structure of *Beowulf*," p. 14.

114. Olson, "Projective Verse," in *The New American Poetry*, ed. Allen, pp. 387–88.

115. Quoted in Creeley, "Introduction," p. 6.

116. David Jones, *The Anathemata* (London: Faber & Faber, 1955), p. 33.

117. "Robert Creeley in Conversation with Charles Tomlinson," *The Review* 10 (January 1964): 26.

118. Jerome Mazzaro, *WCW: The Later Poems* (Ithaca, N.Y.: Cornell Univeristy Press, 1973), p. 65.

119. Gaston Bachelard, *The Poetics of Space*, trans. Maria Jolas (New York: Orion Press, 1964), p. 222.

120. Cf. Gilbert, *James Joyce's Ulysses*, p. 48: "It has been suggested that the presentation of the mind of each personage in *Ulysses* and its past history by the Joycean method of fragmentary revelation corresponds to the manner in which Nature herself disposes the clues of her discovery. The consequences of universal law lie scattered before our eyes in apparent confusion."

6   *Paterson* as Modern Epic

1

Epic intention is rarely accidental; where it reveals
itself it tends to reflect the poet's deepest impulses
in writing the poem.[1]

A. Walton Litz asserts that "in *Paterson* he [Williams] was
squarely confronted with the problem of integrating a number
of lyric passages into some larger structure, of bridging the gap
between lyric talent and epic intent."[2] Many of the poem's
critics do not consider Williams as having been at all successful
at such an integration. Consequently, *Paterson* criticism has
characteristically appreciated and analyzed the poem's parts
and minimized the value of the poem as a whole. Frank
Thompson in his essay "The Symbolic Structure of *Paterson*"
observes (somewhat inconsistently) that "though there are
numerous fine sections, it [*Paterson*] fails totally."[3] Glauco
Cambon asserts that "the foregoing quotations [from *Paterson*]
. . . should certainly help in assessing the levels to which
Williams' poetry can rise, yet a judgment of his major effort as a
total accomplishment will have to be mixed."[4] Robert Creeley
talks of his "equivocal" reaction to *Paterson*, but then goes on to
say that "sections of that poem are fabulous."[5] John Malcolm
Brinnin, in discussing the poem's "obsession with freedom"

and "stretches of dullness," remarks that "these failures would not seem so great if the successful parts of the poem were not so luminous."[6] John Ciardi comments that "partial failure does not preclude partial or even great success."[7] William Pratt in *The Imagist Poem* describes *Paterson* as an "aggregate Imagist" poem.[8] Jerome Mazzaro writes that "as in much Romantic poetry, the failed long poem becomes a vehicle for a series of small lyrical successes, and often in the work's course, the reader comes across powerful and exquisite sections."[9]

Hart Crane was also considered by a number of critics to be a poet with a specifically lyric talent and his long poem *The Bridge* (1930) encountered objections similar, if not identical, to those subsequently raised in relation to *Paterson*. Notwithstanding the fact that Crane thought of his poem as "an epic of the modern consciousness"[10] and compared its "historic and cultural scope"[11] to the *Aeneid, The Bridge* was persistently criticized as a collection of lyrics[12] and Crane's moral and intellectual stance was thought to be incompatible with the writing of an epic.[13] The fact that remarkably similar critical statements were directed toward both *The Bridge* and *Paterson*, although the works are considerably different, further supports the contention that an appreciable amount of *Paterson* criticism may be a product of the aesthetic controversy which we discussed in Chapter 1, or, at the very least, symptomatic of a modern prejudice against the long poem. This prejudice may be traced back to *The Poetic Principle*, in which Poe asserts that "a long poem does not exist. . . . 'A long poem,' is simply a flat contradiction in terms." Poe maintains that *Paradise Lost* can only be regarded as "poetical" if it is considered "merely as a series of minor poems" and he even suggests that the *Iliad* was intended as a "series of lyrics."[14]

The Bridge was Hart Crane's first attempt at a large structure ("For the Marriage of Faustus and Helen" and "Voyages" are both under 150 lines), whereas, as we saw in Chapter 4, Williams experimented with extended patterns throughout his career. Furthermore, it is clear that a long poem had been in the back of Williams's mind for a considerable number of years before the publication of Book I. He told Edith Heal that "I had known always that I wanted to write a long poem" (IWW, 81). In his *Autobiography* he writes that "the first idea centering upon the poem, *Paterson*, came alive early" (AUTO, 391). In a number of letters he makes reference to the long incubation period of the poem: "That magnum opus I've always wanted to do" (SL, 163 [1936]); "a mass of material I have been collecting for years" (SL, 230 [1944]); "the whole of the four books has been roughly sketched out for several years" (SL, 253 [1947]). During an interview with John Thirlwall he admits that he "always wanted to write a poem celebrating the local material."[15] In 1929 he was already referring to *Paterson* as a long poem.[16]

Primarily because of its length, *Paterson* has often been simply described, without comment, as an "epic" poem.[17] However, a number of critics have felt it necessary to qualify the term "epic" in relation to *Paterson*, to adopt, in Brian Wilkie's words, a special "*ad hoc* definition."[18] Jerome Mazzaro writes that "at best, it is . . . a lyric-epic."[19] Ray B. West observes that "Williams seems to be attempting to merge the personal aspects of the lyric with the mythical qualities of a larger form, something very close to a modern epic."[20] James Breslin labels the poem "a kind of pre-epic, a rough and profuse start from which some later summative genius may extract and polish,"[21] Thirlwall asserts that "*Paterson* . . . hardly exhibits the anonymity of a genuine epic. If, however, a personal epic may be defined as the record of a 'hero' (i.e., a man of superior talents and/or sensibilities) making an odyssey through the world, *Paterson* is a personal epic."[22] Benjamin Sankey writes that "in a limited sense, of course, *Paterson* is an attempt at a 'national' epic—certainly no *Iliad*, or even an *Aeneid*, but an epic in roughly the sense that *Leaves of Grass* is sometimes called an epic."[23] John Ciardi writes that " 'Paterson' is in fact epic in intent, if by 'epic' one is willing to understand 'the sustained handling of a society-enclosing subject matter.' "[24]

On the other hand, some critics react against using the generic term, even in a qualified way. Joel Conarroe, for example, maintains:

> The poem as a whole is not an epic, however plastic the genre may be. Like its hero, it is too protean, unpredictable, and multifaceted to fit any neatly ordered category. Moreover, its style is not ceremonial, is not the lofty vehicle of a great subject, as that of even a modern epic should be. Nor is the work a long narrative poem. [25]

In his "Polemical Introduction" to *Anatomy of Criticism,* Northrop Frye observes that "most critical efforts to handle such generic terms as 'epic' and 'novel' are chiefly interesting as examples of the psychology of rumor." [26] However, in the fourth chapter Frye writes, "The purpose of criticism by genres is not so much to classify as to clarify such traditions and affinities, thereby bringing out a large number of literary relationships that would not be noticed as long as there were no context established for them." [27] R. S. Crane in his introduction to *Critics and Criticism: Ancient and Modern* posits a type of criticism which would first ask what is the power of the whole which the writer has achieved or attempted, and would then proceed to determine to what extent the final product follows from the requirements of that whole. [28] Similarly in *A Preface to Paradise Lost* C. S. Lewis asserts that "the first qualification for judging any piece of workmanship from a corkscrew to a cathedral is to know *what* it is—what it was intended to do and how it is meant to be used." [29] Williams himself wrote to Henry Wells in reference to *Paterson:*

> I think you fail sufficiently to take into consideration my role as a theorist. . . . For I think that only by an understanding of my "theory of the poem" will you be able to reconcile my patent failures with whatever I have done that seems worthwhile. [SL, 286]

In light of these statements, it seems appropriate to conclude our discussion of *Paterson* with an evaluation of the poem as a modern epic, for if Williams's remarks are examined, it becomes clear that he thought of the poem as belonging to an "epic" tradition. In 1939 Williams wrote: "The truth is that news offers the precise incentive to epic poetry, the poetry of events. . . . The epic poem would be our 'newspaper.' . . . The epic if you please is what we're after, but not the lyric-epic sing-song. It must be a concise sharpshooting epic style."[30] During the interview with Thirlwall, Williams uses the term "epic" directly in relation to *Paterson:*

> It's hard to say how the idea was hatched. I had a concept that came to me: it was to speak as a person, as a certain person; and I thought to myself: "Well, if I am going to speak about a person it must be an actual person, but a really heroic figure as all epic poems are."[31]

Williams also continually juxtaposes *Paterson* to the *Iliad* and the *Odyssey.*[32] Brian Wilkie contends that "the poet who aims to write a new epic tends not to generalize about form or to be affected by the generalizations of his contemporaries; he is more likely to be thinking. . . of those particular poets who for him represent his epic ancestry."[33] In the course of explaining his "theory of the poem" to Henry Wells in response to two essays Wells had written on *Paterson*, Williams writes: "The poem . . . is the assertion that we are alive as ourselves—as much of the environment as it can grasp: exactly as Hellas lived in the *Iliad*. If I am faulty in knowledge or skill it is of small matter so long as I follow the ball" (SL, 286). In his interview with Thirlwall, Williams explains:

> I was moved, as always, by the violence of history, which may be an accident, but still it gives features to the otherwise pointless force of events. It brings out characteristics of people, and, well, it brings them out so that you have to pay attention to them. All poems have to be built on physical changes, wherever they may be.

If it's an *Iliad*, it's the violence of a war. If it's an *Odyssey*, it's the voyage, the compendium of all that's been built about voyages and places seen.[34]

More specifically, in a 1951 publisher's release of *Paterson IV* Williams calls Paterson Odysseus: "Odysseus swims in as man must always do, he doesn't drown, he is too able, but, accompanied by his dog, strikes inland again (toward Camden) to begin again."[35]

Furthermore, it was seen in Chapter 4 that Williams's experimentation with extended patterns was accompanied not only by a reevaluation of the place and use of poetry in the modern world, but also by a gradual development of his relationship with and attitude toward his audience, his subject matter, and himself, all of which reached a culmination in *Paterson*. It is noteworthy that these changes in attitude and purpose are widely considered to be essential to the epic form, or, at the very least, indicative of an epic tendency, which further supports a consideration of the poem in terms of epic tradition. Northrop Frye, for example, suggests that poetry of the isolated individual is a lyric tendency while poetry of the social spokesman is an epic tendency: "That is, when the poet communicates as an individual, his forms tend to be discontinuous; when he communicates as a professional man with a social function, he tends to seek more extended patterns."[36] T. S. Eliot in *The Three Voices of Poetry* maintains that "the voice of the poet addressing other people is the dominant voice of epic, though not the only voice."[37] In a similar vein, in *A Portrait of the Artist as a Young Man*, Joyce has Dedalus observe:

> The lyrical form is in fact the simplest verbal vesture of an instant of emotion. . . . The simplest epical form is seen emerging out of lyrical literature when the artist prolongs and broods upon himself as the centre of an epical event and this form progresses till the centre of emotional gravity is equidistant from the artist himself and from others.[38]

In attempting an analysis of *Paterson* as a modern epic, we are faced with the apparent necessity of defining our terms. Yet to arrive at a generally acceptable definition of epic in order to see if *Paterson* measures up is not only an impossible but also a superficial and irrelevant task, for works participate in a mode to varying degrees. Thus, rather than define epic or dogmatically classify *Paterson*, the following discussion will consider to what extent the epic tradition is important to an appreciation and understanding of *Paterson* as a whole. We will then turn our attention to an evaluation of Williams's conscious use of epic traditions and conventions in the poem. The last section of this chapter considers the power which *Paterson* has as a whole: "We *listen* to the poem as it moves from beginning to end, but as soon as the whole of it is in our minds at once we 'see' what it means."[39]

2

We have yet had no genius in America, with tyrannous eye, which knew the value of our incomparable materials, and saw, in the barbarism and materialism of the times, another carnival of the same gods whose picture he so much admires in Homer; then in the Middle Age; then in Calvinism. Banks and tariffs, the newspaper and caucus, Methodism and Unitarianism, are flat and dull to dull people, but rest on the same foundations of wonder as the town of Troy and the temple of Delphi, and are as swiftly passing away.[40]

Critical reaction to *The Bridge* (and later to *Paterson* itself) typifies the dogmatic attitude toward epic poetry which Williams repudiated in the writing of *Paterson:* the insistence that an epic must necessarily "have a point of view," be a "judgment of human action," or a product of "a firm moral and poetic tradition," and have "a readily paraphrasable content" and an "argument to be realized and discussed."[41] Nevertheless, critics who have attempted to determine *Paterson*'s genre have generally examined the poem from a traditional and prescriptive point of view.

Some of these same critics not only prescribe rules and standards for epic poetry, they also assert that an epic poem is no longer possible in our day. After pronouncing *The Bridge* to be a magnificent failure, Allen Tate goes on to maintain that Crane's treatment of the epic "was doubtless the most satisfactory possible in our time."[42] Similarly, Alvarez maintains that

> it was precisely because he [Crane] belonged so much to his age and place that he failed to write the great long American poem. . . . For he inherited the chaos of his time. . . . In this way he is like Scott Fitzgerald: he responded so fully to his time that he could never go beyond its limitations.[43]

Roy Harvey Pearce, after discussing long poems from Joel Barlow's *Columbiad* to *Paterson*, concludes with the statement that "as epics (in the traditional sense) *Song of Myself* and the rest are disasters mitigated only by the fact that their makers had genius and courage enough to risk disaster." He continues with the hope that "perhaps we will even have one day a kind of community in which we can conceive of an authentic hero, whom the poets among us will finally be able to memorialize and reaffirm in a true epic."[44] Brinnin likewise asserts:

> As an epic, *Paterson* shares with a number of other modern poems the fact that its structure, suggested partly by an available cultural situation, is nevertheless mostly the device of an author who, in despair, creates what he has failed to inherit—a body of myth, a roster of dramatis personae, a religious sanction. The official façades of democracy and Christianity cannot disguise the fact that the contemporary world is characterized more by disparity than by unity. Consequently, the poet is denied the advantage of a homogeneous community where the deeds of religious and political heroes reflect common ideals.[45]

Breslin contends that "Williams's attempt to put the totality of his world in a single work pushed him toward the epic, the most sublime of all literary forms; yet, as he well knew, the serene tone, graceful continuity, and monumental beauty of the epic were impossible in his fragmented world."[46] Because these critics adhere to traditional, prescriptive attitudes toward the nature of epic, they conclude that an epic cannot be written today in what they consider to be a society of "historical and spiritual dislocation."[47] Their statements are in effect asserting that the success of an epic depends on the kind of society in which the poet is writing rather than on the poet's creative process. As we shall see, Williams challenges the prescriptive attitudes toward epic as well as the contention that the times preclude the successful completion of one.

This is not to say that Williams was unaware of the difficulties involved in the writing of what he referred to in a letter to Wallace Stevens as "the impossible poem *Paterson*" (SL, 230). In *The Descent of Winter* he writes that "the difficulty of modern styles is made by the fragmentary stupidity of modern life" (IMAG, 259). Williams admits in his *Autobiography* that *Paterson* "called for a poetry such as I did not know" (AUTO, 392). In a letter to Henry Wells in 1950 he describes the poem as "a failing experiment, toward assertion with broken means" (SL, 286), and in the "Preface" to *Paterson* he refers to the "defective means" with which he has to work. However, he firmly believed, as he told José García Villa in 1950,

> a man wonders why he bothers to continue to write. And yet it is precisely then that to write is most imperative for us. That, if I can do it, will be the end of *Paterson*, Book IV. The ocean of savage lusts in which the wounded shark gnashes at his own tail is not our home.
>
> It is the seed that floats to shore, one word, one tiny, even microscopic word, is that which can alone save us. [SL, 292][48]

The difficulties involved in writing a modern epic necessarily become a part of the subject matter of the poem and as Williams wrote to Marianne Moore in 1951 in reference to her adverse reaction to *Paterson IV*, "At times there is no other way to assert the truth than by stating our failure to achieve it" (SL, 304).

Moreover, as we saw in Chapter 5, Williams vigorously rejects the premise that the poem is essentially a replica of the actual world. He clarifies his position on this subject through the use of Shakespeare's aphorism about holding up the mirror to nature, which he felt had done a great deal of harm "in stabilizing the copyist tendency of the arts" (IMAG, 121). Williams does not consider the representation of actuality to be a concern of poetry. He asserts in his *Autobiography* that

> it is NOT to hold the mirror up to nature that the artist performs his work. It is to make, out of the imagination, something not at all a copy of nature, but something quite different, a new thing, unlike any thing else in nature, a thing advanced and apart from it. [AUTO, 241]

It must be kept in mind that in this statement Williams is referring specifically to the form of the poem, not to its content. Denise Levertov makes a similar point when she writes:

> Our period in history was (is) violent and filled with horrors, and I never for a moment considered it was "not poetic," not the concern of poetry, to speak of them. . . . But the poems against which I was reacting were not dealing with these matters either: they simply seemed, in their formlessness, their lack of care for the language, for delving deep, for precision, to be imitating the chaos surrounding them. The best poems of recent years that are *about* that chaos were not. . . . They *have* the "inner harmony" that is a contrast to the confusion round about them.[49]

In 1932 Williams wrote to Kay Boyle that poetry

> is not formed "like" the society of any time; it might be formed in a manner opposite to the character of the times, a formal rigidity of line in a period of social looseness. That is, the outstanding genius of such a time might, in his attic, be writing that sort of poetry. [SL, 131]

Williams was determined that *Paterson* would "not be the symptom of a chronic bellyache" (SL, 130). An example of writing in "a manner opposite to the character of the times" is found in *Paterson* II, ii, 66–67, where the structure counteracts and thereby elevates the subject matter. Williams interpreted this passage to Thirlwall by explaining that "it is a contrast between the vulgarity of the lovers in the park and the fineness, the aristocracy of the metrical arrangement of the verse. I do have measure here, but the very subject hides it from the uninitiated."[50] This is a clear and compact example of the distinction we made in the beginning of Chapter 5 between the material and dominant theme of the poem. The material theme encompasses the factors of a fragmentary and vulgar environment, but the dominant theme of the poem is articulated through a structure which is both diagnostic and therapeutic.[51] Many of *Paterson*'s critics have not been able to surmount the "block" that the subject matter may present to the "uninitiated." Yet, as Williams writes in his essay "Against the Weather": "Both materials and structure have a meaning that is to be discovered, one in relation to the other, not in an esoteric, special sense but in a general sense hidden by the other, a full sense which the partial, selective sense seeks to hide and is put there to hide" (SE, 208).

Although *Paterson* has generally been subjected to traditional generic criticism, Williams's critical thinking in relation to the poem has much in common with modern genre theory. For example, in *Romantic Poets and Epic Tradition* Brian Wilkie asserts that "the great paradox of the epic lies in the fact that the partial repudiation of earlier epic tradition is itself traditional."[52] Similarly, Karl Kroeber in *Romantic Narrative Art* maintains:

> *The Prelude*, then, is epic in its rejection of the traditional principles of epic narrative. . . . It is precisely . . . reversals of conventional epic standards, not Wordsworth's half-century of labour on his poem or references to and echoes of previous epic

poems, that command for *The Prelude* the title of epic. . . . Genuine literary epic, that is, epic written by a poet conscious of earlier examples of the form, must be inspired by the pressing sense that the great literary monuments of the past convey only a partial, a limited, and hence a misleading consciousness of the human predicament.[53]

Thomas Greene introduces *The Descent from Heaven* with the statement:

The perpetuation of a genre involves a continuity of essence but not of accidents, of spirit rather than convention, that the spirit will develop its forms from the language and traditions and affinities of a given milieu, that no imported forms can mechanically impose themselves without a sense of artificiality; that the norms of a genre like the epic have to be violated if its vitality in a sophisticated society is to remain vigorous.[54]

Wellek and Warren likewise assert:

The literary kind is an "institution"—as Church, University, or State is an institution. It exists, not as an animal exists or even as a building, chapel, library, or capitol, but as an institution exists. One can work through, express himself through, existing institutions, create new ones, or get on, so far as possible, without sharing in polities or rituals; one can also join, but then reshape, institutions.[55]

In the section on "Measure" in Chapter 5 it was suggested that Williams uses the word "foot" in order to emphasize the relationship between his new measure and traditional prosody; to stress that measure is retained, although the nature of the "foot" has changed from fixed to variable. Similarly, Williams maintains that *Paterson* belongs to an epic tradition, notwithstanding the fact that the poem substantially differs from traditional literary epics. In both instances Williams consciously chose to retain conventional terminology in order to be able to stress that while his work represents a break with the past it is also part of a continuing tradition. Williams insists upon the existence of a vital association between *Paterson* and the classical epics and simultaneously asserts that the poem is a rebuttal, "a reply to Greek and Latin with the bare hands." Although he writes on his unpublished *Paterson* worksheets that "I shall never be satisfied until I have destroyed the whole of poetry as it has been in the past" (BUFFALO), he also explains that "it is to cleanse the tradition that we attack or should attack, to wipe out its anachronisms, and to command respect and attention. Not only for ourselves but for the tradition, for the renewing of the establishment" (BUF-FALO). In "The Poem as a Field of Action" he writes that "it may be said that I wish to destroy the past. It is precisely a service to tradition, honoring it and serving it that is envisioned and intended by my attack, and not disfigurement—confirming and *enlarging* its application" (SE, 284). In *Paterson* Williams writes that "clearly, it is the new, uninterpreted, that/remoulds the old, pouring down" (II, iii, 101).

Williams's simultaneous repudiation and honoring of the past can best be understood in relation to his interpretation of what it means to be "classic" and his conviction that the greatest respect he can pay to the literature of the past is to write well, here, today: "I speak of an approach to a possible continent, such poems as would signalize a complete break with the past, fit to lay beside the work of the past which they would thus affirm by their newness."[56] In the first place, Williams does not accept that the "classic" describes only that which was created in another time and another place and has no relevance to work which is done in the modern world. He writes in *Yes, Mrs. Williams* that

> it is a trait of the tradition of learning and of the attempt of the race of man to find security in the world to adore the old. The best of it is believed caught and held—so we all talk and even believe, in spite of ourselves in the old as of great value—even superlative beyond our grasp—the classic.[57]

Williams unequivocally asserts that the "classic" can exist now:

> To me the classic lives now just as it did then—or not at all. The "Greek" is just as much in Preakness as it was in Athens. Everything we know is a local virtue—if we know it at all—the only difference between the force of a great work and a lesser one being lack of brain and fire in the second. In other words, art can be made of anything—provided it be seen, smelt, touched, apprehended and understood to be what it is—the flesh of a constantly repeated permanence. [SL, 130]

Williams was no doubt acquainted with "A Backward Glance O'er Travel'd Roads" in which Whitman similarly observes:

> The ranges of heroism and loftiness with which Greek and feudal poets endow'd their god-like or lordly born characters—indeed prouder and better based and with fuller ranges than those—I was to endow the democratic averages of America. I was to show that we, here and to-day, are eligible to the grandest and the best—more eligible now than any times of old were.[58]

Williams was also acquainted with the work of Antonin Artaud (see III, iii, 164) and his point of view bears a striking resemblance to that of Artaud's concerning the "idolatry of fixed masterpieces:"

> Masterpieces of the past are good for the past: they are not good for us. We have the right to say what has been said and even what has not been said in a way that belongs to us. . . . It is our veneration for what has already been created, however beautiful and valid it may be, that petrifies us, deadens our responses, and prevents us from making contact with that underlying power, call it thought-energy, the life force, the determinism of change.[59]

In an essay on James Joyce, Williams defines the classical method as a "paying attention to the immediacy of its [the writing's] own contact" (SE, 28). The classic has nothing to do with the quality of the available subject matter but rather with the writer's treatment of his materials, his stance toward reality: "Their [Homer's and Scheherazade's] compositions have as their excellence an identity with life since they are as actual, as sappy as the leaf of the tree which never moves from one spot" (IMAG, 101). The classic poem is that which is a product of a vital contact with the materials at one's disposal. As Williams directs and reminds himself in *Paterson:* "—of this, make it of *this*, this/this, this, this, this" (III, iii, 168) and "it can begin again, again, here/again . here" (IV, iii, 234). Paterson admonishes himself to "be reconciled, poet, with your world, it is/the only truth!" (II, iii, 103). Williams writes about admiring Laforge (Jules Laforgue?) for taking "what he finds most suitable to his own wants, what at least he has, and made it *the* thing. It is what the man of force will always do" (SE, 37). Similarly, in an essay on Gertrude Stein, he writes that "what actually impinges on the senses must be rendered as it appears, by use of which, only, and under which, untouched, the significance has to be disclosed. It is one of the major problems of the artist" (SE, 119). Robert Duncan in his introduction to *Bending the Bow* pays tribute to Williams for his formulation of this principle:

> Williams is right in his *no ideas but in things;* for It has only the actual universe in which to realize Itself. We ourselves in our actuality, as the poem in its actuality, its thingness, are facts, factors, in which It makes Itself real. Having only these actual words, these actual imaginations that come to us as we work.[60]

Williams insists that the poet must establish contact with the things of the environment in order to capture in the poem what he calls in *Spring and All* "that eternal moment in which we alone live" (IMAG, 89). However, as we have seen, it is not simply a matter of including the available subject matter in the poem. The poet must create a new, unique form which, as a product of a genuine contact with the subject matter, will affirm and communicate the life of the occasion:

> It cannot be *said* what we are and what we do. It can only be

proved by our creation of formal configurations that we *were* and so remain. . . . Until your artists have conceived you in your unique and supreme form you can never conceive yourselves, *and have not, in fact, existed.*[61]

In reference to the *Divina Commedia* and *El Libro de Buen Amor* Williams accordingly observes:

> In the structure the artist speaks as an artist purely. There he cannot lie. The artist as a man of action perpetuates his deed and records himself as a reality in the structure of his work—for which the content is merely useful. . . . Look at the structure if you will truly grasp the significance of a poem. [SE, 204, 207]

In *Against Interpretation* Susan Sontag likewise insists that "in art, 'content' is, as it were, the pretext, the goal, the lure which engages consciousness in essentially *formal* processes of transformation."[62]

On a number of occasions Williams likens the poem to a machine which needs redesigning in each period. He wrote to Kay Boyle in 1932 that "whatever form we create during the next ten years will be, in excellence, like all the classic inventions, a new thing, a thing intrinsic in the times" (SL, 130). Accordingly, Williams told Edith Heal in reference to *Paterson* that "I had to invent my form, if form it was. I was writing in a modern occidental world; I knew the rules of poetry even though I knew nothing of actual Greek; I respected the rules but I decided I must define the traditional in terms of my own world" (IWW, 83–84).

Williams further contends that through the form of his poem the poet is able to reveal a correspondence between all things, here and there, past and present. We use the word "correspondence" in its etymological sense that implies that "the word was formed to express mutual response, the answering of things to each other" (*OED*). Jack Spicer in his letter to Lorca employs the word in this way and sheds light upon our use of it in relation to Williams:

Things do not connect; they correspond. That is what makes it possible for a poet to translate real objects, to bring them across language as easily as he can bring them across time. That tree you saw in Spain is a tree I could never have seen in California, that lemon has a different smell and a different taste, BUT the answer is this—every place and every time has a real object to *co-respond* with your real object—that lemon may become this lemon, or it may even become this piece of seaweed, or this particular color of gray in this ocean. One does not need to imagine that lemon; one needs to discover it.[63]

Williams believed that by creating a structure which is a product of a genuine contact with his world, revealing "the flesh of a constantly repeated permanence," the materials of his poem thereby enter into correspondence with the facts and factors of other times and other places giving "the feeling of completion by revealing the oneness of experience" (IMAG, 107). On a worksheet for *Paterson* Williams writes:

all places remain the same: all are "Paterson"
to me if I make them so
              whether Hongkong or the past: their
details are interchangeable if I have the eyes for it. [YALE]

In Book V of the poem itself he proclaims that "anywhere is everywhere:/You can learn from poems/that an empty head tapped on/sounds hollow/in any language!" (V, iii, 273). In a reply to T.S. Eliot's statement in "Ash Wednesday" that "place is only place," Williams asserts:

When we experience an actuality, when we experience a vivid moment of passion, associated as it must be with some place, i.e. Lesbos—then, our sensibilities kindled, the knowledge that another in a different place, associated with another complete paraphernalia shares with us this experience, then a literature is born.
Not only is a literature born but all places are made insignificant. We live only in one place at a time but far from being bound by it, only through it do we realize freedom. Place then ceases to be a

restriction, we do not have to abandon our familiar and known to achieve distinction but far from constricting ourselves, not searching for some release in some particular place, rather in that place, if we only make ourselves sufficiently aware of it, do we join with others in other places.[64]

Williams's growing awareness of the poem as a "social instrument" (SL, 286) led him to the conviction that America needed a long poem: "*Paterson* . . . is crying to be written; the time demands it" (SL, 214). Williams wrote in 1939 that "now is precisely the time for it [an epic poem]. . . . If ever we are to have any understanding of what is going on about us we shall need some other means for discovering it."[65] Williams also conceived of *Paterson* as the ultimate regenerative activity in which he, as a writer, could engage: "The brunt of the four books of *Paterson* . . . is a search for the redeeming language by which a man's premature death . . . might have been prevented. . . . The poet alone in this world holds the key to their final rescue."[66]

Williams clearly did not agree that the conditions in the modern world hinder a poet interested in writing a "classical," and by extension, an "epic" poem. In addition, he emphatically held that prescriptive rules actually get in the way of writing a poem for "there is never a poetic form of force and timeliness except that which is in the act of being created, there is no poetic form in theory, in the rules, there is no grammar of poetry—there is only poetry—it is the very essence of the thing that this is so" (SL, 133).[67] Similarly, Nikos Kazantzakis in reference to his poem *The Odyssey: A Modern Sequel* writes:

> Nothing, in truth, is more superficial or more barren than the discussion as to whether or not the *Odyssey* is an epic poem and whether the epic is a contemporary art form. Historians of literature come only after the artist has passed; they hold measuring rods, they take measurements and construct useful laws for their science, but these are useless for the creator because he has the right and the strength—this is what creation means—to break

them by creating new ones. When a vital soul feels, without previous aesthetic theories, the necessity to create, then whatever shape his creations take cannot help but be alive. Form and Substance are one. So far as I am concerned, there has been no age more epical than ours. It is in such ages which come between two cultures—when one Myth dissolves and another struggles to be born—that epic poems are created.[68]

To be "classical," to write an epic poem today, the poet must turn his back on the actual materials and forms of the past, but perpetuate the classical method of contact and of invention of new forms to transmit the life of his world. By these processes, the local becomes the universal, all beings, worlds, and things enter into correspondence: "The work the two-thousand-year-old poet did and that we do are one piece. That is the vitality of the classics" (IMAG, 101).

3

One of the obvious values of genre study is precisely the fact that it calls attention to the internal development of literature. . . . Whatever the relations of literature to other realms of value, books are influenced by books; books imitate, parody, transform other books—not merely those which follow them in strict chronological succession.[69]

In our discussion of the Eliot/Williams controversy in Chapter 1 it was observed that Williams opposes those writers who compose in the forms of the past or whose greatest originality is a product of a conscious deviation from the accepted, fixed forms, in favor of a poetry whose form and content arises from the present, from the demands of the occasion. Accordingly, as we have seen, the content, measure, and overall organization of *Paterson* is a product of a direct contact and engagement with the factors, the people, and the general dynamics of his environment as well as the new, relativistic concepts of reality with which Williams became familiar. Nevertheless, although Williams repudiates the forms and materials of the classical epic, he does make use of certain epic traditions and conventions in *Paterson* in order to assert that the old values and conditions have been supplanted by new values and conditions.

M. H. Abrams in *A Glossary of Literary Terms* enumerates the features and conventions which are commonly shared by literary epics and which are ultimately derived from the Homeric epics.[70] This section will briefly examine the appearance of these features and conventions in *Paterson*. It will be seen that Williams uses the familiar aspects of traditional epic as a vehicle for his novel intention, to facilitate a recognition of the new, and, as he wrote on a worksheet for the poem, to carry "the old genius of Hellas into new channels" (BUFFALO).

The epic narrator commonly begins with a statement of the argument which is narrative in form. *Paterson*, on the other hand, having a nonlinear format, begins with a statement of themes in the form of a catalogue in which each phrase encompasses an aspect of the poem. The phrases "a reply to Greek and Latin with the bare hands" and "a plan for action to supplant a plan for action" suggest that Williams is consciously confronting the epic tradition in order to assert not only the relationship of people to the world in this century and the riches of the present age, but also the new kind of object that the poem itself has become. *Paterson* is an invention, a reply, a new "plan for action."

The statement of themes in the traditional epic is followed by the epic question which relates directly to the cause of the ensuing narrative and is answered by the telling of the tale. However, Williams's version of the epic question "Rigor of beauty is the quest. But how will you find beauty when it is locked in the mind past all remonstrance?" is general and abstract in keeping with *Paterson*'s open form and the pressing needs of the modern age. From the outset, through the statement of themes and the epic question, the reader is encouraged to think of the poem in terms of the epic tradition and is also somewhat prepared for the novelty of what is to come. *Paterson* does not provide an explicit answer to this question in its content or in a conclusion of the story, but rather, as Williams states in his *Autobiography,* "it is the poem itself that is the answer" (AUTO, 392). Brinnin aptly observes that Williams "strives for a poem that will, in its own process, answer the question it continually poses."[71] *Paterson* affirms the value of continual process over products and final conclusions: "We get to the end of the story and people expect perhaps a triumphant development at the end, which does not occur in life and does not occur in the poem [*Paterson*]."[72]

The epic traditionally ranges from heaven to the underworld and its setting is ample in scale. *Paterson* is equally inclusive. All of Williams's early plans and drafts for the poem indicate his desire to range from the "archaic persons of the drama" to the "modern town" (CLP, 10–11), from "the elemental character of the place" to what "any one man may achieve in a lifetime" (Author's Note). He told Thirlwall that *Paterson* was "to show the life of the people beginning with giants and ending with the most sophisticated people I know."[73] Williams chose Paterson to be the focal point of his epic precisely because "a city is a typical thing of the modern world, it's a place where men are most operative. . . . The concept of the city, as I conceived it, was man at his most accomplished."[74] As we saw in Chapter 2, Williams intended Paterson to be a microcosm, a world/city. Accordingly, the preface to *Paterson* begins with the creation of the world/city/man out of chaos and Book I describes the primal forms which begin the history of the place. The contrast between the literal setting of *Paterson* and the settings of the traditional epics encourages and in fact demands a recognition of the universality of the local: "I want to see the unknown shine, like a sunrise. I want to see that overpowering mastery that will inundate the whole scene penetrate to that last jungle. It can be detected in the remote province of a Paterson as well as elsewhere" (SL, 313).

Since gods and supernatural beings usually play an active part in the traditional epic, it is significant that Williams's unpublished worksheets for Book I indicate that he had been thinking about the role of the gods in the classical tradition. Book I was originally titled "The Delineaments of the Gods" and began by introducing the man Paterson and having him discourse upon the gods: "It's understandable that the gods should be without morals since for them there is no one upstairs said he" (BUFFALO). However, Williams did change his initial focus from the gods to the giants probably in order to make use of the creation myth discussed in Chapter 3. The suggestion of this myth provides the poem with a vertical dimension and lends universal importance and proportions to the quotidian details of life in Paterson, New Jersey. The giant in *Paterson* "persists incognito" among the population, who are unaware of his existence and of their unity in his flesh. His function is metaphorical, whereas in the traditional epic, the gods literally play a very active part in the course of events. This obvious contrast facilitates a recognition of the new conditions, preoccupations, and problems of the modern population,

> Who because they
> neither know their sources nor the sills of their
> disappointments walk outside their bodies aimlessly
>   for the most part,
> locked and forgot in their desires—unroused. [I, i, 14]

Abrams writes that an epic poem is "centered on a heroic or quasi-divine figure on whose actions depends the fate of a tribe, a nation, or the human race."[75] Northrop Frye similarly observes:

> The function of the epic in its origin, seems to be primarily to teach the nation, or whatever we call the social unit which the poet is addressing, its own traditions. These traditions are chiefly concerned with the national religion and the national history, and both are presented in terms of the activities of "Giant forms," or

beings at once human and divine, who are called "gods" in the religious context and "heroes" in the historical one.[76]

A clue to the significance of the opening of *Paterson I* is found in one of Williams's meditations in *Kora in Hell:* "Giants in the dirt. The gods, the Greek gods, smothered in filth and ignorance. . . . It's all of the gods, there's nothing else worth writing of. They are the same men they always were—but fallen" (KORA, 50–51). By introducing Paterson and his female counterpart as giant forms, Williams is obviously insisting upon their equally heroic stature. In fact, Williams clearly thought of the entire population of Paterson in terms of "Giants in the dirt": "And the giants live again in your silence and/ unacknowledged desire" (I, ii, 36). He told Thirlwall that the main theme of *Paterson* is "the contrast between the mythic beauty of the Falls and Mountain and the industrial hideousness."[77] The process of the poem is an assertion that behind the "filth and ignorance" and the "industrial hideousness" lies a bountiful reality which rivals the "mythic beauty" of the landscape.

Williams intended Paterson to be an heroic character: "Well, if I am going to speak about a person it must be an actual person, but a really heroic figure as all epic poems are. . . . I took the grand image of the man whom I wanted to celebrate as Paterson."[78] He is also a representative, microcosmic figure, "an image which concerns all men,"[79] "a sort of Everyman."[80] An early draft for Book II indicates the intended inclusiveness of Williams's hero:

> He is a poet—who quotes
> from his own works, a woman-by proxy
> a high diver, an engineer, a cripple
> a hydrocephalic, an acromegalia
> interested in theology, a nigger wench
> with fine features, the rain
> and a pigeon: may his bones rest
> in peace. [YALE]

In these lines we can easily recognize references to Cress, Sam Patch, Peter the Dwarf, and the Beautiful Thing. Pronouns shift constantly throughout *Paterson* and more often than not, Williams does not identify the pronoun's referent: "When I speak of Paterson throughout the poem, I speak of both the man and the city" (IWW, 83). Parker Tyler observes that "Dr. Williams' situation is Finnegan's situation. It is that of the epic, or myth, hero who *dreams his action* to the extent that it ceases to be individually his and becomes also that of others."[81]

Williams indicates from the outset that the fate of the area depends upon Paterson. The population of the city is represented as the dreams of the giant: "his dreams walk about the city" (I, i, 14); "the subtleties of his/machinations . . . animate a thousand automatons" (I, i, 14); "The giant in whose apertures we/cohabit" (I, ii, 34). When the poem shifts from the giant to the man the population is then dependent upon the thoughts of the poet Paterson: "Inside the bus one sees/his thoughts sitting and standing" (I, i, 18); "that they may live/his thought is listed in the Telephone/Directory" (I, i, 18). The quest for "Rigor of beauty" is a poet's quest and hence Paterson's quest. Williams refers to the "perverse confusions" which arise if the poet is not successful, if he fails "to untangle the language."[82]

Periodically throughout the poem Paterson is called "Faitoute" ("Do-all"). In Book I Williams introduces "a national hero," Sam Patch (one of Paterson's historical analogues), as a man of action "who dives from cliffs and the edges of waterfalls."[83] However, in Book III Paterson finally rejects the type of heroic action performed by Patch in his decision to "find my meaning and lay it, white,/beside the sliding water: myself/comb out the language—or succumb" (III, iii, 173). As John Ciardi points out, " 'Paterson' is the process of an intellectual Ulysses, of the intellectual-hero rather than of the action-hero, of the reflective man seeking to evoke and to enter the meaning of the landscape of his life."[84]

Williams includes in *Paterson* a number of allusions and

references to Homer's *Odyssey*. For example, in the library scene in Book III Paterson's loaning of blood to the past brings to mind Odysseus's blood offering in Book XI of the *Odyssey*. Williams associates Paterson's visit to the Beautiful Thing whose room is in the cellar of a house with a descent to hell. At the end of Book III there is a reference to the "whirlpool-mouths" of Charybdis as another descent is made, this time by a dog, toward "Acheron." Odysseus's encounter with the Sirens ("Put wax in your/ears against the hungry sea"), with Nausicaa ("there were some/girls, far down the beach, playing ball"), and his reunion with Argos at his arrival back in Ithaca are alluded to within the last four pages of Book IV. These references encourage and invite the reader's recognition of Paterson as a modern Odysseus.

Of greatest significance is the parallel between Odysseus's struggle to reach his homeland and reinstate himself, and Paterson's struggle as a poet to be reconciled with his world and to resist the call of the "blood dark sea/of praise" (IV, iii, 236). Nevertheless, as Williams noted in a letter to Srinivas Rayaprol in 1950, "Naturally today the conditions have to be differently understood" (SL, 290). It is the process of the quest itself, rather than an arrival at a specific goal, that retains the most value in *Paterson: "La Vertue/est toute dans l'effort"* (IV, iii, 221). According to D. H. Lawrence, this is the "American heroic message. . . . She [the soul] is to go down the open road, as the road opens, into the unknown . . . accomplishing nothing save the journey, and the works incident to the journey."[85] However, it is noteworthy in terms of reaching an understanding of the modern epic hero that it is also the *process* which becomes most important in Kazantzakis's sequel to Homer's *Odyssey*, and in his introduction to the poem Kazantzakis presents a similar "heroic message:"

> For me, the *Odyssey* is a new epical-dramatic attempt of the modern man to find deliverance by passing through all the stages of contemporary anxieties and by pursuing the most daring hopes.

What deliverance? He does not know as he starts out, but he creates it constantly with his joys and sorrows, with his successes and failures, with his disappointments, fighting always. . . . Odysseus struggles by looking ahead unceasingly, his neck stretched forward like the leader of birds migrating.[86]

4

We know nothing and can know nothing
but
the dance, to dance to a measure
contrapuntally,
          Satyrically, the tragic foot. [V, iii, 278]

In a letter to Kay Boyle in 1932 Williams conjectures that the new poetic form created in the following ten years "will take its shape from the character of its age, not the 'social' character, if so positively, not satirically. It will not be the symptom of a chronic bellyache or—something else" (SL, 130). Williams similarly rejects the use of satire in an essay written in 1930 on "The Work of Gertrude Stein," in which he applauds Stein's rejection of satire or flight as an answer to the "triviality, crassness and intellectual bankruptcy" of the environment. He observes that "Stein, or any other artist, must for subtlety ascend to a plane of almost abstract design to keep alive. To writing, then, as an art in itself" (SE, 118–19).[87] Williams's letter to Boyle and his essay on Stein indicate that at that time he rejected satire as a technique on the basis of what he considered to be its derisive nature and generally negative stance toward the subject matter of the work of art. However, the fact that in *Paterson* Williams skilfully expresses a satiric point of view through the use of irony in such a way that the overall effect is one of affirmation rather than derision suggests that he reevaluated and broadened his conception of the use of satire. Williams's inclusion of a passage from *Studies of the Greek Poets* at the end of *Paterson I* substantiates his exposure to and active interest in the concept of satire as a relevant adjunct to writing which deals with "distorted" subject matter:

> Here again, by their acceptance of this halting meter [lame or
> limping iambics], the Greeks displayed their acute aesthetic sense
> of propriety, recognizing the harmony which subsists between
> crabbed verses and the distorted subjects with which they dealt—
> the vices and perversions of humanity—as well as their agreement
> with the snarling spirit of the satirist. [I, iii, 53]

Significantly, Williams titled the first typed versions of *Paterson* "Detail and Parody for the Poem PATERSON."[88]

In *Paterson* V Williams once again refers to Greek drama in
the form of the Satyr play:

> .   .   or the Satyrs, a
> pre-tragic play,
>   a satyric play!
>   All plays
> were satyric when they were most devout.
>   Ribald as a Satyr!
>
> Satyrs dance! [V, ii, 258]

Todd Lieber comments that the satyric/satiric pun suggests an
"element of absurdity or mock-heroism."[89] However, this pun,
coupled with Williams's specific reference to the Greek Satyr
play, is of greater and more complex significance.

Book V of *Paterson* is primarily concerned with the fusion of
opposites and of seemingly irreconcilable differences in attitude (old age/youth; past/present; virgin/whore; life/death;
male/female) through the power of the imagination:

> Peter Brueghel the artist saw it
> from the two sides: the
> imagination must be served—
> and he served
>   dispassionately [V, iii, 265]

This accounts for Williams's dedication of Book V to the memory of Henri Toulouse-Lautrec who was "amusing and tragic at the same time."[90] In an interview with Williams, Walter Sutton asked him if he was interested in Toulouse-Lautrec because "he is the artist of the whorehouse, as you call him, or because of the nature of his work." Williams replied,

> Well, I was attracted to Toulouse-Lautrec by his social position, which I sympathized with. A whore is just as much a human being as a saint, and I wanted to emphasize that. He is a man that respected the truth of the design. For God's sake, what the hell difference is it to him that she's a whore? He was indifferent to it, and the poet is also indifferent to it.[91]

There is a passage in V, ii, 258–60 in which Williams presents what he describes as a number of "fractured images like the beginning of cubism."[92] This passage is included as a separate poem, titled "Tribute to the Painters," in *Pictures from Brueghel*. Williams honours Stein, Klee, Durer, Da Vinci, Freud, Picasso, Juan Gris, and Beethoven, because they embody a certain bipolarity in their work or utilize paradoxical techniques. For example, he draws attention to the seriousness of Gertrude Stein's use of vocables (supposedly meaningless words) and to Paul Klee's technique, which superficially resembles the work of a child. Williams's statement that "all plays/were satyric when they were most devout" indicates that his use of the image of the Satyr play, which is a fusion of tragedy and farce, is of the same order:

> Beyond tragedy and farce
> to the fusion of these opposites
> is
> back
> back to the original goat-song out of which both
> tragedy and satyr-play, those "siamixed" twins,
> by separation arose.[93]

In the Dionysiac festival at Athens three tragedies were

followed by a Satyr play, in which the chorus was dressed to represent Satyrs:

> The material for a satyric drama, like that for a tragedy, was taken from an epic or legendary story, and the action . . . had generally an element of tragedy; but the characteristic solemnity and stateliness of tragedies was somewhat diminished, without in any way impairing the splendour of the tragic costume and the dignity of the heroes introduced. The amusing effect of the play did not depend so much on the action itself, as was the case in comedy, but rather on the relation of the chorus to that action. That relation was in keeping with the wanton, saucy, and insolent, and at the same time cowardly, nature of the Satyrs.[94]

What clearly interests Williams in the Satyr play is its integration of the playful and the devout and its affirmation of the possibility of being satiric without devaluing the subject matter. The facts that the Satyr play was always written by a tragic writer and that the same writer never wrote both tragedies and comedies attest to the ultimately serious nature of the work. The pun on the word "satyric" confirms Williams's recognition of the positive, redemptive aspects of satire. This is, perhaps, even more obvious in the first draft for this section of *Paterson:*

> —all poems are Satyric even when they
> are most devout: reverse the deaths!
> Tragedy is a play! there is no sense to art
> otherwise. Unless we play, unless it is a play
> we are not serious . .
> When we play
>   we are most serious
>   most devout;
> Satyric! [YALE]

Williams's pun on the word "play" in these lines is equally significant in relation to our present theme. In *Homo Ludens: A Study of the Play Element in Culture*, Johan Huizinga maintains that "all poetry is born of play"[95] and observes:

The contrast between play and seriousness is always fluid. The inferiority of play is continually being offset by the corresponding superiority of its seriousness. Play turns to seriousness and seriousness to play.[96]

Huizinga rejects any hypothesis concerning the nature of play which suggests that "play must serve something which is *not* play" and focuses his inquiry on "what play is *in itself.*"[97] Williams similarly insists that the poem is an end in itself, and has a meaning independent of its specific content: "It isn't what he *says* that counts as a work of art, it's what he makes, with such intensity of perception that it lives with an intrinsic movement of its own to verify its authenticity" (SE, 257). Susan Sontag points out that "the sense in which a work of art has no content is no different from the sense in which the world has no content. Both are. Both need no justification; nor could they possibly have any."[98] The process, the "play" of the poem itself is the answer to Paterson's quest: "In 'play' life expresses itself in its fullness; therefore play as an end means that life itself has intrinsic value."[99]

The Satyr play also functioned as a counterbalance to the three tragedies which preceded it by providing a recognition of another mode of perception, another point of view. Williams was interested in achieving such a balance within *Paterson*, and on a worksheet for the poem he writes:

In the old days kings often kept hunchbacks and semi-idiots about them, provided they had that requisite quality of the imagination, giving them the privilege to speak their minds . . . at all times, to interrupt, to deal insults even, on occasion, touching the royal person. . . . Poets, fools. There is a clear justice in this association. [BUFFALO]

In *Paterson*, which was to "embody the whole knowable world" (AUTO, 391), Williams incorporates many levels of subject matter from the foolish to the intensely serious, as well as playful and serious techniques, thereby affirming that one mode is a necessary counterpart of the other and can generate its opposite: "An old bottle, mauled by the fire/gets a new glaze, the glass warped/to a new distinction, reclaiming the/ undefined" (III, ii, 142–43). In *The Inverted Bell*, Joseph Riddel observes that "*Paterson*, in its first four books, has been . . . a 'satyric play,' filled with monsters and grotesques, those figures of 'wonder' which have dotted the history of Paterson and allowed its citizens to define their own normality in relation to outrageous difference."[100]

The chorus of satyrs in the Satyr play performed a dance which was very violent and rapid in its movement and quite probably a parody of noble and graceful dances. When it was suggested to Williams in reference to the last five lines of Book V that "perhaps the satyrs represent the element of freedom, of energy within the form," he agreed: "Yes. The satyrs are understood as action, a dance. I always think of the Indians there."[101] The Satyr play and dance represent to Williams the freedom to play with, to parody, and to satirize not only traditional forms but his own subject matter in a positive rather than a negative way:

> Thus a poem is tough by no quality it borrows from a logical recital of events nor from the events themselves but solely from that attenuated power which draws perhaps many broken things into a dance giving them thus a full being. [SE, 14]

Williams uses the image of the Satyr play and dance in Book V in order to clarify the purpose behind the satiric point of view he expresses in *Paterson*, which he conveys primarily through the use of irony. In fact, if *Paterson* is to be described as a modern epic, it has to be regarded as one which primarily functions in an ironic mode. The New Criticism developed an extended use of the term "irony" which particularly emphasizes the positive nature of ironical techniques, in keeping with the dualistic spirit of the Satyr play. I.A. Richards in

Principles of Literary Criticism defines irony as the "equilib-
rium of opposed impulses:"

> Irony in this sense consists in the bringing in of the opposite, the
> complementary impulses; that is why poetry which is exposed to it
> is not of the highest order, and why irony itself is so constantly a
> characteristic of poetry which is.[102]

As we shall see in the remainder of this section, Williams uses
the technique of irony in *Paterson* in order to convey a sense of
the double-edged nature of existence and "to consolidate life,
to insist on its lowness, to knit it up, to correct a certain
fatuousness in the round-table circle" (SE, 88).

Susan Sontag maintains that "the knowledge we gain
through art is an experience of the form or style of knowing
something, rather than a knowledge of something (like a fact or
a moral judgment) in itself."[103] Accordingly, Williams's ironic
style in *Paterson* also demonstrates a mode of playful perception, a way of knowing the world, which leads to renewal and
recovery:

> We know nothing and can know nothing
>   but
> the dance, to dance to a measure
> contrapuntally,
>   Satyrically, the tragic foot. [V, iii, 278]

In his essay "The Epic of a Place," John Ciardi makes the
connection between Williams's use of the Symonds quotation
at the end of Book I and his subsequent allusions to satyrs in
Book V: "Nor can one fail to note that 'the tragic foot' is not only
the cleft foot of the satyr (a figure both of deformity and of sex)
but a reference once more to the 'deformed foot' of Hipponax."[104]

In *The Enchafed Flood*, a work which attempts to define the nature of the Romantic artist, W.H. Auden writes that "the characteristic of the Romantic period is that the artist, the maker himself, becomes the epic hero, the daring thinker, whose deeds he has to record."[105] It was observed in Chapter 1 that *Paterson* is considered by a number of critics to be firmly planted in the "Romantic" tradition. Paterson has been called a "Romantic" hero and the poem has been described as a record of "the growth of the poet's mind."[106] However, as we subsequently saw in Chapter 5, in the creation of Paterson Williams "objectifies" himself and maintains what is essentially an ironic distance between himself and his protagonist. One of the ways in which he establishes this distance is by casting Paterson in the role of epic hero while simultaneously proposing a relationship between the poet and the dog. In this way Williams avoids any idealization of himself, the epic hero, or the role of a poet. T.R. Whitaker in his chapter on *Paterson* refers to "the modern poet's often ironic celebration of himself as hero-everyman"[107] and Todd Lieber further observes that Williams's "mock-heroic self-portrayal allows the poet to stand back and take an objective view of himself, and it keeps him from becoming carried away with his own heroism."[108] Sherman Paul maintains that "innocence is both reality and pose in Williams, becoming the latter when he consciously uses the former."[109]

As a number of critics have observed, Paterson as hero is pulled in opposite directions. The impulse to retreat ("Mr./ Paterson has gone away/to rest and write" [I, i, 18]), is poised against the impulse to reach out into the body of the world ("Outside/outside myself/there is a world/he rumbled, subject to my incursions" [II, i, 57]). James Breslin disagrees with J. Hillis Miller's main contention that subject/object tension disappears in Williams's work and insists that

this tension is the starting point for most of his major work. Williams remained a self-divided man, alternately repelled by and drawn to the "filthy" present. But as an artist he learned how to use these tensions creatively; and to miss them is to miss the dynamic play of voice in his work.[110]

Breslin maintains that "the conflict between self-assertion and ego-loss" gives us the major conflict of the poem [*Paterson*]."[111] James Guimond similarly observes that there is in Paterson a conflict between two kinds of mind: one which is open to the newness of the world and the other which reacts with indifference and fear.[112] As we saw in Chapter 5, Williams uses the techniques of interlace and juxtaposition to undercut Paterson's heroic pretensions thereby incorporating into the poem his own awareness of the double-edged nature of existence and the possibility of more than one kind of experience. Paterson is not an anti-hero or a mock-heroic hero. He is more accurately described as an ironic hero, not only because of Williams's ironic treatment of him as protagonist, but also because of Paterson's gradual recognition and acceptance of his own opposite and contradictory impulses and attitudes:

> Escape from it—but not by running
> away. Not by "composition." Embrace the
> foulness
>
>   —the being taut, balanced between
> eternities [III, i, 126]

James Guimond observes that Williams's technique in *Paterson* "has certain affinities with the ironic methods that Demuth used in his urban landscape paintings."[113] He goes on to maintain that

in *The Cantos* and *The Waste Land* meaning is often derived from the ironic juxtaposition of a partial, brutalized present and a fuller, more sensitive past age. . . . Thus the present is seen as an ironic diminuation [*sic*] of past excellence. In Demuth's paintings and Williams' poems the present image is—aesthetically—an ironic diminuation [*sic*] of its own potentiality. Morally, the ironic contrast is between actual men's works and their powers or responsibilities. Or as Webster's puts it, "irony . . . a result that is the opposite of what might be expected or considered appropriate" (*New World* ed.).[114]

Williams's use of irony in *Paterson* does not undermine or devalue his subject matter as such, but rather, emphasizes the wealth and abundance with which we are surrounded, for his irony is directed toward the fact that, notwithstanding the richness of the present age, there is a surfeit of vulgarity and degradation in our society. Through a variety of techniques Williams indicates that the problem lies not with the modern world and therefore with the materials of the poem, but with the lack of imagination, the lack of language, the fear and indifference which suffers "an orchestral dullness" (II, ii, 78) to overlay the world. *Paterson,* as Williams wrote on a worksheet for the poem, is designed to offset these factors which "make of the age in which we live something less than the near Paradise it might well be, with Plenty staring us in the face on all sides" (BUFFALO; see facsimile 2). In Book IV the poet's task in the world today is associated with Marie Curie's boiling down of the pitchblende

> to get, after months of labor
>
> a stain at the bottom of the retort
> without weight, a failure, a
> nothing. And, then, returning in the
> night, to find it
>
> LUMINOUS! [IV, ii, 209]

In the course of his quest for "Rigor of beauty" Paterson himself ironically discovers that

> beauty is unheeded   tho' for sale and
> bought glibly enough

But it is true, they fear
it more than death, beauty is feared
more than death, more than they fear death [III, i, 129]

Not only is beauty unheeded, but there are people who
actively try to destroy it:

Beautiful thing

—intertwined with the fire. An identity
surmounting the world, its core—from which
we shrink squirting little hoses of
                                        objection—and
I along with the rest, squirting
at the fire. [III, ii, 145]

In *The Anatomy of Criticism* Northrop Frye maintains:

It is in satire and irony that we should look for the continuing
encyclopaedic tradition, and we should expect that the containing
form of the ironic or satiric epic would be the pure cycle, in which
every quest, however successful or heroic, has sooner or later to be
made over again.[115]

Not only does Williams incorporate into *Paterson* an ironic
perspective through a variety of structural and thematic
techniques, the containing form of the poem is ironic, for a goal
is not reached and the quest not completed. Furthermore, as
Paterson develops it becomes apparent that there is, in fact, no
specific goal and that by its very nature the quest is a
continuous process and can never be accomplished: "Odysseus
swims in as man must always do, he doesn't drown, he is too
able, but, accompanied by his dog, strikes inland again (toward
Camden) to begin again."[116] Accordingly, Book V of *Paterson* is
a new beginning which accommodates the changes that have
occurred in Williams and in the world:

Paterson . . . .

```
                    has returned to the old scenes
                                        to witness

            What has happened
                        Since Soupault gave him the novel
                                    the Dadaist novel

            to translate—
                        The Last Nights of Paris.
                                    "What has happened to Paris
            since that time?
                        and to myself"? [V, i, 243]
```

Paterson does not offer a fixed solution. The hero cannot achieve his quest because the need which a "redeeming" language fulfills is constantly changing. The world is in a continual state of flux and no solution can be final. As Robert Creeley explained in an interview with Charles Tomlinson,

> There is no unity of view, let's say, in the more classical sense. It's not something that Williams, I think, even considered interesting. . . . He knew that you change your mind every time you see something, and—what is it he says?—"A new world is only a new mind." So the context is continually what you can feel and where you are.[117]

Paterson ironically discovers that life, the journey, is its own goal: "Virtue is wholly/in the effort to be virtuous   ." (IV, iii, 221) and "The dream/is in pursuit!" (V, ii, 259).

Richard Lattimore points out that "the *Iliad* was composed for a Hellenic audience, of the upper class, among which many claimed to trace their ancestry back to the heroes of the Trojan War."[118] Gilbert Highet similarly maintains that Homer "composed for an aristocratic audience which was deeply interested in the heroic past."[119] The classical epic poet was writing within a continuous cultural and literary tradition which served to make the past relevant to his audience by showing how the present is the culmination of that past. This is

an explicit motivation of Virgil's *Aeneid*, written in deliberate
imitation of the Greek epics:

> And he [Aeneas] suffered
> Much, also, in war, till he should built his town
> And bring his gods to Latium, whence, in time,
> The Latin race, the Alban fathers, rose
> And the great walls of everlasting Rome.[120]

Paterson, on the other hand, is synchronic rather than
diachronic—it relates the audience to the present through an
imaginative apprehension of the strictly American past and the
"things" of the present itself, disregarding European antecedents and background. For, as Williams writes in *In the
American Grain*, "what we are has its origin in what *the nation
in the past has been*; that there is a source in AMERICA for
everything we think or do" (IAG, 109). In his *Autobiography*
Williams describes how, during his visit to the West Coast, he
had been impressed by the fact that the cities "faced the
Orient; that Europe had no more than a legendary hold on
them" (AUTO, 382). Nevertheless, he found that "the young in
the colleges yearn for France, for New York, Boston, for that
'culture,' and look (through the eyes of New England teachers)
to a past, feeling themselves yokels" (AUTO, 383). He asserts
that "there is for them only one metaphor: Europe—the past.
All metaphor for them, inevitably so, is the past: that is the
poem" (AUTO, 385). Eric Mottram observes that, "like Whitman, Williams refused to let an epic structure be the metaphor
of the past as a European past or any kind of non-American past
in the manner of the *Cantos* or the *Four Quartets*."[121] The sea
which Paterson turns his back on at the end of Book IV is,
among other things, representative of the tyranny of the past:

> The sea of savage lusts, nostalgic
> with its cry, Thallassa, Thallassa! [*sic*]
> to draw us in, to draw the past

down on us. Until we drown in our
regrets and losses [YALE]

Paterson swims out of this sea and, as Williams explains to
Edith Heal, "*Paterson IV* ends with the protagonist breaking
through the bushes, identifying himself with the land, with
America" (IWW, 34). In *In the American Grain* Williams
depicts Edgar Allen Poe's embrace of the New World in terms
of a similar image: "His greatness is in that he turned his back
and faced inland, to originality, with the identical gesture of a
Boone" (IAG, 226). It was observed in Chapter 1 that *Paterson*
was written as a deliberate reply to *The Waste Land* and in
Book III there is a specific rejection of Eliot's stance toward the
past: "Who is it spoke of April? Some / insane engineer. There is
no recurrence. / The past is dead" (III, iii, 169). In the lines at
the end of Book IV there may be another ironic echo of Eliot:
Prufrock hesitates over eating a peach and eventually
"drowns," while Paterson picks some beach plums after saving
himself from the sea, i.e., from the compulsion of older forms
and the European past. In a letter to Robert Creeley in 1950
Williams defines "bad art" as "that which does not serve in the
continual service of cleansing the language of all fixations upon
dead, stinking dead, usages of the past."[122] Hugh Kenner
accurately observes that

> he [Williams] has a sense of that unique thing, the American
> community, a community built upon no past or fragments of a past,
> permeated by a dielectric [*sic*] that all but baffles communication,
> united by symbols held unexpectedly in common, parodying itself
> in every printed word; not the remnants of former order the best
> modern poetry has learned to express by using shards of older
> forms, the "unreal city" of *The Waste Land* or the spezzato paradise
> of *The Cantos,* not a great order smashed but a new one so far
> voiceless.[123]

In a letter to Williams found among the unpublished manuscripts for *Paterson V*, Cid Corman observes that "it is not

nature that dances, but we, each one of us, that 'dances' it into 'being.' A poem is a presentation, or an introduction, if you will, into being. Of being" (YALE). *Paterson* is "a reply to Greek and Latin with the bare hands" and "a plan for action to supplant a plan for action" because the poem itself is a "model of consciousness."[124] Rather than supplying us with information about the world, *Paterson* demonstrates a way of knowing the world and offers a perspective upon how our lives can be made valuable—here, today:

> And if when I pompously announce that I am addressed—
> To the imagination—you believe that I thus divorce
> myself from life and so defeat my own end, I reply:
> To refine, to clarify, to intensify that eternal moment
> in which we alone live there is but a single force—
> the imagination. [IMAG, 89]

NOTES TO CHAPTER 6

1. Brian Wilkie, *Romantic Poets and Epic Tradition* (Madison: University of Wisconsin Press, 1965), p. viii.

2. A. Walton Litz, "WCW," in *The Literary Heritage of New Jersey* (New Jersey Historical Series, Vol. 20, Princeton, 1964), p. 105.

3. Frank Thompson, "The Symbolic Structure of *Paterson*," *Western Review* 19 (1955): 292.

4. Glauco Cambon, *The Inclusive Flame*, (Bloomington: Indiana University Press, 1963), p. 213.

5. "Robert Creeley in Conversation with Charles Tomlinson," *The Review* 10 (January 1964): 27.

6. John Malcolm Brinnin, "WCW," in *Seven Modern American Poets*, ed. Leonard Unger (Minneapolis: University of Minnesota Press, 1967), p. 116.

7. John Ciardi, "The Epic of a Place," *Saturday Review of Literature* 41, no. 4 (11 October 1958): 37.

8. William Pratt, *The Imagist Poem* (New York: Dutton, 1963), p. 38.

9. Mazzaro, "Dimensionality in Dr. Williams' 'Paterson,' " *Modern Poetry Series* 1, no. 3 (1970): 98–117.

10. Hart Crane, *The Complete Poems and Selected Letters and Prose* (New York: Liveright Publishing Corp., 1966), p. 252.

11. Ibid., p. 254.

12. See Allen Tate, "Hart Crane," in *Prose Keys to Modern Poetry*, ed. Karl Shapiro

(New York: Harper & Row, 1962), p. 218; Alfred Alvarez, *The Shaping Spirit* (London: Chatto & Windus, 1958), p. 110; Walter Sutton, "Dr. Williams' *Paterson* and the Quest for Form," *Criticism* 2 (Summer 1960): 258; Ivor Winters, *In Defense of Reason* (Denver: University of Denver Press, 1947), p. 591.

13. See Tate, "Hart Crane," p. 216; Alvarez, *The Shaping Spirit*, pp. 110–11; Yvor Winters, *Primitivism and Decadence* (New York: Haskell House, 1969), p. 6.

14. Edgar Allen Poe, "The Poetic Principle" in *Prose Keys to Modern Poetry*, ed. Shapiro, p. 14. Aristotle was perhaps the first critic to assert that length implies some loss of unity and that "the concentrated effect is more pleasurable than one which is spread over a long time and so diluted" ("The Poetics," in *Criticism*, ed. Charles Kaplan [Scranton, Penn., n.d.], pp. 50–51).

15. John C. Thirlwall, "WCW's *Paterson*," *New Directions in Prose and Poetry 17* (Norfolk, Conn.: New Directions, 1961), 307.

16. In "A Novelette" Williams writes that "The poem *Paterson* must be finished" (IMAG, 279).

17. In the *Anatomy of Criticism* (Princeton: Princeton University Press, 1971), p. 246, Northrop Frye writes that "we have the three generic terms drama, epic, and lyric, derived from the Greeks, but we use the latter two chiefly as jargon or trade slang for long and short (or shorter) poems respectively."

18. Wilkie, *Romantic Poets and Epic Tradition*, p. vii.

19. Mazzaro, "Dimensionality in Dr. Williams' 'Paterson,' " p. 116.

20. Ray B. West, "The Modern Writer," *College English* 15, no. 4 (January 1954), p. 213.

21. James Breslin, *WCW* (New York: Oxford University Press, 1970), pp. 172–73.

22. Thirlwall, "WCW's *Paterson*," p. 271.

23. Benjamin Sankey, *A Companion to WCWs's Paterson* (Berkeley: University of California Press, 1971), p. 11.

24. Ciardi, "The Epic of a Place," p. 37.

25. Joel O. Conarroe, *WCW's Paterson* (Philadelphia: University of Pennsylvania Press, 1970), p. 14.

26. Frye, *Anatomy of Criticism*, p. 13.

27. Ibid., pp. 247–48.

28. R. S. Crane, "Introduction," in *Critics and Criticism* (Chicago: University of Chicago Press, 1952), pp. 15–16.

29. C. S. Lewis, *A Preface to Paradise Lost* (London: Oxford University Press, 1943), p. 1.

30. Quoted in Mike Weaver, *WCW* (Cambridge: Cambridge University Press, 1971), p. 120. The "lyric-epic sing-song" is undoubtedly a reference to *Leaves of Grass*.

31. Quoted in Thirlwall, "WCW's *Paterson*," p. 307.

32. In Linda Wagner, *The Prose of WCW* (Middletown, Conn.: Wesleyan University Press, 1970), pp. 151–52, Wagner erroneously maintains that Williams "would probably not have welcomed comparisons between it [*Paterson*] and earlier epics. . . . In fact, he did not intend to write an epic at all, only a poem to encompass his world."

33. Wilkie, *Romantic Poets and Epic Tradition*, pp. 19-21.

34. Quoted in Thirlwall, "WCW's *Paterson*," p. 309.

35. Quoted in ibid., p. 264.

36. Frye, *Anatomy of Criticism,* p. 55.

37. T. S. Eliot, *The Three Voices of Poetry* (New York: Cambridge University Press, 1954), p. 7.

38. James Joyce, *A Portrait of the Artist as a Young Man* (New York: The Viking Press, 1962), p. 214.

39. Frye, *Anatomy of Criticism,* p. 77.

40. Ralph Waldo Emerson, *The Complete Works of Ralph Waldo Emerson* (Boston: Houghton, Mifflin, 1903) 3:37.

41. See Tate, "Hart Crane," in *Prose Keys to Modern Poetry,* ed. Shapiro, p. 219; Alvarez, *The Shaping Spirit,* pp. 110–11.

42. Tate, "Hart Crane," p. 221.

43. Alvarez, *The Shaping Spirit,* p. 109.

44. Roy Harvey Pearce, *The Continuity of American Poetry* (Princeton: Princeton University Press, 1961), p. 133.

45. Brinnin, "WCW," p. 110.

46. Breslin, *WCW,* 170.

47. Brinnin, "WCW," p. 46.

48. The "ocean of savage lusts" is doubtless a reflection of the "sea of savage lusts" in an early draft for *Paterson IV* (see Chap. 6).

49. Denise Levertov, *The Poet in the World* (New York: New Directions, 1973), pp. 4–5.

50. Quoted in Thirlwall, "WCW's *Paterson,*" p. 276.

51. See "WCW: Two Judgments," in *WCW,* ed. J. Hillis Miller (Englewood Cliffs, N.J.: Prentice-Hall, 1966), where Kenneth Burke asserts that Williams "was an imaginative physician and a nosological poet" (p. 51) and refers to Williams's "diagnostic eye" (p. 57).

52. Wilkie, *Romantic Poets and Epic Tradition,* p. 10.

53. Karl Kroeber, *Romantic Narrative Art* (Madison: University of Wisconsin Press, 1960), pp. 102–103.

54. Thomas Greene, *The Descent from Heaven* (New Haven: Yale University Press, 1963), p. 5.

55. René Wellek and Austin Warren, *Theory of Literature* (New York: Harcourt, Brace, 1949), p. 235.

56. William Carlos Williams, "An Approach to the Poem," *English Institute Essays, 1947* (New York: Columbia University Press, 1948), p. 58.

57. William Carlos Williams, *Yes, Mrs. Williams* (New York: McDowell, Obolensky, 1959), p. 136.

58. Walt Whitman, "A Backward Glance O'er Travel'd Roads," in *The Collected Writings of Walt Whitman,* vol 2, *Prose Works 1892,* (New York: New York University Press, 1964), p. 727.

59. Antonin Artaud, *The Theater and its Double,* trans. Mary C. Richards (New York: Grove Press, 1958), pp. 74, 78.

60. Robert Duncan, *Bending the Bow* (New York: New Directions, 1968), p. vii.

61. Williams, "An Approach to the Poem," p. 60.

62. Susan Sontag, *Against Interpretation* (New York: Farrar, Straus & Giroux, 1966), p. 25.

63. Jack Spicer, "Letter to Lorca" in *The New American Poetry*, ed. Donald M. Allen (New York: Grove Press, 1960), p. 414.

64. William Carlos Williams, "The Fatal Blunder," in *Quarterly Review of Literature* 2, no. 2 (1944–45): 125–26.

65. Mike Weaver, *WCW* (Cambridge: Cambridge University Press, 1971), p. 120.

66. William Carlos Williams, "A Note on Paterson: Book III" (Norfolk, Conn.: New Directions, 1949) (back flap of dust jacket).

67. This statement does not contradict Williams's insistence that one needs to understand his "theory of the poem" for there is a difference between the prescriptive theory which Williams inveighs against in this letter and his own formulation of what his poetry attempts. In fact, one of the main contentions of his own "theory" is that there should not be any prescriptive rules.

68. Nikos Kazantzakis, *The Odyssey: A Modern Sequel*, trans. Kimon Friar (New York: Simon and Schuster, 1967), p. xii.

69. Wellek and Warren, *Theory of Literature*, pp. 245–46.

70. M. H. Abrams, *A Glossary of Literary Terms* (New York: Holt, Rinehart and Winston, 1971), pp. 49–51.

71. Brinnin, "WCW," p. 114.

72. Quoted in Thirlwall, "WCW's *Paterson*," p. 281.

73. Quoted in ibid., p. 272.

74. Quoted in ibid., p. 307.

75. Abrams, *A Glossary of Literary Terms*, p. 49.

76. Northrop Frye, *Fearful Symmetry: A Study of William Blake* (Boston: Beacon Press, 1947), p. 316.

77. Quoted in Thirlwall, "WCW's *Paterson*," p. 277.

78. Quoted in ibid., pp. 307–308.

79. Quoted in ibid., p. 308.

80. Robert Lowell, "*Paterson II*," *The Nation* 166 (June 19, 1948): 692.

81. Parker Tyler, "The Poet of *Paterson* Book One," *Briarcliff Quarterly* 3, no. 11 (October 1946): 171.

82. Williams, "A Note on Paterson: Book III."

83. Ibid.

84. Ciardi, "The Epic of a Place," p. 37.

85. D. H. Lawrence, "Whitman," in *Prose Keys to Modern Poetry*, ed. Shapiro, p. 247.

86. Kazantzakis, *The Odyssey*, p. xii.

87. Williams expresses a similar idea in *Paterson V*, where he proposes that "the cure began, perhaps / with the abstraction / of Arabic art" (V, ii, 259). Because of the religious strictures against representational art, the Arab artists compensate with abstract, geometrical design and by using Arabic script itself as an art form.

88. Thirlwall, "WCW's *Paterson*," p. 264.

89. Todd M. Leiber, *Endless Experiments* (Columbus: Ohio State University Press, 1973), p. 241.

90. Thirlwall, "WCW's *Paterson*," p. 288.

91. Walter Sutton, "A Visit with WCW," *Minnesota Review* 1 (Spring 1961): 322.

92. Thirlwall, "WCW's *Paterson*," p. 293.

93. Norman O. Brown, *Closing Time* (New York: Random House, 1973), p. 59.

94. *Harper's Dicitionary of Classical Literature and Antiquities,* ed. Harry Thurston Peck (New York: American Book Co., 1896), p. 1419.

95. Johan Huizinga, *Homo Ludens* (Boston: Beacon Press, 1970), p. 129.

96. Ibid., p. 8.

97. Ibid., p. 2.

98. Sontag, *Against Interpretation*, p. 27.

99. Quoted by Norman O. Brown in *Life Against Death* (New York: Vintage Books, 1959), p. 33.

100. Joseph N. Riddel, *The Inverted Bell* (Baton Rouge: Lousiana State University Press, 1974), p. 276.

101. Stanley Koehler, "The Art of Poetry VI: WCW," *Paris Review* 8, no. 32 (Summer–Fall 1964): 130.

102. I. A. Richards, *Principles of Literary Criticism* (New York: Harcourt, Brace, 1926), p. 250.

103. Sontag, *Against Interpretation*, p. 22.

104. Ciardi, "The Epic of a Place," p. 39.

105. W. H. Auden, "The Artist as Don Quixote," from *The Enchafed Flood,* in *Prose Keys to Modern Poetry,* ed. Shapiro, p. 200.

106. Conarroe, "The 'Preface' to *Paterson,*" p. 42.

107. Thomas R. Whitaker, *WCW* (New York: Twayne Publishers, 1968), p. 129.

108. Lieber, *Endless Experiments*, p. 228.

109. Sherman Paul, *The Music of Survival* (Chicago: University of Chicago Press, 1968), p. 45.

110. Breslin, *WCW*, p. 23.

111. Ibid., p. 181.

112. James Guimond, *The Art of WCW* (Chicago: University of Illinois Press, 1968), p. 187.

113. Ibid., p. 50.

114. Ibid., p. 53.

115. Frye, *Anatomy of Criticism*, p. 322.

116. Thirlwall, "WCW's *Paterson,*" p. 264.

117. "Robert Creeley in Conversation with Charles Tomlinson," *The Review* 10 (January 1964): 27.

118. *The Iliad of Homer*, trans. Richard Lattimore (Chicago: University of Chicago Press, 1951), p. 31.

119. Gilbert Highet in Introduction to *The Odyssey to Homer*, trans. S. H. Butcher and A. Lang (New York: The Modern Library, 1950), p. xi.

120. *The Aeneid of Virgil*, trans. Rolfe Humphries (New York: Charles Scribner's Sons, 1951), p. 3.

121. Eric Mottram, "The Making of *Paterson,*" *Stand* 7, no. 3 (1964): 27.

122. "WCW to Robert Creeley," in *The Poetics of the New American Poetry,* ed. Donald M. Allen and Warren Tallman (New York: Grove Press, 1973), p. 140.

123. Kenner, "With the Bare Hands," in *WCW*, ed. Tomlinson, p. 188.

124. Sontag, *Against Interpretation*, p. 27.

Bibliography

Works by William Carlos Williams Cited

"The American Idiom." In *New Directions* 17, edited by J. Laughlin. New York: New Directions, 1967.

"An Approach to the Poem." In *English Institute Essays, 1947*. New York: Columbia University Press, 1948.

The Autobiography of William Carlos Williams. New York: New Directions, 1967.

The Collected Earlier Poems. London: MacGibbon & Kee, 1967.

The Collected Later Poems. London: MacGibbon & Kee, 1965.

"An Essay on *Leaves of Grass*." In *Leaves of Grass One Hundred Years After*, edited by Milton Hindus. Stanford: Stanford University Press, 1955, pp. 22–31.

"The Fatal Blunder." *Quarterly Review of Literature* 2, no. 2 (1944–45): 125–26.

"Four Unpublished Letters by William Carlos Williams." *Massachusetts Review* 3, no. 2 (Winter 1962): 292–96.

"Free Verse." *Princeton Encyclopedia of Poetry and Poetics*, Edited by Alex Preminger. Princeton, N.J.: Princeton University Press, 1974, pp. 288–90.

Imaginations: Five Experimental Prose Pieces. Edited by Webster Schott. London: MacGibbon & Kee, 1970.

In the American Grain. London: MacGibbon & Kee, 1966.

"In Praise of Marriage." *Quarterly Review of Literature* 2, no. 2 (1944): 145–49.

I Wanted to Write a Poem. Edited by Edith Heal. London: Cape Editions, 1967.

Kora in Hell: Improvisations. San Francisco: City Lights, 1969.

"The Later Pound." *The Massachusetts Review* 14, no. 1 (Winter 1973): 124–29.

"Letter to an Australian Editor." *Briarcliff Quarterly* 3, no. 2 (October 1946): 205–208.

"Letters to Denise Levertov." *Stony Brook,* no. 1/2 (Fall 1968): 162–68.

Many Loves and Other Plays. Norfolk, Conn.: New Directions, 1961.

"New Direction in the Novel." *New Democracy* 5 (November 1, 1935): 81–83.

"A Note on Paterson: Book III." *Paterson* (Book Three). Norfolk, Conn.: New Directions, 1949 (on back flap of dust jacket).

Paterson. New York: New Directions, 1963.

Pictures from Breughel and Other Poems. London: MacGibbon & Kee, 1968.

"Poetry and the Making of Language." *The New Republic* 133, no. 18 (October 31, 1955): 16–17.

Selected Essays of William Carlos Williams. New York: New Directions, 1969.

The Selected Letters of William Carlos Williams. Edited by John C. Thirlwall. New York: McDowell, Obolensky, 1957.

"A Study of Ezra Pound's Present Position." *The Massachusetts Review* 14, no. 1 (Winter 1973): pp. 118–23.

A Voyage to Pagany. New York: Macaulay, 1928.

"*White Mule* Versus Poetry." *The Writer* 50, no. 8 (August 1937): 243–45.

Yes, Mrs. Williams: A Personal Record of My Mother. New York: McDowell, Obolensky, 1959.

Other Works Cited

Abercrombie, David. *Studies in Phonetics and Linguistics.* London: Oxford University Press, 1971.

Abrams, M.H. *A Glossary of Literary Terms*. New York: Holt, Rinehart and Winston, 1971.

Adams, Robert Martin. *Surface and Symbol: The Consistency of James Joyce's Ulysses*. New York: Oxford University Press, 1967.

Aiken, Conrad. *A Reviewer's ABC*. New York: Meridian Books, 1958.

Allen, Donald M., ed. *The New American Poetry*. New York: Grove Press, 1960.

Allen, Donald, and Creeley, Robert, eds. *The New Writing in the USA*. Harmondsworth, Middlesex: Penguin Books, 1967.

Allen, Donald, and Tallman, Warren, eds. *Poetics of the New American Poetry*. New York: Grove Press, 1973.

Alvarez, Alfred. *The Shaping Spirit: Studies in Modern English and American Poets*. London: Chatto & Windus, 1958.

Aristotle. "The Poetics." In *Criticism: Twenty Major Statements*. Edited by Charles Kaplan. Scranton, Penn.: Chandler, n.d., pp. 20–51.

Artaud, Antonin. *The Theater and Its Double*. Translated by Mary Caroline Richards. New York: Grove Press, 1958.

Auerbach, Erich. *Mimesis: The Representation of Reality in Western Literature*. Princeton, N.J.: Princeton University Press, 1973.

Bachelard, Gaston. *The Poetics of Space*. Translated by Maria Jolas. New York: Orion Press, 1964.

Barnett, Lincoln. *The Universe and Dr. Einstein*. New York: Bantam Books, 1972.

Barrett, William. *Irrational Man: A Study in Existential Philosophy*. New York: Doubleday, 1958.

Bennett, Joseph. "The Lyre and the Sledgehammer." *Hudson Review* 5, no. 2 (Summer 1952): 295–307.

Berry, Francis. *Poetry and the Physical Voice*. London: Routledge and Kegan Paul, 1962.

Beum, Robert. "The Neglect of Williams." *Poetry* 80 (August 1952): 291–93.

Breslin, James E. *William Carlos Williams: An American Artist*. New York: Oxford University Press, 1970.

————. "William Carlos Williams and the Whitman Tradition." *Literary Criticism and Historical Understanding: Selected Papers from the English Institute.* Edited by Phillip Damon. New York: Columbia University Press, 1967.

Brinnin, John Malcolm. "William Carlos Williams." *Seven Modern American Poets.* Edited by Leonard Unger. Minneapolis: University of Minnesota Press, 1967.

Brown, Norman O. *Closing Time.* New York: Random House, 1973.

————. *Life Against Death: The Psychoanalytical Meaning of History.* New York: Vintage Books, 1959.

————. *Love's Body.* New York: Random House, 1966.

Burke, Kenneth. "The Methods of William Carlos Williams." *The Dial* 82 (February 1927): 94–98.

Cage, John. *Silence.* Cambridge, Mass.: M.I.T. Press, 1969.

Cambon, Glauco. *The Inclusive Flame: Studies in American Poetry.* Bloomington: Indiana University Press, 1963.

Campbell, Joseph, and Robinson, Henry Morton. *A Skeleton Key to Finnegans Wake.* London: Faber & Faber, 1947.

Ciardi, John. "The Epic of a Place." *Saturday Review of Literature* 41, no. 4 (October 11, 1958): 37–39.

Cixous, Hélène. *The Exile of James Joyce.* Translated by Sally A.J. Purcell. New York: David Lewis, 1972.

Coleridge, Samuel Taylor. *Selected Poetry and Prose.* Edited by Elisabeth Schneider. New York: Holt, Rinehart and Winston, 1964.

————. *Specimens of the Table Talk.* London: John Murray, Albermarle St., 1858.

Conarroe, Joel O. "The 'Preface' to *Paterson.*" *Contemporary Literature* 10, no. 1 (Winter 1969): 39–53.

————. *William Carlos Williams' Paterson: Language and Landscape.* Philadelphia: University of Pennsylvania Press, 1970.

Corrigan, Matthew. "Malcolm Lowry, New York Publishing, & the 'New Literacy.'" *Encounter* 35, no. 1 (July 1970): 82–93.

Crane, Hart. *The Complete Poems and Selected Letters and Prose.* New York: Liverwright, 1966.

Crane, R.S. "Introduction." *Critics and Criticism: Ancient and Modern.* Chicago: University of Chicago Press, 1952.

Creeley, Robert. "Introduction." *Selected Writings of Charles Olson.* New York: New Directions, 1966.

Davie, Donald. "Answer to Question 1 on American Rhythm Questionnaire." *Agenda* 11, nos. 2–3 (Spring–Summer 1973): 40.

———. *Ezra Pound: Poet as Sculptor.* New York: Oxford University Press, 1964.

———. "The Legacy of Fenimore Cooper." *Essays in Criticism* 9, no. 3 (1959): 222–38.

Deutsch, Babette. *Poetry in Our Time.* New York: Doubleday, 1963.

Dewey, John. "Americanism and Localism." *The Dial* 68, no. 6 (June 1920): 684–88.

Dijkstra, Bram. *The Hieroglyphics of a New Speech: Cubism, Stieglitz, and the Early Poetry of William Carlos Williams.* Princeton, N.J.: Princeton University Press, 1969.

Dorn, Edward. *Gunslinger 1 & 2.* London: Fulcrum Press, 1970.

Duncan, Robert. *Bending the Bow.* New York: New Directions, 1968.

Dupeyron-Marchessou, Hélène. *William Carlos Williams et le Renouveau du Lyrisme.* Paris: Presses Universitaires de France, 1967.

Eberhart, Richard. "General Points." *Agenda* 11, nos. 2–3 (Spring–Summer 1973): 41–44.

Eliade, Mircea. *Myths, Dreams and Mysteries: The Encounter Between Contemporary Faiths and Archaic Reality.* Translated by Philip Mairet. London: Collins, 1968.

———. *Patterns in Comparative Religion.* Translated by Rosemary Sheed. Cleveland: World, 1963.

Eliot, Thomas Stearns. "Notes Towards a Definition of Culture." *Partisan Review* 11 (Spring 1944): 145–57.

———. *The Three Voices of Poetry.* New York: Cambridge University Press, 1954.

———. *The Use of Poetry and the Use of Criticism.* London: Faber & Faber, 1933.

Ellman, Richard. "From Renishaw to Paterson." *The Yale Review* 39, no. 3 (March 1950): 543–45.

Emerson, Ralph Waldo. *The Complete Works of Ralph Waldo Emerson,* vol. 3. Boston: Houghton, Mifflin, 1903.

Fiedler, Leslie A. "Some Uses and Failures of Feeling." *Partisan Review* 15, no. 8 (August 1948): pp. 924–31.

———. *Waiting for the End*. New York: Stein and Day, 1964.

Frye, Northrop. *Anatomy of Criticism*. Princeton, N.J.: Princeton University Press, 1971.

———. *The Educated Imagination*. Bloomington: Indiana University Press, 1964.

———. *Fables of Identity: Studies in Poetic Mythology*. New York: Harcourt, Brace & World, 1963.

———. *Fearful Symmetry: A Study of William Blake*. Boston: Beacon Press, 1947.

———. *The Modern Century*. Toronto: Oxford University Press, 1967.

———. *The Well-Tempered Critic*. Bloomington: Indiana University Press, 1963.

Gilbert, Stuart. *James Joyce's Ulysses*. Harmondsworth, Middlesex: Penguin Books, 1963.

Greene, Thomas. *The Descent from Heaven: A Study in Epic Continuity*. New Haven, Conn.: Yale University Press, 1963.

Grigsby, Gordon K. "The Genesis of *Paterson*." *College English* 23, no. 4 (January 1962): 277–81.

Guimond, James. *The Art of William Carlos Williams: A Discovery and Possession of America*. Chicago: University of Illinois Press, 1968.

Gunn, Thom. "Poetry as Written." *Yale Review* 48, no. 2 (December 1958): 297–305.

Hall, Donald. "Supplement: On Rhythm from America." *Agenda* 11, nos. 2–3 (Spring–Summer 1973): 45–48.

Harper's Dictionary of Classical Literature and Antiquities. Edited by Harry Thurston Peck. New York: American Book Co., 1896.

Hill, Geoffrey. "Redeeming the Time." *Agenda: Special Issue on Rhythm* 10, nos. 4–11, no. 1 (Autumn–Winter 1972/3): 87–111.

Hobbes, Thomas. *Leviathan: Or the Matter, Forme & Power of a Commonwealth, Ecclesiasticall and Civill*. Cambridge: Cambridge University Press, 1904.

Homer. *The Iliad of Homer*. Translated by Richard Lattimore. Chicago: University of Chicago Press, 1951.

———. *The Odyssey of Homer*. Translated by S.H. Butcher and A. Lang. New York: Modern Library, 1950.

Honig, Edward. "The *Paterson* Impasse." *Poetry* 74 (April 1949): 37–41.

Hopkins, G.M. *The Correspondence of Gerard Manley Hopkins and Richard Watson Dixon*. Edited by Claude Colleer Abbott. London: Oxford University Press, 1935.

———. *The Letters of Gerard Manley Hopkins to Robert Bridges*. Edited by Claude Colleer Abbott. London: Oxford University Press, 1935.

———. *The Poems of Gerard Manley Hopkins*. Edited by W. H. Gardner and N. H. MacKenzie. London: Oxford University Press, 1967.

Huizinga, Johan. *Homo Ludens: A Study of the Play-Element in Culture*. Boston: Beacon Press, 1970.

Jarrell, Randall. *Poetry and the Age*. London: Faber & Faber, 1955.

Johnson, Samuel. *History of Rasselas: Prince of Abyssinia*. Oxford: Clarendon Press, 1927.

Jones, David. *The Anathemata*. London: Faber & Faber, 1955.

Joyce, James. *A Portrait of the Artist as a Young Man*. New York: Viking Press, 1962.

———. *Ulysses*. New York: Modern Library, 1942.

Juhasz, Suzanne. *Metaphor and the Poetry of Williams, Pound, and Stevens*. Lewisburg: Bucknell University Press, 1974.

Kartiganer, Donald M. "Process and Product: A Study of Modern Literary Form." *The Massachusetts Review*, 12, no. 2 (Spring 1971): 297–328.

Kazantzakis, Nikos. *The Odyssey: A Modern Sequel*. Translated by Kimon Friar. New York: Simon and Schuster, 1967.

Keats, John. *The Letters of John Keats: 1814–1821*, Vols. 1 and 2. Edited by Hyder Edward Rollins. Cambridge: Harvard University Press, 1958.

Kenner, Hugh. *The Pound Era*. Berkeley: University of California Press, 1971.

Knight, G. Wilson. *The Wheel of Fire: Interpretations of Shakespearean Tragedy*. New York: Meridian Books, 1957.

Koch, Vivienne. *William Carlos Williams*. Norfolk, Conn.: New Directions, 1950.

————. "William Carlos Williams: The Man and the Poet." *The Kenyon Review* 14, no. 3 (Summer 1952): 502–10.

Koehler, Stanley. "The Art of Poetry VI: William Carlos Williams." *Paris Review* 8, no. 32 (Summer–Fall 1964): 110–51.

Kroeber, Karl. *Romantic Narrative Art*. Madison: University of Wisconsin Press, 1960.

Langbaum, Robert W. *The Poetry of Experience*. New York: W. W. Norton, 1963.

Lawrence, David Herbert. *The Complete Poems of D. H. Lawrence*. London: Heinemann, 1964.

————. *Phoenix*. Edited by Edward D. McDonald. New York: Viking Press, 1936.

Levertov, Denise. *The Poet in the World*. New York: New Directions, 1973.

Lévi-Strauss, Claude. *A World on the Wane*. Translated by John Russell. London: Hutchinson, 1961.

Lewis, C. S. *A Preface to Paradise Lost*. London: Oxford University Press, 1943.

Leyerle, John. "The Interlace Structure of Beowulf." *University of Toronto Quarterly* 37 (1967–68): 1–17.

Lieber, Todd. M. *Endless Experiments: Essays on the Heroic Experience in American Romanticism*. Columbus: Ohio State University Press, 1973.

Litz, A. Walton. "William Carlos Williams." In *The Literary Heritage of New Jersey*. New Jersey Historical Series, vol. 20. Princeton, 1964, pp. 83–130.

Lombardi, Thomas W. "William Carlos Williams: The Leech-Gatherer of *Paterson*." *Midwest Quarterly* 9 (July 1968): 333–49.

Lowell, Robert. "*Paterson* I." *Sewanee Review* 4 (Summer 1947): 500–503.

————. "*Paterson* II." *The Nation* 166 (June 19, 1948): 692–94.

McLuhan, Marshall. *From Cliché to Archetype*. New York: Pocket Books, 1971.

————. *The Interior Landscape: The Literary Criticism of Marshall McLuhan*. New York: McGraw Hill, 1969.

————. *The Mechanical Bride*. New York: Vanguard, 1951.

————. *Understanding Media: The Extensions of Man*. New York: New American Library, 1964.

Martz, Louis L. "*Paterson:* A Plan for Action." *Journal of Modern Literature* 1, no. 4 (May 1971): 512–22.

———. *The Poem of the Mind.* New York: Oxford University Press, 1966.

Marx, Leo. *The Machine in the Garden: Technology and the Pastoral Ideal in America.* New York: Oxford University Press, 1964.

Mazzaro, Jerome. "Dimensionality in Dr. Williams' 'Paterson.' " *Modern Poetry Series* 1, no. 3 (1970): 98–117.

———, comp. *Profile of William Carlos Williams.* Columbus, Ohio: Charles E. Merrill, 1971.

———. *William Carlos Williams: The Later Poems.* Ithaca: Cornell University Press, 1973.

Miller, J. Hillis. *Poets of Reality.* Cambridge, Mass.: Harvard University Press, 1965.

———, ed. *William Carlos Williams: A Collection of Critical Essays.* Englewood Cliffs, N.J.: Prentice-Hall, 1966.

Mottram, Eric. "The Making of *Paterson.*" *Stand* 7, no. 3 (1964): 17–34.

Mumford, Lewis. *The City in History: Its Origins, Its Transformations, and Its Prospects.* New York: Harcourt, Brace & World, 1961.

Nash, Ralph. "The Use of Prose in *Paterson.*" *Perspective* 6, no. 4 (Autumn 1953): 191–99.

Nelson, Cary. *The Incarnate Word: Literature as Verbal Space.* Urbana: University of Illinois Press, 1973.

Neussendorfer, Sister Macaria. "William Carlos Williams' Idea of a City." *Thought* 40 (Summer 1965): 242–74.

Nowottny, Winifred. *The Language Poets Use.* New York: Oxford University Press, 1962.

Olson, Charles. *Causal Mythology.* San Francisco: Four Seas Foundation, 1969.

———. *The Maximus Poems.* New York: Jargon/Corinth Books, 1960.

———. *Mayan Letters.* Edited by Robert Creeley. London: Cape Editions, 1968.

———. "*Paterson (Book Five).*" *Evergreen Review* 2, no. 9 (Summer 1959): 220–21.

"One Man's River." Anon. rev., *Times Literary Supplement*, no. 3, 263 (September 10, 1964): 842.

Ong, Walter J., S. J. "Hopkins' Sprung Rhythm and the Life of English Poetry." In *Immortal Diamond: Studies in Gerard Manley Hopkins*. Edited by Norman Weyland, S.J. New York: Sheed & Ward, 1949, pp. 93–174.

Ostrom, Alan. *The Poetic World of William Carlos Williams*. Carbondale: Southern Illinois University Press, 1966.

Paul, Sherman. *The Music of Survival*. Chicago: University of Illinois Press, 1968.

Pavese, Cesare. *Selected Poems*. Translated by Margaret Crosland. Harmondsworth, Middlesex: Penguin Books, 1971.

———. *This Business of Living: Diary 1935–1950*. Edited & translated by A.E. Murch. London: Peter Owen, 1961.

Pearce, Roy Harvey. *The Continuity of American Poetry*. Princeton, N.J.: Princeton University Press, 1961.

Pearson, Norman Holmes. "Williams, New Jersey." *The Literary Review* 1 (Autumn 1957): 29–36.

Peterson, Walter Scott. *An Approach to Paterson*. New Haven, Conn.: Yale University Press, 1967.

Poe, Edgar Allan, *Complete Works of Edgar Allan Poe*, vol. 1. New York: Fred De Fau & Co., 1902.

Pound, Ezra. *ABC of Reading*. New York: New Directions, 1960.

Pratt, William. *The Imagist Poem: Modern Poetry in Miniature*. New York: Dutton, 1963.

Quinn, Sister M. Bernetta. *The Metamorphic Tradition in Modern Poetry*. New Brunswick, N.J.: Rutgers University Press, 1966.

———. "*Paterson*: Landscape and Dream." *Journal of Modern Literature* 1, no. 4 (May 1971): 523–48.

Raban, Jonathan. "Chance, Time and Silence: The New American Verse." *Journal of American Studies* 3, no. 1 (July 1969): 89–101.

Ramsey, Paul. "William Carlos Williams as Metrist: Theory and Practice." *Journal of Modern Literature* 1, no. 4 (May 1971): 578–92.

Richards, I.A. *Principles of Literary Criticism*. New York: Harcourt, Brace, 1926.

Riddel, Joseph N. *The Inverted Bell: Modernism and the Counter-*

poetics of William Carlos Williams. Baton Rouge: Louisiana State University Press, 1974.

"Robert Creeley in Conversation with Charles Tomlinson." *The Review* 10 (January 1964): 24–35.

Sankey, Benjamin. *A Companion to William Carlos Williams's Paterson.* Berkeley: University of California Press, 1971.

Sapir, Edward. *Language: An Introduction to the Study of Speech.* New York: Harcourt, Brace, 1921.

Scholes, Percy A. *The Oxford Companion to Music.* Edited by John Owen Ward. London: Oxford University Press, 1970.

Shakespeare, William. *The Complete Works.* Edited by G. B. Harrison. New York: Harcourt, Brace & World, 1952.

Shapiro, Karl. *In Defense of Ignorance.* New York: Vintage Books, 1960.

———, ed. *Prose Keys to Modern Poetry.* New York: Harper & Row, 1962.

Shelley, Percy Bysshe. "A Defense of Poetry." *English Literary Criticism.* New York: Scribner's, 1896, pp. 160–99.

Solt, Mary Ellen. "William Carlos Williams: Idiom and Structure." *The Massachusetts Review* 3, no. 2 (Winter 1962): 304–18.

———. "William Carlos Williams: Poems in the American Idiom." *Folio* 25, no. 1 (1960): 3–28.

Some Imagist Poets: An Anthology. Boston: Houghton Mifflin, 1915.

Sontag, Susan. *Against Interpretation and Other Essays.* New York: Farrar, Straus & Giroux, 1966.

Spears, Monroe K. *Dionysus and the City: Modernism in Twentieth-Century Poetry.* New York: Oxford University Press, 1970.

Spengler, Oswald. *The Decline of the West: Perspectives of World-History,* vol. 2. Translated by Charles Francis Atkinson. New York: Alfred A. Knopf, 1947.

Stead, Christian Karlson. *The New Poetic.* London: Hutchinson, 1964.

Stevens, Wallace. *Letters of Wallace Stevens.* Edited by Holly Stevens. New York: Alfred A. Knopf, 1966.

Sutton, Walter. "A Visit with William Carlos Williams." *Minnesota Review* 1 (Spring 1961): 309–24.

————. "Dr. Williams' *Paterson* and the Quest for Form." *Criticism* 2 (Summer 1960): 242-59.

Tanner, Tony. "Notes for a Comparison Between American and European Romanticism." *Journal of American Studies* 2, no. 1 (April 1968): 83–103.

————. *The Reign of Wonder: Naivety and Reality in American Literature*. Cambridge: Cambridge University Press, 1965.

Taupin, René. *L'Influence du Symbolisme Français sur La Poésie Amériçaine* (De 1910 Á 1920). Paris: Líbrairie Ancienne Honoré Champion, 1929.

Thirlwall, John C. "William Carlos Williams as Correspondent." *The Literary Review* 1 (Autumn 1957): 13–28.

————. "William Carlos Williams' *Paterson:* The Search for The Redeeming Language—A Personal Epic in Five Parts." *New Directions in Prose and Poetry 17*. Norfolk, Conn.: New Directions, 1961.

Thompson, Frank. "The Symbolic Structure of *Paterson.*" *Western Review* 19 (1955): 285–93.

Tomlinson, Charles, ed. *William Carlos Williams: A Critical Anthology*. Harmondsworth, Middlesex: Penguin Books, 1972.

Turville-Petre. *Myth and Religion of the North: The Religion of Ancient Scandinavia*. New York: Holt, Rinehart and Winston, 1964.

Tuve, Rosemond. *Allegorical Imagery: Some Medieval Books and their Posterity*. Princeton, N.J.: Princeton University Press, 1966.

Tyler, Parker. "The Poet of *Paterson* Book One." *Briarcliff Quarterly* 3, no. 11 (October 1946): 168–75.

Van Nostrand, A.D. *Everyman His Own Poet*. New York: McGraw Hill, 1968.

Vazakas, Byron. *Transfigured Night*. New York: MacMillan, 1946.

Vinaver, Eugène. *The Rise of Romance*. Oxford: Oxford University Press, 1971.

Virgil. *The Aeneid of Virgil*. Translated by Rolfe Humphries. New York: Scribner's, 1951.

Wagner, Linda Welshimer. *The Poems of William Carlos Williams: A Critical Study*. Middletown, Conn.: Wesleyan University Press, 1964.

————. *The Prose of William Carlos Williams.* Middletown, Conn.: Wesleyan University Press, 1970.

Wallace, Emily Mitchell. *A Bibliography of William Carlos Williams.* Middletown, Conn.: Wesleyan University Press, 1968.

"Ways of Looking at a Poem and a Poet." Anon. rev., *Times Literary Supplement*, no. 3, 613 (May 28, 1971): 611.

Weatherhead, A. Kingsley. "William Carlos Williams: Prose, Form, and Measure." *Journal of English Literary History* 33 (March 1966): 118–31.

Weaver, Mike. *William Carlos Williams: The American Background.* Cambridge: Cambridge University Press, 1971.

Webster's New Collegiate Dictionary. Springfield, Mass.: G. & C. Merriam, 1973.

Weimer, David R. *The City as Metaphor.* New York: Random House, 1966.

Wellek, René. *Concepts of Criticism.* New Haven, Conn.: Yale University Press, 1963.

Wellek, René, and Warren, Austin. *Theory of Literature.* New York: Harcourt Brace, 1949.

West, Ray B. "The Modern Writer." *College English* 15, no. 4 (January 1954): 207–15.

Whitaker, Thomas R. *William Carlos Williams.* New York: Twayne Pub., 1968.

Whitehead, Alfred North. *Science and the Modern World.* New York: Macmillan, 1947.

Whitman, Walt. *The Collected Writings of Walt Whitman: Prose Works 1892*, vol. 2. New York: New York University Press, 1964.

————. *Leaves of Grass.* New York: New American Library, 1958.

————. *Walt Whitman of the New York Aurora.* Edited by Joseph Jay Rubin and Charles H. Brown. Pennsylvania: Bald Eagle Press, 1950.

Wilkie, Brian. *Romantic Poets and Epic Tradition.* Madison: University of Wisconsin Press, 1965.

Winters, Yvor. *In Defense of Reason: Primitivism and Decadence.* Denver: University of Denver Press, 1947.

————. *Primitivism and Decadence: A Study of American Experi-*

mental Poetry. New York: Haskell House, 1969.

Wordsworth, William, and Coleridge, Samuel Taylor. *Lyrical Ballads 1805*. London: Collins, 1968.

Zukofsky, Louis. *An "Objectivists" Anthology*. Le Beausset: To, 1932.

Index